# *Death Lore: Texas Rituals, Superstitions, and Legends of the Hereafter*

# *Death Lore: Texas Rituals, Superstitions, and Legends of the Hereafter*

Edited by Kenneth L. Untiedt

Publications of the Texas Folklore Society LXV

UNT PRESS

University of North Texas Press

Denton, Texas

10 9 8 7 6 5 4 3 2 1

Permissions:
University of North Texas Press
P.O. Box 311336
Denton, TX 76203-1336

The paper used in this book meets the minimum requirements of the American National Standard for Permanence of Paper for Printed Library Materials, z39.48.1984. Binding materials have been chosen for durability.

Library of Congress Cataloging-in-Publication Data

Death lore : Texas rituals, superstitions, and legends of the hereafter / edited by Kenneth L. Untiedt.
p. cm. — (Publications of the Texas Folklore Society ; 65)
Includes bibliographical references and index.
ISBN 978-1-57441-256-7 (cloth : alk. paper)
1. Death—Social aspects—Texas. 2. Thanatology—Texas. I. Untiedt, Kenneth L., 1966– II. Texas Folklore Society.
HQ1073.5.U62T49 2008
306.909764—dc22

2008029767

*Death Lore: Texas Rituals, Superstitions, and Legends of the Hereafter* is Number LXV in the Publications of the Texas Folklore Society

# CONTENTS

# PREFACE

Upon hearing the proposed topic for this PTFS, many people responded to me with the same reaction: Why? Death does seem like a rather unusual subject for an entire publication, doesn't it? Not if you check your local library. The shelves are stocked with books on burial customs, studies of the process of dying, cemeteries, and cultural and religious beliefs about the afterlife from all over the world. Still, people weren't sure about the idea when they first heard it. Death is almost something you just don't talk about. At the same time, no one really seemed turned off by the subject. Most were quite interested. They all began to immediately suggest ideas for papers, or they at least shared death-related stories. I understand the mixed feelings, but I hope that no one gets too hung up on the morbid topic, or feels that it was chosen solely for its creepiness or some cheap shock value.

There are many reasons why I made death lore the focus of an entire volume. First, it's a fascinating topic. Everyone has ideas about what happens when we die, and no one really knows for sure. Death is a mystery, and it will remain so forever. No matter how much we can learn about disease and why people die, what happens after is purely a matter of belief—and faith, in many cases. Also, as an organization that preserves and presents folklore, we haven't done much research on the lore surrounding death. There've been a few articles—some on cemetery or funeral customs, roadside graves, and ghosts, as well as this year's throwback article by Hortense Warner Ward: "The Yellow Flower of Death," from the 1948 PTFS *The Sky Is My Tipi*—but only relatively few in sixty-four previous books. And there is a lot to write about. Again, check your local library. With so much lore surrounding the one event that affects us all, why haven't we done more on it?

Perhaps it's because the topic is so personal. This volume produced some very interesting submissions, but not all were chosen for publication. Some were simply *too* personal. We all have our own individual views of death, how we should honor the dead, and what happens after we die, but I wanted to include articles that not only showed the private feelings and experiences of the contributors, but also ones that expressed the common view, the lore of the folk that we could all relate to. Many of these stories and articles reveal intimate memories of loved ones passing, as well as customs, rituals, superstitions, and beliefs of the afterlife that are deep-rooted and, therefore, will surely live on through generations to come.

Death lore involves our most sacred, oldest traditions—yet, it is vital to our everyday twenty-first-century lives, and even to the future. Rhett Rushing told me of a blog he does that provides regular updates on Texas ghost stories for the San Antonio *Express-News.* A recent (May 4, 2008) article in the Nacogdoches newspaper, *The Daily Sentinel,* told of a Waco cemetery that had been relocated in the late 1960s to make way for the Texas Ranger Hall of Fame and Museum. It seems the gravestones were relocated, but not all of the remains of the deceased. As you'll learn in this volume, strict rituals are to be followed when graves are moved, and because those rituals were ignored, the present generation is being connected to ancestors long forgotten.

Because death lore covers so much, I've done something I haven't done for any previous publication: I've included an Introduction, which serves as the first chapter. This Introduction is not intended to be the end-all source for every custom or belief related to death; instead, it is an overview of the most common lore, along with some historical background. The second chapter looks at cemeteries—how they hold mysterious and yet valuable information about our past, and also how they function as sacred places which should be treated with respect and care. The next chapter focuses on how people die and what happens afterwards, including the rituals we practice before and after death, as well as the ceremonies and, yes, even the humor that comfort us when we've lost loved ones. The fourth chapter explores unanswered questions about death; it covers not only ghostly accounts of the spirit world, but also bizarre deaths and other experiences we can't explain. The final chapter is more philosophical, offering contemplative views of the value of visiting the dead, and reflections about time spent with the living. This book offers a variety of death lore, and I hope you find it thought-provoking and useful.

As always, I thank all of the contributors who wrote articles for this book. I also thank my colleagues at Stephen F. Austin State University, as well as some key administrators who helped the TFS keep running smoothly over the past year: Jerry Williams, Interim Chair of the Department of English and Philosophy, and Brian Murphy, Dean of the College of Liberal and Applied Arts. And of course, many thanks go to all the folks at the UNT Press.

This publication is dedicated to Janet Simonds. Her work as office secretary is invaluable to me. She assists with nearly every stage of the publication of these books, but she has been especially helpful with this one. In addition to formatting the submitted texts, corresponding with contributors, and reworking the photos for articles, she also designed the cover—exactly the way I envisioned it. Her hard work allows me to focus on editing, which can be challenging while dealing with the countless issues that face an untenured faculty member in a department that has had more than its share of complications and administrative difficulties recently. When you come to Nacogdoches at Easter in 2009, remember to tell Janet what a good job she does.

Kenneth L. Untiedt
Stephen F. Austin State University
Nacogdoches, Texas
May 18, 2008

# INTRODUCTION

## The Lore of Death

by Kenneth L. Untiedt

Contrary to what Captain Kirk told us at the beginning of every *Star Trek* episode, space is not the final frontier. Nor is the ocean, which many scientists believe warrants more research and promises more potential life-sustaining solutions for our planet than does any place outside our atmosphere. No, death is the real final frontier. It is the true unknown, and it is the only adventure everyone must ultimately face. A select few people have been to outer space, and their travels have been thoroughly documented. Each day scientists answer more of the questions we have about our material world and the universe in which we live. However, no one knows for sure what will happen when death occurs. The mysteries of death make the lore that surrounds it unique for two reasons. First, because death is universal and occurs without regard to culture, gender, social status, ethnic background, country of origin, or any other factor, it is the focus of more folklore than anything else. Also, because no one knows what awaits them after their inevitable death, much of the folklore related to dying is generated by fear.

Some burial customs and superstitions regarding death go back centuries—indeed, to earliest man. Contemporary cultures maintain a strong connection to this lore, more so than to any other kind. Younger generations are more likely to retain death rituals and customs than they are other life cycle events, such as births and rites of passage celebrations. With divorce rates averaging well over fifty percent, couples may adhere to wedding customs the first time, but the second or third time around, most folks don't worry as much about following tradition. Especially here in America, as families continue to spread apart in a vastly transient society, fewer people embark on cross-country trips to see newborns or celebrate sixteenth birthday parties, sometimes for grandchildren or other relatives they've visited in person only a few times. The baby can be seen via a live video feed on the Internet from anywhere in the world, and videotapes or DVDs and digital photographs are easy to produce and share, again because of computer technology. A death in the family, however, still calls for a personal appearance. We don't honor the dead through a web cam.

One reason death customs continue when others fade away is that we are able to rely on an organized, regulated institution to help keep them alive: the funeral industry. Funeral homes, no matter how corporate they've become, still promise to assist families with every part of the burial process—even providing counseling on how to grieve properly, but also almost certainly explaining all the most common rituals and burial customs, at least for that particular local culture. A more important reason, though, is that death is final. We remember little if anything of other life cycle events such as our own birth, learning to walk, or first days of school. And almost everyone looks forward to those occasions that, in many cases, have become more about clever marketing and commercialism (Sweet Sixteen birthday parties) than they are about achieving something meaningful. On the other hand, no one overcomes death, and the loss of a loved one often affects people more powerfully—and personally—than any other event.

To understand more about dying and what might follow, people study the folklore related to death. They can learn about rituals from cultures all around the world, as well as how they originated and have changed. Many books (and now web sites) repeat much of the same information, providing only variations of many different cultures over time. One can compare specific examples of superstitions, rituals, customs, and beliefs of ancient man, as well as those within contemporary cultures. Each culture's beliefs surrounding death are an important starting point for such study, for they are at the heart of all death lore (and all folklore in general). Shared beliefs are a substantial part of what defines a culture. The idea that people *believe* in something is what makes them continue the practice with which it is associated. While the origins may have been lost, people find comfort in the rituals, superstitions, and customs that support what the larger group believes.

Man's attempt to learn more and satisfy curiosities about his surroundings and his future demonstrate his civilized nature. His comprehension of his inevitable death and his desire to understand it is what separates him from other animals. According to Edward Martin, "The earliest belief of what may be termed 'mind' was that a ghost dwelt inside the body, making the body alive and conscious. At death this ghost or spirit permanently withdrew from the body."[1] Simple reasoning explains why primitive man first imagined such a spirit exists. "On a cold morning he could see his breath. He did not understand the oxidation process. Vapor arising from fresh blood meant the same to him, for too much loss of blood meant death."[2] However, most people even today believe there is a spirit within us that will venture on to some other place—either good or bad. Perhaps every known religion has incorporated such beliefs. According to Martin, "This belief in a conscious 'spirit' that leaves the body at death still persists in present-day religions."[3] These beliefs from those early times continue to shape our customs and superstitions, regardless of whether the original purposes for them have long since been forgotten or replaced with others. Nothing in science can disprove them, for there is no way to objectively study the afterlife. Death is *the* great unknown.

Effie Bendann notes there are numerous problems with the various methods of studying death customs of ancient or primitive cultures. Comparison of similar practices in different cultures does not always include the reasoning behind such practices. Other schools of thought, including psychological studies and the theory of diffusion, present their own unique limitations to fully understanding a particular culture's death-related lore.[4] Bendann contends that the best method scholars can offer is a purely historical approach of looking at individual periods in specific societies to examine which customs have survived and how they've been altered over decades, or even centuries. Such a study will reveal "the fact that there are certain common features in all areas, such as the causes of death, the significance of burial, the dread of the spirit, the specific attitude toward the corpse, mourning rites, taboos, the potent power of the name, and feasts for the dead."[5] These features are essentially universal, and this introduction provides an overview of the origins of some of the most familiar death-related lore.

Why do people have so many beliefs, superstitions, and customs and rituals about dying? The main reason is that we fear death more than anything else, although a secondary reason is respect—for the dead, and for what happens after we die. The fear of dying consistently ranks among the top of people's most common fears. We may say that we don't fear death, but the origins for the rituals and customs themselves suggest otherwise. According to Bertram Puckle, "Fear of the dead is the origin of almost every funeral custom which has come down to us today; from the pomp of the procession to the laudatory epitaph on the tombstone, to propitiate the acute sensibility of the departed."[6] Effie Bendann refers to the "dread of the spirit," which she clarifies is a fear of whatever inhabited the deceased and not the corpse itself.[7] Archeological research shows that "the big idea of burials was to defend the survivors from the very dangerous discontented souls or ghosts of the recently dead."[8] It's the spirit that we really worry about. The corpse we can study—we can see it, and examine it from a medical standpoint. What was inside, and presumably leaves for another unknown world, is what we don't understand and, therefore, fear.

While fear is the main impetus for death lore, our modern, more educated culture also takes into consideration an increasingly evident respect for the process of dying. Healthcare professionals understand that terminally ill patients are fearful of their impending deaths.[9] Nurses commonly have a more intimate relationship with dying patients than do doctors, and the healthcare industry realizes how important the nurse's role is in assisting the dying with their transition. Therefore, nurses are schooled in ways to communicate more compassionately with patients so they can better attend to those who know their lives are ending and ease their worries. Such training can help prevent nurses from revealing to their patients their own superstitions or fears about death; it can also help them with the grieving process and personal feelings which they feel naturally after having bonded with the patients.[10] Everyone involved in another's death needs to believe in something to resolve the anxieties and emotions it triggers.

Our fear of death leads to countless superstitions about it. These superstitions, in turn, generate customs, rituals, festivals, and other lore to protect against—and celebrate—the dead. Except in some cases of the terminally ill under close care of a doctor, no one knows when death will occur. Therefore, folklore regarding signs of approaching death comprises entire chapters of books. Puckle states, "Many of the superstitions . . . are obviously nothing more than a chain of associated ideas. . . . 'Death warnings' as they are called, have nearly all an obvious origin."[11] Some death warnings are commonly known in many cultures, as are the reasoning behind them. Breaking a mirror is believed to cause seven years bad luck because ancient people thought the reflection was the soul, and breaking the mirror would destroy it; the sign of impending death when a bird flies into a house stems from birds being able to fly to the heavens, and the superstition that they would carry away a person's soul.[12]

Modern man understands polished glass and the source of a mirror's reflection, as well as the limitations of a bird's flight, but other superstitions remain just as popular despite how commonplace their occurrences are. The following are but three examples: "A white moth inside the house or trying to enter means death";[13] "If you shiver it is said by the gossips that 'someone is walking over your grave,'" and "If you dream of nursing a baby and the baby cries, you will either die yourself or lose a near relative."[14] No matter how often such simple events occur, some people maintain their beliefs that death is sure to follow.

Whether we can predict it or not, death *is* inevitable, and once it occurs we want loved ones to find peace in whatever comes afterward. We take measures we hope will ensure that they can arrive at any eternal destination that awaits them. Each culture has specific rituals to facilitate the transition of the deceased to the afterlife, from the preparation of the corpse to its burial and all else related to death. Early Jews believed the dead were unclean, hence their rituals of purifying the corpse as well as its burial clothes.[15] According to Puckle, "No doubt the origin of the custom of washing, anointing and clothing the corpse in garments suitable to its rank was instituted in the dim ages, when it was believed that the departed required such attentions to enable them to appear at their best in a future material state."[16] Each culture's rituals for preparing corpses have their own reasoning. Margaret Coffin states, "Southern Negroes, like many others, used a cooling board for laying out their dead and, in the past, placed a plate of salt and ashes beneath the board. The ashes were put there to absorb disease and, at the committal service, were placed in the grave."[17] Many Native Americans (among other peoples) go a step further and believe the deceased must have all their body parts intact to travel in the next world.

Once prepared, the body must find its way to the next destination, which most often involves burial in the ground (although some cultures—or individuals within cultures that typically practice burial—prefer cremation). Martin claims many customs originated to prevent the spirit from reentering the body after it had left. He notes that a corpse is carried feet first so the body can not look back and see the spirit following, thereby allowing the spirit to again inhabit the body.[18] Others believe the feet should go first so the deceased, being envious of the living, will not look back and "beckon one of the family to follow it in death."[19] The reason for removing a corpse from a home through a window or another opening other than the door is to confuse the spirit so that it can not follow; covering the body with dirt is another way of keeping the spirit away.[20] Of course, burials also once kept wild animals from desecrating the corpse, as well as prevented unsanitary conditions as the body decomposed, concerns still valid in some cultures.

It has long been thought that blocking a funeral procession would impede the deceased's journey, so attempts are made to keep the hearse from stopping on its way to the cemetery.[21] Contemporary right-of-way customs are still observed and, in fact, enforced by laws, no matter how dangerous they've become in light of our modern transportation and roadways. Police escorts are often used, even in metropolitan areas and on streets and highways where vehicles must cross high-traffic intersections, all at the peril of those charged with providing safe passage for the funeral procession.

Preparing the dead for burial has generated multiple professions: undertakers, of course, but also "layers out of dead" for public display.[22] Now, any such occupations are considered highly professional, requiring advanced study and licensing to perform services legally. Another profession historically partnered with death is that of the cabinet maker. The practice of being placed in some type of enclosure—a coffin, or a "chest"—prior to being interred is Biblical, coming from Genesis 1:26: "He (Joseph) dieth and is chested."[23] Being buried in this manner was once a distinction of wealth or status; for the poor, a coffin was used only to transport the deceased to the grave site.[24] The purpose of encasing the deceased in a coffin, the earliest of which were made of stone, was to preserve them for resurrection.[25] The first European-Americans often had no coffins, but were buried instead wrapped only in cerecloth shrouds.[26]

Standard "ready-made" coffins were available by the War of 1812, but the term "casket" did not come into use until the mid-1800s.[27] Scraps from the materials used to make coffins were frequently placed inside out of the superstition that they would endanger the carpenter or anyone else who touched them.[28] Related customs involve placing personal items—from weapons to tools to valuables, including putting coins on the eyes of the body—in the coffin, so the deceased may use them in the afterlife.[29] During the late nineteenth century, cast iron materials and coffins booby-trapped with explosives were developed to discourage grave robbers who might be tempted to steal such treasures.[30] The newest models of coffins offer stainless steel outer vaults encased around coffins constructed of the finest wood, fiberglass, or even other metal.

Funerals were once much more intimate affairs than they are today, when they are advertised in the local newspaper and on the

Internet. For some early American communities, funerals were by invitation only. According to Coffin, "In Dutch New Amsterdam and up the Hudson to Albany, the *aanspreecker*, or inviter, performed his own special service. Clothed in black, with long crape ribbons streaming from his hat, he hurried to the homes of relatives and friends of the deceased—for no one attended a funeral uninvited."[31] For some Pennsylvanian Germans, wine and "dead cakes" were delivered when making such invitations; the cakes, which looked like large cookies and often had the deceased's initials scratched in them, "were not eaten but kept as a memento of the person who had died."[32] For less private funerals, bells were used not only to notify members of a community of a death, but also to scare away evil spirits.[33]

Death has played an integral part in the construction of the average home for many cultures. "When the Pennsylvania Germans were ready to build homes, they planned a room called the *doed-kammer* or dead room, where a body lay until time for the funeral. This room had doors broad enough to allow the exit of bearers carrying a casket. The rarely used parlor, always kept neat for a funeral or a wedding, was found in many a New England home, too."[34] The home of the deceased is still where mourners usually congregate, either before or after a funeral. Wakes originated out of watching over the dead in hopes that they might regain consciousness; sometimes, the watchers attempted to "rouse the ghost" by playing practical jokes and "taking various liberties with the corpse."[35] Eventually, these events became times of celebration more than sadness. Irish wakes turned into parties where the corpse was propped up to observe the celebration, and Southern funerals were social occasions where people everywhere within a fifty-five mile radius were expected to attend.[36] Texas is exposed to the customs and rituals of many different cultures, from Halloween celebrations of European tradition (although now much altered from the original) to the Hispanic variation of All Souls Day (Dia de los Muertos).

Regardless of cultural background, black is recognized practically everywhere as the proper mourning attire. The reason again is related to our fear of death. Those closest to the deceased—the undertaker, mourners, and pall bearers—originally wore black so they could be "inconspicuous." Because the dead are envious, no one near the corpse wanted to be recognized and thereby beckoned to follow into death. Black is also thought to prevent contamination, particularly among African Americans.[37] Eventually, the fashion industry throughout Europe and America began setting rules regarding mourning wear. Coffin states:

> By the nineteenth century there were definite rules setting the length of mourning and the clothing to be worn during each period. Two years of deep mourning was expected of widows. During the first year the bereaved wore solid black wool garments . . . with collars and cuffs of folded, untrimmed crape, no other trim. . . . During the second year of mourning, the widow might wear a silk fabric trimmed with crape and use black lace for her collars and cuffs. . . . After a year and a half, she might vary her wardrobe with garments or trim of gray, violet, or white. . . . Children in mourning, those under twelve, wore white in summer and gray in winter, both trimmed with black buttons, ruffles, belts, or bonnet ribbons only.[38]

These fashion standards served to adhere to lore surrounding death, but surely commercialism was also a factor.

Many death rituals and customs related to preparing and burying the dead have nothing to do with fashion, worldly possessions, or concerns about the prevention of disease. They are religious in nature. Some remain virtually unchanged from their original, ancient purpose, while others have been altered greatly over centuries of interpretation and adaptation. Eating flesh of the dead has many purposes for cultures all over the world, from tribes that practice cannibalism to acquire virtues of the deceased to Christian rituals of receiving communion out of respect or remembrance.[39]

The "sin-eater" is a scapegoat figure in many cultures; an individual accepts a small fee and a meal in order to take on the moral trespasses and consequences of the afterlife for someone else.[40] In Christianity, Christ fulfilled such a role when he offered himself as a sacrifice for all men's sins. To honor his act and to prepare for his second coming, Christian burials typically place the dead facing east—the direction from which he will come.

Such beliefs are at the core of all our folklore—we do things because we believe strongly in them. A wide array of death lore exists, more so than any other type of lore. There are many reasons that death lore continues when other lore is forgotten or changes beyond recognition. However, the main reason is that we all fear it so much. This introductory chapter offers only an overview of some of the most common superstitions about death and its customs and rituals. The rest of this volume includes over twenty-five articles that illustrate some of the various aspects of death lore as shaped by the beliefs of Texans.

## ENDNOTES

1. Edward A. Martin. *Psychology of Funeral Service.* 4th edition. Grand Junction, Colorado: Sentinel Printing Co., 1962. 17–18.
2. Ibid. 20.
3. Ibid. 18.
4. Effie Bendann. *Death Customs: An Analytical Study of Burial Rites.* New York: Alfred A. Knopf, 1930. 1–13.
5. Ibid. 16.
6. Bertram Puckle. *Funeral Customs: Their Origin and Development.* London: T. Werener Laurie, Ltd., 1926. 173.
7. Bendann. 57, and 83.
8. "burial customs." *Funk & Wagnalls Standard Dictionary of Folklore, Mythology, and Legend* Volume One: A-I. Maria Leach, editor. New York: Funk & Wagnalls Company, 1949.
9. Carol Ren Kneisl. "Thoughtful Care for the Dying." *American Journal of Nursing* Volume 68 #3, March 1968. 550.
10. Ibid. 550–553.
11. Puckle. 17.
12. Martin. 22–23.

13. Margaret M. Coffin. *Death in Early America: The History and Folklore of Customs and Superstitions of Early Medicine, Funerals, Burials, and Mourning*. Nashville: Thomas Nelson Inc., Publishers, 1976. 59.
14. Puckle. 19.
15. "burial customs."
16. Puckle. 35.
17. Coffin. 79.
18. Martin. 22.
19. "funeral customs."
20. Martin. 22.
21. "funeral customs."
22. Coffin. 81.
23. Puckle. 43.
24. Ibid. 42.
25. Ibid. 43–44.
26. Coffin. 101.
27. Ibid. 105.
28. Ibid. 102.
29. Puckle. 49–51.
30. Coffin. 107.
31. Ibid. 69–70.
32. Ibid. 71.
33. Ibid. 72.
34. Ibid. 73.
35. Puckle. 61–63.
36. Coffin. 85 and 91.
37. "funeral customs."
38. Coffin. 197–199.
39. Puckle. 70–73.
40. Ibid. 69.

# “FINAL” RESTING

# PLACES

San Fernando Cathedral

# LIFE AND DEATH IN OLD BEXAR

**by David LaRo**

I'll begin by explaining this is primarily a discussion of old burials and *old* cemeteries in and around Bexar—San Antonio—and not the NEW, commercial variety. You should realize that Bexar once covered approximately half of present-day Texas, so if I seem to go far afield, that might explain it.

Growing up, I was taught to fear cemeteries, and to avoid them, if possible. Now, I join many folks who seek out cemeteries for various reasons. We visit with the departed, meet kinfolk, exchange or collect genealogical information, and remember our departed ancestors. We may bring food or drink, erect monuments, maintain the grounds, or take rubbings of headstones. Thus do we continue many traditional public and private celebrations.

Genealogists study births, deaths, marriages, and children. Graveyards are a great resource, as well as a powerful expression of culture. Long after some facets of a culture have disappeared, we can study changes within that culture, document practices no longer commonplace, and note physical evidence such as headstones, inscriptions, and decorations.

Many of us are interested in where our people are buried. Some of us want to know *exactly* where, as in, "Mabel, do you see Uncle Ezra's stone?" Others simply take comfort in the European tradition of burial in "sanctified ground." When finding an ancestor in a cemetery, I have often wondered, "Why are you buried here, in this forgotten place?" My experience with historical researchers and archeologists makes me aware of other forgotten places: I enjoy connecting some of it to things we see every day. Many of you will have memories of your own out-of-the-way graveyards.

My hometown of San Antonio has a strong Spanish history. In 1691, the first recorded Europeans to visit San Antonio were Governor Terán de los Ríos and Fr. Massanet, bound for East Texas. Tired from their journey, ready to enjoy an abundant and beautiful river, they stopped to rest for a spell. They named our river *"San Antonio de Padua."* In 1718, Mission *San Antonio de Valero* (later called the Alamo) and the presidio (a military post) were founded by the Spanish government. If these institutions did not exactly thrive, they at least persisted for over a half century. San Antonio really began to hum with activity in 1731, when the *Villa San Fernando* was given by the Spanish government to settlers from the Canary Islands (*Isleños*).

A local archeologist friend believed the first site of Mission *San Antonio de Valero* was near a present-day downtown Italian Catholic church, though that has not yet been proven. Soon, the mission was relocated to a site likely very near the present church of St. Joseph's (many locals call the present church "St. Joske's" because of its location, surrounded on three sides by what was once the historic Joske's of Texas store.) Here the mission remained for some five years until moving to the current site—the site of the 1836 battle we know as the Battle of the Alamo. The presidio was also relocated into what is now downtown San Antonio's Military Plaza.

Are there burials at those early sites, now covered with concrete? To put it another way, did anyone die during those years? Of course. Human remains have been discovered in the grounds now under the old Post Office/Federal Building (across the street from the Alamo), and others have been found near the Alamo wall on Houston Street. Are there still remains under downtown San Antonio? My guess would be in the *hundreds.*

Three East Texas missions were relocated during the 1730s to San Antonio, where they joined existing missions *San José* and *Valero.* They were to form the backbone for a strong missionary effort. History shows us the physical missions had long lives, and several remain active Catholic parishes today, located as they are within a National Park property. In 1738, construction began on the parish church of *San Fernando,* intended to serve the Canary Islands settlers. It was located in the center of town, per Spanish custom. In front of the church was the *camposanto* (sanctified ground, or cemetery). Many years later, when the church was enlarged, it was extended toward the Plaza, a portion of the present chapel resting directly above the site of the earlier *camposanto*. I've visited that church and always wonder just whose remains are below my feet.

By 1740, the Spanish had established five missions along the river—and the parish church—all going about the daily business of ministering, teaching, farming, weaving, ranching, and rescuing heathen souls. There were births, deaths, and marriages. Their normal life span at that time was *considerably* shorter than ours today. At their death, most of the parishioners were buried "in the faith" by their priest. Where possible, they were buried in holy ground. Customarily, only the padre and high officials were normally permitted the honor of burial within the church walls; however, numerous wills contained generous donations to the church for that specific "honor."

If buried within the chapel, parishioners were usually buried "feet toward the altar," while the padres were buried with their heads near the altar and their feet to the congregation. This permitted the risen parishioners, on the day of resurrection, to face the altar while the padres would face the congregation. When exploring a site of a former mission complex, the finding of human remains within the walls of a structure is significant. I have heard stories of burials within the ruins of abandoned churches in order to take advantage of the already sanctified ground.

Other individuals would have been buried near private homes, in gardens, or wherever circumstances dictated. If under siege by marauders, many were simply buried where they fell. Examples of these burials are still being discovered during the course of construction projects. An archeologist found the remains of a young girl buried next to the Spanish Governor's Palace in a little courtyard. Who was she? We'll likely never know. A few blocks north of the Palace, during construction of a new building, workers found two bodies, one atop the other, buried in what had been a private courtyard. The identities of the "couple" were eventually discovered and the local paper published the story. Everyone loves a mystery solved, even if no romance was involved.

In August of 1749, there was a ceremonial burial in Military Plaza of a live pony with full war regalia, weapons and all. The ceremony signified the end of fighting, and thus the "hatchet" was buried . . . to seal the treaty with the Apache. Pursuing peace with the Apache, the Franciscan missionaries wanted to expand their mission "footprint" northward, into the hills where the Apache lived. This was not a popular idea with church officials, the military, or the Indians of that area. However, in 1757, after finally obtaining formal church approval, a group set out. Their plan was to establish a mission—a mission that would be remembered as Mission *San Sabá.*

Remember the *San Sabá* story? At present-day Menard, the Spanish built the mission. Upriver a bit, the protecting presidio was built. The mission was ineffective. Apparently, so was the presidio. Within the year, Mission *San Sabá* was looted and burned to the ground by local natives. One of the missionaries and several of the staff were brutally murdered. Burials at the mission site were lost when the mission's location was forgotten. Fortunately, it was very recently rediscovered, after years of fruitless searching, by the unlikely team of an archeologist and an architect. Will this site someday reveal more graves?

Two other missions, *San Lorenzo* and *Candelaria,* were established a short distance from the *San Sabá* mission. They were short-lived, but within the ruins of the *San Lorenzo* site archeologists located eight burials in a confined area they identified as the chapel.

By 1770, San Antonio had grown to over 3,000 non-indigenous residents. Reasoning tells me many more people did not survive the forty years of recurring episodes of Indian warfare. There could be hundreds of forgotten graves! Keep in mind that as they are discovered by excavation crews, unexpected remains face an uncertain fate. I suspect some are quickly covered over without even slowing construction. Others might delay construction for official reaction. Some are studied by scholars, and then re-buried. Laws may require the remains be returned to living descendants. What to do with the remains can be a dilemma, both legally and spiritually.

Early on, many large ranches had their own family chapel and burial place for their people. The *ranchos* and the presidios had small

**Grave removal project in front of San Fernando Church**

churches where padres came to minister to the residents. Their burials would likely have been nearby. *Vaqueros*, travelers, and freighters were probably buried where they fell, as many were far from home. It is easy to believe that many remote burial sites have been forgotten.

Not all the deceased *could* be forgotten. By 1807, Bexar residents began to experience a terrible odor at the front entrance of San Fernando Church. Parishioners had been buried in crypts in the church and in the church yard for seventy years. The old *camposanto* had reached the end of its useful life. The numbers of dead, laid to rest atop previous burials, had exceeded the saturation point. Parishioners chose to enter the church by a side door to avoid the odor at the front. The church got approval to establish a "new" cemetery, the San Antonio Cemetery, in an area to the west across the San Pedro Creek. The land for this cemetery was given to the city by the government of Spain. This area lies under what is now the Santa Rosa hospital. Non-Catholic residents were buried in a separate area adjacent to and just south of the Catholic burial ground. The "non-Catholic" area is now known as Milam Park, named for Ben Milam, who died during the historic siege of Bexar.

If you get the opportunity, you should visit the San Fernando Cathedral in San Antonio. It is still the "Mother Church" for many San Antonians, and its beauty is impressive. The area just inside the present front entrance rests above the *camposanto* used by the early settlers. An archeologist who worked under the present church during a renovation some years ago described it to me as "almost like digging in bone meal." Markers located within the church document burials of notables within the walls. The earliest marked graves in San Antonio are within this church.

To reach the new San Antonio Cemetery from San Fernando, a burial party had to travel approximately three quarters of a mile and cross San Pedro Creek to the west. In those days, there was not a bridge like the current one, only a low-water crossing. Funeral parties accompanying a carriage bearing the coffin were subject to attack by renegade Indians as soon as they left the town plaza. Many burials were carried out by well-armed mourners. Sometimes, more burials were required than originally intended. On occasion, the party would be attacked as it crossed the creek, and stories tell of the assembled men quickly pushing the coffin into the creek as they turned the cart around and high-tailed it back to the plaza where soldiers and protection were usually found!

Few cities have seen more battles than San Antonio. Most familiar was the Alamo, but there were many others, including the 1813 Gutierrez-Magee expedition, which made its fatal blunder just south of San Antonio. When 4,000 Royalist Spanish forces under Arredondo marched up from Mexico to put down the Green Flag Rebellion, there were some 1,400 rebels waiting for them in ambush. The rebel ambush failed. There followed the Battle of the Medina, a massacre from which only a few rebels escaped. Today, a small marker tells of the battle where the rebel bodies were left on the field, unburied, just a few miles south of the city. The entire city was imprisoned by Arredondo, and another sixty locals were shot (and by his order) left in the public square.

Stories of escape, pursuit, capture, and execution vary greatly with the teller, but the Royalists do not appear as "forgiving" in any of the stories. A letter from Fr. Sambrano on March 9, 1814 (seven months after the battle) begs permission to bury the corpses lying in the Plaza. He explains that "other men far more guilty" are walking around, pardoned, and further, that "young children are learning disrespect for the dead as they throw rocks at the corpses." Forgiveness not being one of the strengths of that day, no permission was given. The bodies on the Medina battlefield remained until then Gov. Trespalacios had them buried under a large oak. Undocumented stories tell of their later burial at an area chapel.

Here's another forgotten burial. At the storming of downtown Bexar in 1835, Ben Milam and his men forced General Cos from the city. During the battle, Milam was felled by a bullet to the head. Old Ben was buried where he fell, in the garden of the Veramendi house. Here he rested in peace for years until he was given the honor of reburial (by a local Masonic Lodge) in the area now called Milam Park. This park, adjacent to the Catholic cemetery of that day, received those departed who were non-Catholics, non-baptized, suicides, and sinners of a varied ilk. Old Ben, it seems, may have fallen into several of these categories, so there he was laid to rest.

Ben's birthday was remembered with a floral wreath by the Daughters of the Republic of Texas for many years at the urging of Adina de Zavala, but eventually, the annual memorial was forgotten. (Adina was the granddaughter of Lorenzo de Zavala, the first Vice-President of the Republic of Texas. She was also a former Vice-President of the Texas Folklore Society.)

At some point in history, Ben's grave joined the other forgotten graves. During 1993, when the city's plan to remodel Milam Park did not include mention of Ben's remains, a few local historians took up the cause. Two of them drove to Austin and searched the archives and discovered the location of the burial site. They then insisted that the city exhume and re-inter him with the honors he deserved. City officials, of course, did not take them too seriously, but did begin to pay attention when news reporters began to

**Old Ben Milam marker—Milam Park**

appear on the excavation site. Old Ben was located when one swipe of a backhoe came up with pieces of his skull. At that time, the project shifted gears into a proper archeological dig. Ben was carefully removed, studied, and then transported across the country for further study by the Smithsonian. He was returned to San Antonio and re-buried near his previous interment with honors from many segments of the community, from Masons to Catholics to politi-

**Ben Milam statue in present Milam Park**

cians. Ben may have traveled farther following his death than he did during his life.

Soon after finding Ben Milam, another unknown burial was discovered in the park: a one-legged, pipe-smoking Protestant with an 1848 *peso* in his pocket! Not as well documented or reported as old Ben, he has *already* been forgotten . . . like so many others. After Texas won its independence from Mexico in 1836, there were still hostile engagements with Mexican troops. The Battle of

**Inside San Antonio National Cemetery**

the Salado as well as the famous Dawson Massacre took place west of and fairly near today's IH-35. During the distractions of various hostilities, it appears the remains of the Dawson Massacre were left on the ground at the spot where they fell. They were later recovered from this soil and re-interred with honors at LaGrange, Texas. After 1850, burials ceased in both the Catholic Cemetery and in adjacent Milam Park. City burials were then conducted in a large plot of over one hundred acres situated on the *east* side of town. Catholic burials were moved to a location farther west named, appropriately, San Fernando.

"Were the existing bodies moved?" you might wonder. At the time, there was a newspaper story which implied they were moved in a single day. There was a news photo which showed hundreds of old grave markers piled high, ready for destruction. Are there remains still under the present Santa Rosa hospital? I suspect there are.

The first cemetery, San Fernando, has now grown into three separate cemeteries. When I last visited the oldest of the three, I

**Clara Driscoll's crypt**

saw no evidence of a high level of care lavished on those grounds, unfortunately. However, there are still many people in that community who take part in regular activities and celebrations there. The initial "East Side" cemetery area now includes thirty-one distinct cemeteries on the 103 acres, and reflects a wide range of efforts expended in upkeep, mostly poor, but certainly showing significant recent improvement.

San Antonio has two National Military Cemeteries. One is located within the East Side cemetery complex and shows an outstanding level of upkeep, which makes me proud. One can walk the cemeteries of the various fraternal organizations and the several churches represented there, but it is not until one walks into the

National Cemetery that any sense of reverence is felt. There, the grounds are very well maintained and care is obvious.

The East Side cemetery complex contains over 26,000 graves, most buried before 1942. In one of these cemeteries, you can find the crypt of Clara Driscoll, called by some the "Savior of the Alamo." Nearby is the smaller marker of Adina de Zavala, who is, of course, credited by others as the moving force in the "Save the Alamo" story. Look for it, if the weeds are not too high to read the inscriptions on the stones.

It was in the very large National Cemetery located on Fort Sam Houston that a "cultural indicator" jumped out at me. On a recent visit during a holiday week, the Hispanic traditions of respect for their ancestors and a love of color seemed to merge there among all the rows of markers. I found that twenty-eight of the thirty decorated graves I checked bore Hispanic names. Flowers, real and artificial, adorned those graves. I had been told that a cemetery with a largely Hispanic census can be recognized from afar by the color one sees. I saw that vividly demonstrated. A much closer inspection is required to distinguish Baptist from Methodist, English from German. At one private Hispanic cemetery in South Bexar County, I noticed home-crafted grave markers. Amateurish? Perhaps, but they were placed there with obvious love and respect. And sweat! Thirty long miles from old Bexar. I hope I never get too old to learn life's worthwhile lessons.

I find differences between urban and rural graveyards. Respect appears to be disappearing from the urban scene. You may feel this as you travel urban areas, but it seems most visible in the places where our ancestors and early leaders are being—literally—trashed. It is not pleasant to consider our societal "progress" while standing in an urban graveyard. I recall a book by Robert Fulghum in which he tells of his annual practice of visiting his own gravesite, chosen by him for the finest and most scenic view. He spends an entire day there, pondering eternity. I'll bet he wouldn't like many of *our* urban plots. Rural graveyards generally have more vases, growing flowers, personal items, and toys left at gravesides. The rural cemetery seems to somehow exemplify the practice of keeping faith with tradition and with our ancestors.

I know of a private, rural cemetery for area residents only, with a "cemetery association" to maintain it. In 1996, it assessed members a fee of $12.80 to cover grounds upkeep. This seems to be common in smaller communities. I even found a "grave house" in this cemetery, unusual in this part of the state.

I recall visiting one very special gravesite which is not within Bexar. It is located on a high bluff looking east over the blue Pacific Ocean. Within a native Hawaiian community lies a little country cemetery not far from the village of Hana, Maui. The graveyard is situated behind a very small and crudely built board and batten church building, but it is *immaculate.* Maybe because it's a "native Hawaiian" cemetery, the sense of reverence is powerful. So intense was it, I did not even take my camera from the car. I found the grave I sought: that of Charles Lindbergh. I stood there in awe, transfixed, for several minutes. Lindbergh selected the spot, I suspect, because it was the most beautiful spot he'd ever seen. His judgment was good. After all, he'd seen a lot of the world. At his feet is a bluff which commands a view of the blue Pacific where the ocean seems to extend forever. Lindbergh rests there, surrounded with reverence and sheer natural beauty. I am glad I made the effort to see that grave.

I believe cemeteries provide a place where we, the living, can visit the graves of our ancestors, commune with them, and remember. As we grow older, memories are among our most important sources of pleasure. It appears, though, from the condition of many of our cemeteries, we are failing to teach our children "graveyard etiquette" and respect. Traditions are being lost. I fear we are losing our link with our past, something I believe is very important to our culture. That loss may be more serious than we realize. Most of us want to know where we come from. Cemeteries are a great place to start.

On a Hill Far Away

While walking on a limestone hill,
Feeling one with all creation—
Watching birds and smelling flowers,
Far from city, care and time—
I spied a grove of cedar trees
Much higher than their brothers,
And slowly climbed the slope to see
Why man had not cut down
Like all the others
These tall green spires
That beckoned me,
As if a ghost had called.

I tripped before I spotted
The rusted barbed wire strands
Which marked its bounds,
A cemetery old,
With hewn stones dotting weedy earth.
And as I walked on hallowed ground,
I felt the gates of time close me all around.

The ancient dates I spied
Did not surprise me so. For it was clear,
Those who mourned their loved ones here
Rest, in other plots,
Maybe close but likely far
From where these lived and died.

Another generation says:

"I know not where her body lies.
No map to lead me there,
Where I can kneel and tell my child,
'Your grandma's mother lies beneath this spot.
And over there she worked to rear her brood.
Near the creek her husband plowed the ground.
And Grandma walked on yonder road
To a schoolhouse now long gone,
Where Grandpa played and read his books
And teased her pigtails bound.'"

I crossed the fence.
The gates behind me closed.
The birds still chirped and flowers bloomed.
I walked in silence still.
The tear upon my cheek fell off
And soaked into the ground
To blend with all creation,
Like the souls upon the hill.

[These words were written by Chris T. Orth, a good friend and a wise man, used with permission of his family.—*LaRo*]

Confederate Field at the Texas State Cemetery

# THE PAST AT REST: TWO HISTORIC AUSTIN CEMETERIES

by L. Patrick Hughes

The looks of disbelief and inevitable questions are remarkably similar year after year. "We're going where?" Patiently I explain that classes next week will be held off-campus at the Texas State Cemetery on East Seventh Street and Oakwood Cemetery alongside Interstate 35. "What," my students ask, "do graveyards have to do with this course on Texas history?" "A great deal," I respond, guaranteeing that our cemetery tours will bear physical witness to much that we have discussed in class. I promise to illustrate the remarkably different ways different cultures approach the burial ceremony, and to reveal the meanings of gravestone symbols stretching back thousands of years. Such visits are one of the more effective learning opportunities for those studying the state's rich history and peoples.

The State Cemetery dates from Edward Burleson's death in 1851. Wishing to honor the former vice-president of the Republic of Texas, state legislators arranged for his interment on land owned by Andrew Jackson Hamilton, himself a future governor. Three years later, the state purchased eighteen acres from Hamilton to serve as the final resting place for Texas heroes and high-ranking government officials. Based on the nineteenth century concept that cemeteries could serve as museums for the living as well as resting places for the departed, the Board of Control has managed the facility over the intervening years as the "Arlington of Texas."

It certainly has that look and feel, especially in the southeastern section where row after symmetrical row of identical white headstones mark the graves of over two thousand Confederate veterans, widows, and relatives. Interestingly, an acre in the northeast corner was set aside following the War Between the States for federal troops who perished during the Reconstruction occupation of the

Lone Star State. These remains were subsequently moved to the national cemetery at Fort Sam Houston in San Antonio. At Republic Hill, situated on a rolling hillside covered with stately oaks from which downtown Austin is visible, three hundred of the most prominent figures of Texas history lie in peaceful rest. Many were reinterred from various sites across the state and nation over the last century. In contrast to Oakwood, the State Cemetery has been well maintained and has throughout the decades exuded the intended aura of exclusivity and its official status.

Funeral processions pass through the Rose Gate and the Columbarium fashioned from granite blocks with niches for burial urns. A series of reflection ponds separated by waterfalls greets guests emerging from the Visitors Center, inspired by the long barracks at the Alamo. The Hilltop affords an overview of the entire cemetery, while the *Plaza de los Recuerdos,* a memorial consisting of thirty-one massive limestone tablets, commemorates several thousand individuals who have made significant contributions to Texas since its inception. Over all, atop a one hundred-and-fifty-

**Entrance to Texas State Cemetery**

foot tall flagpole waves a state flag the size of a four-car garage, visible all the way from Interstate 35.

Republic Hill is and will always be the heart of the State Cemetery. In peaceful quiet, the panoramic sweep of Texas history rolls by monument after monument. Here lie Stephen F. Austin, General Albert Sidney Johnston, and Governor Edmund J. Davis, with their stories of colonization and revolution, the sacrifice of Texans on every battlefield of the Civil War, and the tumultuous years of Reconstruction. The headstones of "Ma" and "Pa" Ferguson, Alvin J. Wirtz, Allan Shivers, and Ralph Yarborough bring the twentieth century alive. Their monuments evoke remembrances of wars with the Ku Klux Klan, the Lower Colorado River Authority's transformation of Hill Country life, and the life-or-death struggles between liberals and conservatives for control of the Lone Star State's Democratic party. "Three Legged Willie" Williamson, Josiah Wilbarger, Bigfoot Wallace, Edwin Waller, J. Frank Dobie, Walter Prescott Webb, and Barbara Jordan: each has a story and a lesson to impart to those who wish to truly know this place called Texas.

A visit to Oakwood Cemetery is a different but equally rewarding experience. Created by the Republic of Texas in 1836 and deeded to the City of Austin twenty years later, Oakwood witnessed its first burial in 1841 with the interment of a Negro man reportedly killed by Indians. Nearly twenty-seven thousand burials have taken place in the intervening years. Herein lie the famous, the infamous, and the commoners of a century-and-a-half. Unlike modern facilities characterized by sterile uniformity, manicured landscaping, and perpetual care, Oakwood projects the image of startling diversity, irregular maintenance, and the corrosive effects of time—qualities far more appealing to historians and folklorists. It is a sixty-two acre oasis amid the noise and frenetic activity of a Sunbelt boomtown. Every spring oceans of bluebonnets spread across acre after acre of Oakwood. From this sea of blue arise headstones and monuments of every conceivable shape, size, and material. Oaks, cedars, magnolias, pecans, and crepe myrtles provide cooling shade and a home for honeybees, squirrels, and every manner of bird.

**J. Frank and Bertha Dobie's monument at the Texas State Cemetery**

If history is a compilation of what a particular people have done, it permeates every corner of this hidden jewel. At Oakwood you will find it at the graves of Joseph Baker, secretary to the *ayuntamiento* at San Felipe de Austin, Suzana Dickinson, eyewitness to the fall of the Alamo, and Francis Dietrich, survivor of the Goliad Massacre during the revolution against Mexico. The statue memorializing George D. Hancock, a participant in the Somervell Expedition that chased Mexican invaders back to the Rio Grande in 1842, reminds those that stand before it of the fragility of nationhood during the years of the Republic.

Here also lie E. M. Pease, A. J. Hamilton, and Oran M. Roberts. At their graves students of the state's past learn of the conflicting stances these governors took on secession, the Civil War, and Reconstruction. Linked together by the turbulent events of the 1860s and 1870s, how appropriate it seems that they now rest within several hundred yards of one another over a century later. Nearby are the plots of cattle baron George W. Littlefield, and Governor James Stephen Hogg alongside philanthropist daughter Ima. Not to be omitted are those who greatly influenced

**Texas State Cemetery's Monument Hill**

local affairs in Austin, such as city marshal/gunslinger Ben Thompson and Mayor Tom Miller, who led the capital city through the Great Depression, the New Deal, and World War II.

Unlike the State Cemetery with its restrictive admittance regulations, the headstones at Oakwood speak of us all, not just the few and famous. Here may be discovered the rainbow of nationalities, races, cultures, and religious beliefs that make Texas such a land of contrasts. Textbooks describe the floodtide of Anglo-Americans from Dixie who crossed the Sabine in the nineteenth century in search of new opportunities and the fulfillment of Manifest Destiny. Oakwood provides the physical evidence. The Egglestons left Georgia pushing on towards their nation's newest frontier, as did members of the Bugg household, who took great pride in having been among the first families in colonial Virginia. Benjamin Grumbles, a veteran of the War of 1812, and Abner H. Cook, designer and builder of the Governor's Mansion, came from the Carolinas. Kentucky-born George W. Terrel arrived via Tennessee while Virginia-born Mary Murphy came from Alabama.

**A Celtic Cross at Oakwood Cemetery**

Hebrew inscriptions characterize the southwest corner plot of Oakwood bought and maintained by Temple Beth Israel since 1876 for those of the Jewish faith. Here rest for the ages Texans who came from Eastern Europe in the "new immigration" of the latter 1800s. Some were young. Elias Olenick came from Poland only to be murdered on the streets of Austin in 1877. None was longer-lived than Prussian-born Spinze Badt who died in 1888, at the age of 112!

Sadly, Oakwood offers less information about others who contributed mightily to the progress of our state. Hispanic grave markers predating 1900 cannot be found at this municipal facility. This, however, is the norm rather than the exception. According to Professor Terry Jordan in *Texas Graveyards: A Cultural Legacy,* Hispanics in colonial times traditionally buried their dead in unmarked graves. When the use of markers was adopted in the nineteenth century, family members fashioned them almost exclusively from rapidly deteriorating wood as opposed to limestone or granite.

Longer-lasting memorials came only with the advent of concrete in the latter 1800s. Even then, however, biographic information was kept to an absolute minimum—name, date of birth, and date of death. Only two markers in the older section designated for Hispanics include place of birth. This characteristic of older Hispanic memorials means that little about their immigration and mobility patterns can be discerned here.

The situation with black Texans buried at Oakwood is even more disappointing. While a portion of land in the northwest corner of the cemetery was set aside for the use of black Austinites, all graves are unmarked. This includes those of George W. Long, the first person interred at Oakwood, and Jacob Fontaine, a prominent figure in the black community following the Civil War. Arkansas-born Fontaine, for whom the State of Texas erected a historical marker, came to Austin in 1864 as a slave. Following emancipation, he established First Baptist Church, Colored once "Jim Crow" segregation came to the state capital. Information on the others buried before the establishment of a separate cemetery designated for blacks is nonexistent.

Visually, the Anglo and new Hispanic sections of Oakwood could not be more different from one another. Ninety-nine percent of Anglo gravestones were commercially manufactured of limestone, granite, or marble. There are many recurring shapes and styles, but there is a feeling of sameness when contrasted to Hispanic memorials. Remarkably diverse, these are almost exclusively folk markers fashioned by family members or amateur craftsmen. Latin crosses made of wood, pipe, metal, and stone proliferate. Some are plain, others quite elaborate. There are crude markers with hand-scratched inscriptions in Spanish, but also those with glass marbles or tiny shells pressed into still-wet concrete. Visitors will find examples of *relicaritos,* miniature shrines with religious icons, as well as *nichos,* recessed niches often containing a photograph of the deceased. Monuments created by overlaying a stone base with either simple or intricate patterns of ceramic tiles are among the most colorful. Visit this area of Oakwood at the beginning of November and you will find a number of gravesites where family members have left handcrafted *coronas* (paper wreaths) or *pan muerto* as part of Dia de los Muertos (Day of the Dead, or All Souls' Day).

Symbols and images traditionally found in Southern cemeteries, many of which date back to ancient Mediterranean cultures, have made their way to Oakwood as well. The rose, emblematic of the Great Mother Earth, fertility, and the assurance of rebirth into the afterlife, and the dove, representative of the Holy Spirit, are without question the most numerous. Scrolls are traditionally used to portray the "book of life," while an upright cypress tree conveys the message of "hope." Sculpted fingers point skyward, so that strangers might know where the souls of the departed have traveled, and clasped hands symbolize the deceased's welcome to heaven. The reclining lamb, conveying infant mortality, assures bereaved parents that the Shepherd watches over all, young and old alike. Sheared columns and uprooted trees signify lives ended prematurely, while shattered urns give visual testimony to "abundant life" or an aged individual. The hourglass, most appropriately, reminds one and all that our time on earth is finite.

Each new tour of the Oakwood facility by students results in the discovery of tombstone symbols heretofore overlooked. While the ubiquitous Woodmen of the World tree stump markers are impossible to miss, locating a headstone with a sculpted passion flower, representing Christ's suffering, is a genuine feat. Equally challenging to find are usages of the chalice (the sacraments), poppy (eternal rest), horn (resurrection), and skull and crossbones (death). Over the years, however, students have been most drawn to and intrigued by one particular marker—a large carved monument featuring the "eye of God" inside a sun-drenched triangle. Below are three links of chain containing the letters "F," "L," and "T." These, I explain, are symbols often found on the monuments of members of two fraternal organizations, the Masons and the Odd Fellows. Three chain links signify the divine trinity and the letters stand for "friendship," "love," and "truth." The eye reminds gravesite visitors of God's eternal presence.

Cemeteries, as Professor Jordan argued so persuasively in his seminal work, are for us the living as much if not more than those who have passed over to what lies beyond. They serve at one level as resting places for the physical remains of the departed but, just as certainly, they are sources of exploration, contemplation, appreciation, and inspiration. How better to honor their memories than to discover, as best we can, the way they lived, the contributions they made, and what they believed, practiced, and endured? Whether it be at these two unique Austin cemeteries or any other of the tens of thousands from one end of the state to the other, drop in for a visit and be at one with the past at rest and the immutable cycle of life. There is much to be learned and appreciated.

**A stubborn Spanish Dagger plant at the grave of the author's mother**

## EDEN CEMETERY

by Margaret A. Cox

I grew up with a healthy respect for graveyards. My grandmother sold tombstones during the 1940s, and I have memories of visiting graveyards with her as a young child. She often took rubbings of monument designs to get ideas for her customers. When I first learned to read, I pronounced the word: "gravy-yard." This was corrected very shortly. I remember my grandmother walking past graves, sighing and saying, "I love to walk among the bones of my ancestors."

One grave in the Eden, Texas, cemetery has no headstone. The entire length and width of the grave is covered in a block of cement, about three feet high. I asked my grandmother about this grave, which looked like none of the others in the entire cemetery. She said she thought the old judge had covered his wife so she couldn't come out and haunt him later on. He said she had been a mean old thing in life, and he didn't want to take any chances.

The cemetery in Eden was located near my grandmother's home. We children could sit on the front porch and watch the funeral processions pass by. Some cousins warned us not to count the cars following the hearse, or we would be the next person to die. I always tried to avert my eyes when funerals were in progress after that.

Since my mother was buried in 1986 at Eden Cemetery, a Spanish dagger bush has repeatedly grown over her grave. It has been dug up several times, but always grows back, as though my mother and her "green thumb" wish it to be there. Perhaps she wants the bush to hide her name on her headstone.

A friend told me of a funeral where something quite unexpected occurred. She said her mother passed away and was laid out in an open coffin in the viewing room. According to custom, friends and relatives passed by for a final viewing of the departed before the service. My friend told me her mother had been born in the Old South and was partly reared by a black nurse. This old lady, I picture to resemble Scarlett O'Hara's Mammy from Gone with the Wind, was the last person to pass by the coffin. As she began weeping and wailing, her poor heart wore out from the stress, and she keeled over and died right there beside the coffin.

This caused a flurry of activity. It was time to move the coffin into the sanctuary for the service. The mourners were waiting in their pews. The organ music was soaring. The large, dead lady on the floor couldn't be moved until a medical person was summoned to declare her dead, so all the undertaker could do was to cover her gently and leave her where she had fallen in the viewing room. I can imagine the amazement of all the folks at the funeral on that day as the news was whispered from pew to pew.

Edward Hall family, 1895, near Fischers Store, Comal County, Texas. The wiggly child on her father's knee grew up to be the author's grandmother, Annie Hall Murray, Eden tombstone saleslady.

Sandra West is laid to rest in her Ferrari sports car. *San Antonio Express-News Collection, UTSA's Institute of Texan Cultures, #E-0041-179-16a, Courtesy of the Hearst Corporation*

# BURIED IN TEXAS: ANY AND EVERY WHICH WAY

by Henry Wolff, Jr.

Sandra Ilene West was accustomed to having her way. She took that stubbornness to the grave with her in one of the more unusual burials ever in Texas, not to mention it being the most spectacular. The millionairess widow of ranch and oil heir Ike West, Jr. of Vanderbilt was buried on May 19, 1977, in San Antonio, wearing a favorite silver-colored lace nightgown and seated as she instructed in her expensive, powder-blue 1964 Italian Ferrari sports car. The seat was slanted comfortably, also according to her wishes.

Visiting the grave, as I did on a hot, dry, early August day in 1996, one finds it difficult to see just where she—and the car—is buried, there being only a slight rise in the surface near a modest flat tombstone with just her name inscribed, and the years of her birth and death: "Sandra West, 1939–1977." More striking are the huge tombstones for some of the old stalwarts of the West family, including the first-generation Texas brothers Ike, Sol, and George, all of whom left their mark on the history of Texas ranching.

Sandra Ilene was buried next to her husband, Ike West, Jr. (1934–1968), who had died in a motel room on the Las Vegas strip after having been discharged from a Los Angeles hospital where he had undergone a crash program of weight reduction. His tombstone is equally nondescript. A coroner's inquest determined that Mrs. West had died of an accidental overdose of drugs on March 10, 1977, in her Beverly Hills, California, home after a period of "highly bizarre behavior." She was said to have been known to close friends as a practical joker. Her body was temporarily entombed in Texas for two months until a ruling was handed down by the Los Angeles Superior Court that her request in a five-year-old handwritten will was "unusual, but not illegal." The court did order the Ferrari to be placed in a six-by-eight-by-seventeen-foot box to preserve dignity. A crane was used to lift the box from a flatbed truck before a crowd of newsmen and several hundred curious onlookers who had gathered at the Alamo Masonic Cemetery. Concrete was then poured around and over the box in what mortuary spokesman Porter Loring termed the most unusual funeral that he had ever handled.

While there have been many unusual burials in Texas, the interment of Sandra Ilene West was definitely like no other, and well documented, unlike some odd burials of earlier times. One of the state's earliest settlers, a man who had his squatter's claim to Texas soil legalized when he was accepted by Stephen F. Austin to become one of the Old Three Hundred, James Briton (Brit) Bailey was a character of his time who supposedly ended up in his final resting place in a standing position. According to legend, he had requested that his body be buried standing up so that no man could look down on him. He was to be facing west since that was the direction that he always aimed, presumably when he came to Texas from North Carolina. He asked that his rifle be placed by his side since he didn't know what man he might meet on the other side. Known as a fighter who was fond of his whiskey, Bailey asked also that his jug be filled to the brim and placed at his feet. When he died of natural causes about 1833 and was buried on Bailey's Prairie near Brazoria, it is said that his wife carried out his requests one by one until she came to the jug. Some versions of the story say the preacher showed up about that time, others that she felt that it just wasn't a proper way to go to the hereafter. At any rate, Old Brit didn't get buried with his whiskey, and ever since there have been stories about his ghost coming out to search the prairie for the jug, especially on cold wintry nights.

In *Backwoods to Border*, the Texas Folklore Society publication of 1943, Gloria Swanson told of her mother having seen Bailey's light, which appeared as a ball of fire that would rise out of the ground and wander over the country. "The men would saddle their horses and follow it," she said. "Sometimes they would ride all night long, and usually near daylight they would see it return to the spot from which it had risen and sink into the ground." Swanson said some believed it was the light of Bailey's gun firing as he goes hunting at night. Others thought it was from a lantern that he carries to guide himself through the swamps of the coastal prairie.

**A Texas State Historical Marker in Brazoria County marks the Brit Bailey Plantation where the Irishman was buried standing up, facing west, gun at his side**

With burials or anything else that involves word-of-mouth accounts that have been passed from generation to generation, it is sometimes difficult to determine just how much of a story should be considered to be true. I had heard of a somewhat eccentric DeWitt County ranchman who had also supposedly been buried standing up near Cheapside, but I was never able to confirm that he was buried in any other than the "traditional" way.

Another who entertained the possibility of being buried standing up was the pioneer Texas physician and naturalist Gideon Lincecum, who ended up being buried with his beloved black English violin in the Mount Zion Cemetery at Long Point in

Washington County, the violin having been a gift from an employer sixty-three years before and on which Lincecum played the tune "Killiecrankie" every Christmas dawn until his death on November 24, 1874. His remains were removed to the State Cemetery in Austin during the Texas Centennial Celebration in 1936, along with other Texas notables, and that is where he now rests, presumably with the old violin.

The thought of being buried standing up came to him when he was living among a colony of ex-Confederates in Tuxpan, Mexico, where he was injured in a cart accident in 1871 while loading pickets to repair a hog fence. In preparing for death, he concocted an idea for "a cheap funeral" that would have had him being placed in a river standing up near a substantial sandstone cliff to serve as his tombstone. "Near the center of the cliff, out of reach of the depredator, will be seen, when you come here, Grandpa's name, date of his birth and demise cut in rock," he said in a letter to a grandson, Frank Lincecum Doran, also known as "Bully." "Immediately under this inscription, and at the bottom of the deep river," Lincecum continued, "if you take the trouble to go down there, you will find the remains of your Grandpa, fastened to a heavy piece of iron, being lashed to the feet, the form standing erect."

He had suffered severe shock and was in great pain when he wrote the letter, and when his youngest daughter, Sallie, learned what he had written, she protested. "You object to the place I have selected for my final resting place," he replied. "That seems strange to me for I was of the opinion that it was one of the brightest thoughts that my mental apparatus had ever generated. Name and age and place of nativity emblazoned on the face of a rock 60 feet high, 200 yards long and overhanging the beautiful Tuxpan. There, out of the way of the rushing tramp of villainous humanity the old carcass, the vehicle that transported the vital spark by a tortuous route from Georgia to the Tuxpan; and the mind, the mental attribute of the living principle which made itself known to external nature, can go though the process of decomposition undisturbed. Why, the idea is not only chaste and beautiful, but it really approximates the sublime." Lincecum recovered and returned to Texas where his being buried with his violin also approximates the sublime, although not in a way quite as unusual as he had envisioned in Mexico.

While to some of us being buried standing up would seem a tiring way to face eternity, Ramey A. Smith had a more relaxing idea when he asked to be buried at Shirley, in Hopkins County, beneath a tree and facing the road. It has since been said the local attorney wanted to be buried on his side so he could watch the cars go by. "I think that was added as a joke," says Faye Gilley of Sulphur Springs. Her father's first cousin, Smith was buried after his death on August 18, 1949, facing north because of his request to be beneath the tree, which has since died or been cut down, leaving him in a rather unusual position with all the other burials facing east. But, he is in a position to see the road.

Not all directional burials are by choice, like when Simp Dixon, a survivor of the Peacock-Lee Feud in North Texas and like-minded cousin of the outlaw John Wesley Hardin, was shot and buried in February 1870 by a squad of United States soldiers in Limestone County. In his book, *John Wesley Hardin, Dark Angel of Texas,* western historian Leon Metz notes that Dixon was buried in the Fort Parker Memorial Cemetery near Mexia "oblique to the others because he was 'crossways with the world.'"

Other unusual burials have more to do with what was buried with the deceased, among the oddest stories being one that has long been told around Erath and Palo Pinto counties about Earl Allen and his telephone. A prominent ranchman who died on March 13, 1924, Allen is buried in a Davidson Cemetery mausoleum at the old coal mining town of Thurber, supposedly with phone in hand. He had never married and had a reputation for drinking, according to John Paul Black of Baird, a distant cousin. Allen's father, William Marion Allen, was a great uncle of Black's and had come from Missouri to Texas by covered wagon with a load of apples in 1857. He went into ranching and was on the board of the Johnson Coal Co.

Thurber resulted from the coal camp that grew up around the mine and is said to have once had a horseshoe-shaped bar that was the largest in any saloon between Fort Worth and El Paso. It isn't known whether the hard drinking reputation of the town had an influence on young Allen, who was born around 1889, but Black notes that the man did gain a reputation for drinking and frequently visited friends in Thurber who kept homemade "grappe" wine.

"He loved the wine," Black says, "but when he drank it he would sometimes pass out for a day or two." Legend has it that he feared being buried underground or alive, and stated in his will that he was to be buried in a mausoleum with a telephone in his hand. "If after three days he hadn't called for them to come get him," Black notes, "he could be considered legally dead and they could disconnect the phone." Whether it actually happened, or not, Black says he can't say for sure. "I never talked to a telephone man who put it in," he says, "or one who took it out." Some say it was just a joke among Allen and his friends. "He is probably chuckling inside that vault today," Black suggests, pointing out that it was quite an accomplishment even if it was just a joke, since folks around Thurber and thereabouts are still telling the story.

Many people are buried with something they consider special, or something of significance that someone decides to put in the casket, like when I buried my father with his western hat since it represented one of the things that he liked to do best while he was on this earth. He was an old-time cow trader and I figured that he would be looking for some trading pens, an auction barn, or a little grass pasture in the hereafter.

Mary Ann Novak of Shiner placed a double-five domino in her father's hand, that being "his favorite rock." Willie J. Kutac died at the age of eighty on July 21, 1988, after collapsing while preparing to drink a glass of tea at the Shiner Senior Citizens Center where they usually play dominoes after dinner. That is what he was thinking about when he said his last words: "Who is going to be my partner today?" Mrs. Novak said her father had told her several months before that if something should happen to be sure and put a double five in his hand.

Perhaps a Stetson hat or a favorite domino is not as unusual as Brit Bailey's rifle and a missing whiskey jug, Lincecum's black violin, or Earl M. Allen's telephone, but each is equally significant in its own way. In an August 14, 1996, article in the *Houston Chronicle's* "Texas" magazine on burial habits in the state, Carol Rust mentioned Major Joseph Dark of Chambers County and his request to have his trusty shotgun placed in the casket beside him, a gun he had successfully used in 1861 to defend his home and which he also carried to war. When his grave had to be moved from a bluff being eroded by the Trinity River, the metal parts of the gun were found among his bones.

Among the more unusual objects to be buried with someone in Texas is a necklace of twenty-four slugs, worn to the grave by Dr. Sophie Herzog when she was buried at Brazoria in 1925. As a widowed mother of fourteen, she had established a medical practice there in 1895, and worked as a surgeon for the St. Louis, Brownsville and Mexico Railroad. Dr. Herzog, who would sometimes travel by hand car, is said to have prided herself on her ability to extract bullets, which she collected and had Percy Brown Jewelers in Houston fashion into a necklace with gold links between the slugs. "This, she told people," according to James A. Creighton in *A Narrative History of Brazoria County,* "brought her good luck."

While some have gone to the grave with something unusual, some have gone with something less than usual. Storyteller Richard Young told Carol Rust of the *Houston Chronicle* a tale that he had heard in Waco around 1950, of a woman who was too poor to afford a decent burial for her husband, so she decided to sell his clothes to raise money; when she learned the casket would be open only from the waist up, she sold his last pair of pants. "After he was buried, a ghost began to appear to his wife," Young said. "It was her husband, wanting his pants."

A burial can also be unusual because of what a person is put away in, like a circus worker that Louis Staggs of Kenedy tells about. The worker had been killed by the rogue elephant Black Diamond when the circus played the oilfield boom town of Mirando City in southeastern Webb County in 1925, and he was buried "rolled in canvas." "I was ten years old," Staggs recalls. "He was buried in a little cemetery that had great big rocks at the gate." Staggs says his parents had built the first hotel in the town.

Black Diamond, incidentally, was executed by a firing squad at Kenedy on October 16, 1929, when the Al G. Barnes Circus had arrived there after the bull elephant killed a woman spectator at a circus parade in Corsicana. He is said to have previously killed at least three other people, two of them circus workers. His head is in storage at the Houston Museum of Natural Science, and one of his feet is a footstool at the old Helena Courthouse Museum in Karnes County. The bulk of the elephant was evidently left to the buzzards rather than being buried, which I believe would have been the biggest burial in Texas since he is said to have been second in size only to P. T. Barnum's famous "Jumbo." Margaret Schulte of San Antonio, who owns the Black Diamond Ranch at Kenedy where the elephant was executed, says her father, Martin Schaefer, named the ranch after the elephant and for years had some of Black Diamond's bones in his barn.

There is an elephant supposedly buried at Pheasant Switch between Blessing and Palacios in Matagorda County, where it died while a circus was traveling through by train. Depending on its size, this could be the biggest burial in Texas. There are many unusual animal burials throughout the state, but that is an entirely different subject.

One unusual grave that took me some time to research after I learned about it from Robert Almand, who does tombstone rubbings and had seen it somewhere in LaSalle County, was that of Sam Tyre's arm, thusly noted on the stone, "The Arm of Sam B. Tyre." It was the first I had heard of a single body part being buried, though I have since heard of others. I learned from Odelle Hamilton of Gonzales that Tyre, a distant relation, had come to Texas by wagon train from Arkansas, while a descendant from Port Lavaca, Joe D. Lawhn, says Tyre lost his left arm below the shoulder at the age of twelve while leading some horses. "One got scared and ran away," he says, "dragging him some length and pulling the flesh off the arm above the elbow." A Mexican doctor laid him out on the kitchen table, chloroformed him, and sawed off the arm. However, Tyre could still rope and ride with the best of them throughout his life, according to Lawhn. The arm is buried in the Millett Cemetery some sixteen miles north of Cotulla. Hamilton says the stone is not the original, and Almand remembered the inscription as "Here Lies Sam Tyre's Arm."

There is a skull from the Battle of Vinegar Hill, way back in 1798 in County Wexford, Ireland, that is buried in the McGuill Cemetery at Blanconia in eastern Bee County. Brought over by a relative of Pat McGuill, a descendant of the Irishman from Wexford who settled in Refugio County in the early 1830s, McGuill had the ancient remains in a trunk in his attic when he was reminded of it during the 200th anniversary celebration of the founding of Mission Nuestra Senora del Refugio in 1995. A marker on the grave includes an inscription to the unknown Irish soldier and a sketch of a "pikehead weapon."

I once heard of a small cemetery, possibly somewhere in East Texas, where Republicans are buried on one side of the road and Democrats on the other, but so far have found nothing to confirm it. I also read somewhere that Charles Goodnight was buried in a tin coffin and am still searching for more about it. In his biography of the famous Texas cattleman, J. Evetts Haley describes it as being a "massive casket." He wrote that Goodnight had died "at saddling up time" on the morning of December 12, 1929.

There is a long forgotten reference that I recall reading about James Kerr, the pioneer surveyor general of the Green DeWitt Colony and Stephen F. Austin colonist, having been buried in a hollowed-out log after his death at his home in Jackson County on Christmas day in 1850. Neither have I been able to confirm the burial of a woman's ashes in a tapestry sewing bag, supposedly in the old Hawley Cemetery near Blessing on the Texas coast where yet another legendary Texas cattleman, old Shanghai Pierce, is buried beneath the life-sized statue that he had sculpted in his own likeness.

Being buried in a significant way is not necessarily unusual, although when news stories first began appearing in 1995 about the Aggie caskets being manufactured by Oak Grove International, a Michigan company, it was not yet considered as being ordinary. Now that a number of Aggies have been buried in the seven-foot-long maroon fiberglass caskets with the familiar Texas A&M University seal on the outside and logo sewn into the white satin headliner, it is no longer all that unusual. One of the first to be buried in an Aggie casket was the longtime Nacogdoches veterinarian, Dr. Francis Joseph Schott, a 1937 graduate of Texas A&M University who died Oct. 26, 1995.

Sometimes burial wishes get a bit more complicated, like when George W. Brackenridge of San Antonio, before his death on December 28, 1920, had a four-foot-high stone fence, a foot-and-a-half thick and 150 feet square, erected around the family cemetery on the old home place in Jackson County, now a part of Brackenridge Park at Lake Texana. "If I had built a gate," he is quoted as having said, "someone would use it as a cow pen, and I don't want cattle walking over the graves." When he died, stairs had to be built so the bereaved could enter the cemetery and, I would assume, for his casket to be carried over the fence. There has never been any care given to the inside of the cemetery, a family wish as well, since they were lovers of nature and disliked seeing the normal course of growth disturbed. The Lavaca-Navidad River Authority continues to abide by their wishes.

**Visitors to Brackenridge Cemetery at Lake Texana in Jackson County look over a four-foot stone wall to see the graves, since there are no gates**

Any discourse on unusual Texas burials would not be complete without mentioning some of the more mysterious. I was at the city cemetery in the Lee County seat of Giddings in late August 1992, when they tried to dig up the old outlaw Bill Longley, to find either his bones or a casket filled with rocks. At the time, they found neither, but before they were through the cemetery looked like a huge gopher had been at work. At the urging of Ted Wax of Gonzales, Louisiana, a team of forensic, anthropological, and archaeological experts dug up a number of graves in an effort to determine if the Texas outlaw had actually been buried in the cemetery. There has long been a story that his hanging on October 11, 1878, had been faked, with his casket having been filled with rocks to make the burial look legitimate. Wax thinks Longley could have escaped and was his grandfather, John Calhoun Brown, who had lived a long and

**Archaeologists search a grave in the Giddings Cemetery where remains of the infamous Texas outlaw Bill Longley were recovered in July 1998. Longley was hanged in 1878, and the exact site of his burial had been a mystery for many years**

useful life in Louisiana. The problem is that nobody knew the exact location of where Longley was buried—or the box of rocks.

The search for Longley's grave would continue, and three years after the removal of remains from an unmarked grave in the Giddings Cemetery in July of 1998, forensic anthropologist Dr. Douglas Owsley of the Smithsonian Institution and Dr. Terry Melton of Mitotyping Technologies in State College, Pennsylvania, announced that DNA evidence from the grave matched that of a granddaughter of Longley's sister. The casket had also contained a religious medal and remains of a celluloid flower that Longley was known to have had with him when hanged. No rocks were found.

Then there is the man from space who some believe to have been buried at Aurora, in southeastern Wise County, after a cigar-shaped spaceship crashed into a windmill in April of 1897. While there is evidence it was a hoax perpetuated by a local cotton buyer who gave the story to the *Dallas Morning News,* in his book *Texas: Amazing But True,* historian Jack Maguire also mentions that there was a marked grave for the spaceman in the community cemetery for many years. The stone, which has since disappeared, had the Greek letter Delta carved on it with some circles inside. An investigation at Aurora in 1973 did locate some fragments that supposedly could not be identified as any known metal. Maguire further mentions that nothing has grown since in a formerly fertile garden where the spacecraft is said to have nosed into the ground.

From the eerie, let us return to the sublime. After the death on November 16, 1995, of seventy-year-old playwright Charles Gordone, who was awarded a Pulitzer Prize in 1970 for his play *No Place To Be Somebody,* and who had been a distinguished lecturer at Texas A&M University for eight years, his ashes were spread at sunset in a prairie funeral. I was told by his wife, Susan Kouÿomjian, that "the wind stopped and the birds stopped singing." She had carried his ashes back to the Canadian River and the Spring Creek Ranch near Amarillo where Gordone had done some work on a play he never got to finish, titled "Ghost Riders."

The cowboy poet and singer Buck Ramsey, in an essay about the Elko Cowboy Poetry Gathering for the National Endowment for the Arts in 1996, described how Gordone's friends had wrapped his ashes in a black bandanna and gathered around on a grassy mound overlooking a small valley. "A few people spoke briefly," he wrote, "a few said a poem, sang a song or played a guitar or fiddle while six jolly cowboys rested horseback in a row by the bulged bandanna, fastened by a hackamore knot, resting in the grass." The ranch foreman and Gordone's friend Rooster Morris then "dismounted, cradled the bandanna in an arm, remounted and rode slowly down the grassy slope of the prairie rain wash. His horse shied and bucked for a brief moment. Rooster opened the bandanna, then eased into a dignified gallop as he scattered the ashes to the wind." It was a burial unusual only in that it wasn't the way that we usually think of someone being buried in Texas. That usually being six feet under in the "traditional" way.

Jim Ainsworth

# THERE'S SOMETHING ABOUT OLD COUNTRY GRAVEYARDS

**by Jim H. Ainsworth**

Memorial Day. Homecoming. Decoration Day. Or my personal favorite—All Day Singing and Dinner on the Ground. All the same? Not exactly, but close. Their common thread? They bring people to cemeteries.

I know that Memorial Day at Mt. Zion is not exactly the same as the national Memorial Day, but I explored the similarities. In 1966, Lyndon Johnson declared Waterloo, New York, as the place of origin for Memorial Day. That community first decorated graves of Civil War Veterans in 1865. Being from the South, Johnson should have known better. Southerners were doing it long before that.

In the old days, we would sing (all day)—and, of course, we would have dinner on the ground. When I was a boy, I always wondered if folks hadn't meant to say dinner on the *grounds,* because we mostly ate off of tables, under a tabernacle, on the grounds of the church or cemetery. Only a few threw down old quilts and actually ate on the ground, but my folks said that was more common in the really-old days.

After dinner on the ground came the hard part. I marveled as men *wearing ties* mowed grass with real push mowers (not walk-behinds, but push). They righted stones, added sand to graves, repaired (even painted) fences, sweating through their Sunday best. My daddy sometimes wore a tie with his overalls—never a suit coat, because he didn't own one. Many men did, and they wore those suit coats to keep people from seeing them sweat. It didn't work. Telltale signs would soon appear under their arms and down their backs—even through those coats. Women tried to stay fresh-looking in stockings, dresses, hats, and bonnets as they hauled food and drinks, pulled weeds, and placed flowers on graves.

For me, twilight was the best part. Things had cooled down. The singing was better, somehow, and even cold chicken tasted good washed down with my mama's iced tea. Sometimes, there was homemade ice cream or watermelons. What was the best part? In public, people would say it was the prayer or the church services, or a memorable sermon. But in private, dinner on the ground usually won that contest. For some, it was the music.

Folks went home at dark leaving the cemetery looking better than at any other time of the year. They went home full—full of wonderful southern cooking, of course, but also full of the sounds of music, prayer, church, and memories. Full of the spirit of having done something good and worthwhile.

In later years, the *ground* did give way to tables and tabernacles and air-conditioned fellowship halls. Singing moved inside or was just omitted. Decorating graves? It's still done, of course, but rarely on Decoration Day. Mowing and pulling weeds is contracted out. (Thank goodness.) In the old days, like today, weeds grew back, real flowers wilted and died, plastic ones faded and curled up in the Texas heat. But what stayed behind? What's left when everybody goes home? *Why do we do it?*

Why? Most would give the obvious answer: to honor the loved ones who have passed before us (and to provide a final resting place for ourselves). But with our spoiled selves today, we complain about the heat. We long for our recliners and remotes—especially for central air. Take-out has become food we bring home to eat in front of our televisions, not food we cook to take someplace else.

So, if we are decorating only a little, if we're not mowing or pulling weeds, if the heat is sometimes oppressive, if cooking is a chore rather than a delight . . . why do we continue? Yes, I know that the business of managing, maintaining, and financing of the final resting place for our loved ones and ourselves must be done. Some of us gather annually to report about last year and make important decisions about next year. I recognize and appreciate the importance of all that, those awesome responsibilities, and the volunteers who carry them out year after year. Those volunteers know why they do it. But what about the rest of us?

Several years ago, I heard a poem read at a funeral and fell in love with it. Most of you have probably heard "Do Not Stand." It was thought to be Indian in origin, because so many Native Americans used it. Actually, it was written by Mary Frye of Baltimore in 1932—about her mother. She wrote it on the back of a grocery sack (for you kids, grocery sacks used to be brown paper bags). John Wayne read the poem at director Howard Hawkes' funeral.

> Do not stand at my grave and weep
> I am not there. I do not sleep.
> I am a thousand winds that blow,
> I am the diamond glints on snow,
> I am the sunlight on ripened grain,
> I am the gentle autumn rain.
> When you awaken in the morning's hush,
> I am the swift uplifting rush
> Of quiet birds in circled flight.
> I am the soft stars that shine at night.
> So do not stand at my grave and cry,
> I am not there. I did not die.

I found those verses so comforting. Still do. It's comforting to think that our loved ones are not there. But if they are *not there,* why do we continue to come—to decorate, to maintain?

If you asked members of our group or any of hundreds gathered across the nation in mostly rural areas why we continue to do this—to have memorial days, decoration days—you would get lots of answers. Many would be unable to clearly articulate the reasons why. It's just something they feel, perhaps just an obligation to do the right thing. I think it's more than that. I grew up in the Klondike community. Once in an old Klondike graveyard, my grandfather said it like this: *"There's just something about an old country graveyard."*

What is that something? Especially if, as "Do Not Stand" proclaims, *they are not here.* That poem is correct, because Mary Frye knew that her mother was not in that cold, often wet, and sometimes cracked ground. She had gone to Heaven. Yet, my grandfather, without waxing poetic, said something profound that seems to contradict that. Maybe it was because Mary's mother was buried in Baltimore and my grandfather was talking about an old cemetery in Klondike where he had buried his mother and several of his children. Memorial days are mostly rural traditions now. Maybe there is just something about *rural cemeteries,* but I think it applies to all of them.

I read my grandchildren a book titled *Last Innocent Summer* by Zinita Fowler. The novel revolves around the death of two little girls in Commerce almost seventy years ago. My grandchildren were enthralled, keeping the novel in their memories as we read it in parts over several months and several visits. When we finished, they wanted to find the graves of those two little girls—and we did—in *an old country graveyard.* When we visited, as much as children can, they calmed for a few minutes. They seemed to understand better—so much better that they wanted to read that novel again. As they stood at the children's graves, I thought about what my Papa Lee had said. There's something about an old country graveyard.

As part of the research for writing my first novel, I read northeast Texas novels such as William Humphrey's *The Ordways* and *Home from the Hill.* Many pivotal scenes in those books take place in old country graveyards. There are several scenes in my books in country graveyards. Not morbid scenes, but very important ones.

When I am writing a novel and need inspiration, when I am trying to get my children or grandchildren to understand and appreciate their heritage, when I am experiencing sad or hard times, or when I just want to reflect and meditate, I find that *something* my grandfather spoke of—at an old country graveyard, standing at the graves of my parents, grandparents, and two brothers.

I, like you, now understand what my grandfather meant when he said there's something about old country graveyards. Yes, it is comforting to think that they are not here, but I find it comforting to think that they are. I like to think that they visit only when we do; they leave when we leave, return when we come again. It's our meeting place, our place to reconnect and remember. It's not the *only* place where we hear their voices or feel their presence, but it's the *always* place—because they are always there.

As we visit—
In the wind, we hear their whispers
About the mistakes they made and how we can avoid them.
In the sun, we feel the warm touch of their embrace.
In the rain, we feel cleansed and calmed.
In the snow, we see the brightness of their smiles.
In the sounds of nature, the chirp of a cricket, the buzz of a locust,
The song of a bird, we hear the healing stories of our childhood.
In the birds that fly around old country graveyards,
We see our loved ones' freedom,
And ourselves flying away.

There's something about old country graveyards. And that is why we do it.

A truck loaded with boxes used to relocate remains

# WHO IS DIGGING ON MY GRAVE? THE CORPS OF ENGINEERS?

## (CEMETERY REMOVAL: FACT AND FICTION)

by Charles B. Martin

The opening of a new man-made lake is a wonderful occasion, especially for fishermen, water sports enthusiasts, city water managers, and homeowners who are lucky enough to own land somewhere along the shore. Not so happy are reluctant farmers who don't want to give up their rich bottom land, and "stream" fishermen and canoeists who hate to see another virgin stream or river lost forever. Nevertheless, once the decision is made to build a dam and flood an area, there is no going back to what life was like before the Corps of Engineers moved in. The whole process is a long one, particularly if the federal government is involved. Even so, the process is carried out in a certain order with public hearings, land purchase and condemnation, clearing of trees and brush, removal of buildings, re-routing of roads, and building of the dam, spillways, and recreational areas.

One aspect of the whole process that many people do not often think about is the number of areas to be flooded by the proposed lake. In our society, while we often do not show much respect for the living, we at least still are pretty good about honoring the dead. Thus, the Corps of Engineers will contract with a private agency to remove all the bodies from the graves of affected cemeteries and re-bury them on higher ground at another site. This process is somewhat involved and not at all easy, as was the case in the building of Ray Roberts Lake northeast of Denton, Texas, between 1985 and 1991, when the lake was officially dedicated.

For cemetery relocation two Corps of Engineers offices, the Fort Worth District office and the Southwest Division office in Dallas, determined what needed to be done. A contractor was hired to clean out each cemetery. A surveyor made up drawings from on-the-spot surveys and cemetery association records. The

Corps then estimated how much it would cost and advertised the contract. Interested parties submitted sealed bids by a given date, and the contract was awarded to the lowest bidder. In the case of the Ray Roberts Lake, the lowest bidder bid $163,000 to remove the more than 600 graves from the area to be flooded.

According to the contract for grave relocation, all remains had to be removed in a dignified manner. No mechanical equipment was to be used to open a grave; thus, all graves were dug up with shovels. The men doing the digging were not permitted to work shirtless or in shorts no matter how hot the weather. The first group employed by the Corps quit after two weeks because they feared that some of their own family members would die if they disturbed the graves. A plastic tarp was supposed to be hung over each grave as it was being dug up, but with so many trees, shrubs, and tombstones, this practice was not always followed. All remains, whether bone fragments, coffin fragments, or any items buried with the deceased, were placed in small plywood boxes about three feet long and one-and-a-half feet wide. The human remains and other items in a grave were to be reburied the day they were exhumed or stored overnight in a licensed mortuary.

**Reason Jones' tombstone in the old Jones Cemetery**

In Jones Cemetery, the oldest cemetery, where the last burial was held in 1952, very little remained in any grave. In fact, the cemetery itself had been completely neglected. The fence was down and cattle had grazed among the tombstones, knocking them over and breaking them, and trees, brush, and weeds had completely overrun the cemetery. Many graves contained only bits of rusty coffin nails or handles, fragments of bones, and even glass fragments, indicating that the coffin had a glass sealer lid. Infants' graves often had nothing except perhaps a rusty clasp, which had evidently been pinned at the neck of the baby's gown. In one infant's grave, only a piece of shoe leather with metal grommets for shoe laces was found. From the more recent burials, those in the 1940s and early '50s, a few pieces of metal coffins were unearthed along with bones and clothing fragments.

The most prominent tombstone had the name of Reason Jones (born October 10, 1813, died March 4, 1895). Mr. Jones was buried between his two wives, by whom he sired eleven children each. One wife was buried with a fully loaded Colt revolver, the kind first manufactured between 1889 and 1894. The rusty gun and bullets were placed in the plywood box to be buried at the new site. No workman or observer was permitted to remove anything from a grave, no matter what the condition.

The next of kin was required to sign a permit for the relocation of a grave, assuming the next of kin could be found. If they could be located, they were invited to view the removal. In the case of Jones Cemetery, where so many graves could not be identified and so many others were long forgotten by the next of kin, very few people came. One elderly woman came to the disinterment of her great aunt whom she said had been buried with her rings. Sure enough the rings were found among the few remains but, of course, they had to be reburied in the new grave. Another elderly man, appropriately named Jones, came to witness a removal and provided Mr. Jerry Spraggens, the Corps representative, with all kinds of interesting information about various people buried in the cemetery.

**Reason Jones' tombstone after the grave was relocated**

Workers were usually required to dig down at least six feet in the earth to be sure to recover whatever remains might be left of the deceased. In Jones cemetery where the soil was basically clay, most graves weren't so deep, many only three to five feet deep. The workers could tell that they had reached the bottom when the soil suddenly became much harder. Since most people in earlier times were buried in wooden coffins, there was nothing to be found in the bottom of the grave—even the last bone fragments had "returned to dust." Usually, there was a thin layer of darker soil which contained what was left of the body and the coffin. The worker was then required to scrape one cubic foot of soil from the bottom of the grave and place it in the plywood box to be buried in the new cemetery.

Grave markers in the last century, and even in this one, were often made of wood, which is subject to decay just like the coffins. Thus, many of the old cemeteries to be flooded by the new lake contained numerous unmarked graves. Most of the graves could be identified by tombstones or by plots on cemetery maps. In some cases, the contractor suspected that there might be an unmarked

A trailer used to move headstones

grave within the cemetery and checked the earth to be sure. In Jones Cemetery the contractor noticed a huge bed of iris at the south end of the cemetery. Upon exploration, he found a couple of rough stones, obviously meant to be headstones. Sure enough, there were two graves at that site.

To be completely sure that all graves had been located, the contractor cut several trenches about two feet deep with a back hoe. If he found soft places in the walls of the trench, he could be relatively sure that these were actual graves. At least eighty graves in Jones Cemetery were discovered in this way. These remains, usually a cubic foot of earth, and those from other graves whose residents were unknown, were moved to the new Jones-Bloomfield Cemetery provided by the Corps of Engineers. Before they were covered up, a representative from the Corps of Engineers had to check to be sure that the number on the box corresponded to the number of the grave. Then, if a family member ever comes along and looks at the Jones Cemetery map and says "My relative is buried there," he can be shown exactly where the relative is buried in the new Jones-Bloomfield Cemetery. The contractor in charge of relocating the graves had to provide a small granite stone for each unmarked grave. Granite cylinders imbedded flush with the surface of the earth with a brass plate marked "Unknown" adorn countless graves in the new cemetery.

The best marked graves in Jones Cemetery had granite tombstones, which had been weathered by the elements for many decades. Other tombstones were made of sandstone with letters barely legible. Although the last burial in Jones Cemetery took place over fifty years ago, some tombstones looked more recent than half a century old. Evidently, relatives, hearing that the cemetery was to be moved, hurried to get a stone on their relative's grave before it was moved. One grave had an obelisk marked "C.S.A.," or Confederate States of America. Stones not placed in concrete slowly sank into the soft earth and were embedded two to three feet into the graves. Some crypts marked "Shipley" were just that—crypts built of stones and filled with rocks. The remains were found in sandy soil about two feet below the rocks in the crypts (about four feet down). Perhaps the Shipley survivors did not want animals digging up their loved ones, though this didn't seem to be a worry to anyone else buried in Jones Cemetery.

I visited a second cemetery affected by the lake, Bloomfield Cemetery, which at that time was still active with two fairly new graves, one in 1983 and one in 1984, both with earth sinking in. This cemetery was on a hillside, whose lower end would be flooded by the new lake. The spring of 1985 was a rainy one, and most of the graves had water in them. At least one set of bones was dug up out of a foot of water. Bloomfield Cemetery had a number of large cedar trees which had been planted among the graves. One large tree was growing over the spot where an infant supposedly had been buried. The gravediggers dug down about four feet next to the tree, and then *under* the main root system where they found the necessary coffin fragments. Most excavations at Bloomfield Cemetery the day I visited brought up nothing but coffin and bone fragments.

A man named Jones had also visited this cemetery a few days before and provided certain information which proved helpful to the gravediggers. He said that two people were buried with their heads to the east instead of the west, which is customary. Sure enough, the gravediggers who had found bones but no skulls started digging a little distance to the east and found the skulls. Another grave was thought to have two people in it because of the many large bone fragments. Mr. Jones reported that Dr. J. J. Shipley, the occupant of the grave, was a very big-boned man who weighed about 240 pounds. Upon closer examination the remains proved to be a single set of bones. Mr. Jones also mentioned that families sometimes had the funeral at the cemetery. Two cane-bottomed chairs were found facing each other, as the coffin had been set on them during the funeral service.

Bloomfield Cemetery had a few graves with coffins encased in concrete or steel vaults. One concrete vault was broken on the bottom, evidently dropped by the mortician, or placed on uneven ground and cracked when the earth over it settled. Many of the vaults were full of water which began to leak out when they were lifted from the earth. Removing a vault is the most laborious aspect of cemetery relocation. Bars with four- to five-inch lips are placed on the sides of the vault so that it can be raised up enough (by machine) for straps to be placed under it. Then it is hoisted up with a backhoe and moved to the new cemetery. Water seems to be the greatest enemy to our earthly remains, and to coffins and vaults as well. Bodies buried in sandy soil last longer because the drainage is better.

In the new cemetery bodies that were intact—and not very many were—were buried with the head to the west and the feet to the east according to custom, presumably facing the east to await the second coming of Christ. Evil people are supposed to be facing north or south, but no one had been found in this position. Men were buried to the south of their wives, in keeping with the traditional position of the man on the right side at their wedding and the belief that Eve was created from a rib on Adam's left side.

In the relocation of the older cemeteries, it is interesting to note how little was found in the graves. "Dust thou art and to dust thou shalt return" had literally proved to be the case in most of the older graves. Even the caskets themselves, especially the wooden ones, had returned to dust, leaving if anything a few rusty nail heads. Metal coffins with vaults were unable to keep out the ravages of water and decay, and their inhabitants were faced with the same fate. Thus, no corpses were preserved completely intact, to disintegrate in a split second when they were exposed to the open air as legend says. There is simply no way to preserve a body from the intrusion of moisture and air and subsequent decay. Mr. Coker, owner of a Sanger funeral home, reported that in all the relocations he had witnessed only one corpse had withstood the ravages of time and weather: an elderly man who had been buried in a metal casket and remained fairly well preserved, mustache, suit, and all seeming to outlast the casket. The only intact corpses I have seen that have been dead for many years have either been Egyptian mummies or the bodies from cemeteries in Guanajuato in central Mexico, where certain chemicals in the soil had preserved them like withered mummies.

Mr. Coker also reported that hair does not continue to grow after a person dies, and that dead bodies do not sit up of their own accord. Instead, after death the skin draws up and shrinks, thus making any head or facial hair merely seem longer. Muscles may also draw up, causing minor movements in an appendage, but no muscles are able to cause a body to sit upright.

When one attends a cemetery removal and sees firsthand the eventual fate of all human beings and the failure of metal crypts and coffins to preserve our bodies intact, one wonders if all this trouble to move the graves is really necessary. Can't a body that has "returned to dust" rest as well under the lake as in an unkempt grave trampled by cattle somewhere on the lone prairie? Several hundred American servicemen are entombed in a watery grave in the U.S.S. *Arizona* in Pearl Harbor. Other servicemen have been buried at sea, lost forever somewhere on an ocean floor. At least with the *Arizona,* survivors of the men entombed there can come to the memorial atop the sunken battleship and read the names of their loved ones who rest below the surface. Presumably any survivors from the cemeteries I have described can come to the new Bloomfield-Jones Cemetery and locate the remains of their loved ones. I suppose we somehow manage to take comfort in seeing a final resting place.

Other burials both past and present are equally impermanent. Students of *Hamlet* are told that the gravedigger must make room for more tenants in a crowded cemetery and whatever bones he digs up, including Yorick's skull, are taken to the charnel house. In Guanajuato, in central Mexico, families must rent space in the local cemetery for their loved ones. If the rent is not paid, then the body can be removed to make room for a new tenant. As mentioned earlier, certain chemicals in the soil preserve the bodies and tend to mummify them. Oddly, a museum of the mummies with innumerable shriveled bodies has become one of the popular tourist attractions in Guanajuato today.

**Mummies on display in the Guanajuato museum**

Centuries ago bodies were prepared for burial wrapped in a winding sheet or shroud, thus hastening the decomposition process. From a Christian viewpoint this would be the natural order of things. In some societies, ancient Egypt for example, great attempts were made to preserve the body for eternity, hence the development of an elaborate mummification process. In modern America the funeral industry, with advanced techniques of embalming and the merchandising of hermetically sealed coffins and crypts, has at least been able to delay the natural decomposition process for years to come, at considerable expense to the next of kin. Such commercialization of the funeral industry was exposed several years ago by Jessica Mitford in *The American Way of Death*. Because of the high cost of dying, many people today have opted for cremation or giving their bodies to science.

In one of Thomas Hardy's poems, the speaker asks, "Then, who is digging on my grave?" Both friends and enemies reply that they had already forgotten him. The final response comes from his faithful dog, which unfortunately had not come to visit his master's grave:

> Mistress, I dug upon your grave
> To bury a bone, in case
> I should be hungry near this spot
> When passing on my daily trot.
> I am sorry, but I quite forgot
> It was your resting place.

Perhaps we, too, realize too well that we will also be soon forgotten; thus, we find comfort in tombstones and grave markers to give us some bit of immortality.

The presence of bodies, coffins, graves, and tombstones helps us to come to grips with the reality of death in the midst of real life. Fiction also confronts us with our own mortality, from the allegorical descent of Everyman into the grave with his only companion, Good Deeds, to Ophelia's insultingly simple "maimed rights," to Heathcliff's demonic passion for the dead Cathy Earnshaw. To save time I will examine only the last of these in more detail. After Linton's death, Heathcliff says to Nelly:

> I got the sexton, who was digging Linton's grave, to remove the earth off her coffin lid, and I opened it. I thought, once, I would have stayed there, when I saw her face again—it is hers yet . . . but he said it would change, if the air blew on it, and so I struck one side of the coffin loose, and covered it up . . . and I bribed the sexton to pull it away, when I'm laid there, and slide mine out too. I'll have it made so, and then, by the time Linton gets to us, he'll not know which is which!

Strangely enough, he can still recognize her beautiful features, though she has been dead and buried for eighteen years. Furthermore, the coffin is still intact, and the screws evidently offer no resistance when Heathcliff opens the lid. Her body does not suddenly disintegrate when exposed to the outside air. If all goes well for Heathcliff, their bodies will be united in death and eventually in dust. Hopefully, these three restless souls will not be threatened with a lake, or they may end up in one turbulent plywood box with three cubic feet of human clay.

GET THERE:

# RITUALS, CEREMONIES AND THE PROCESS OF DYING

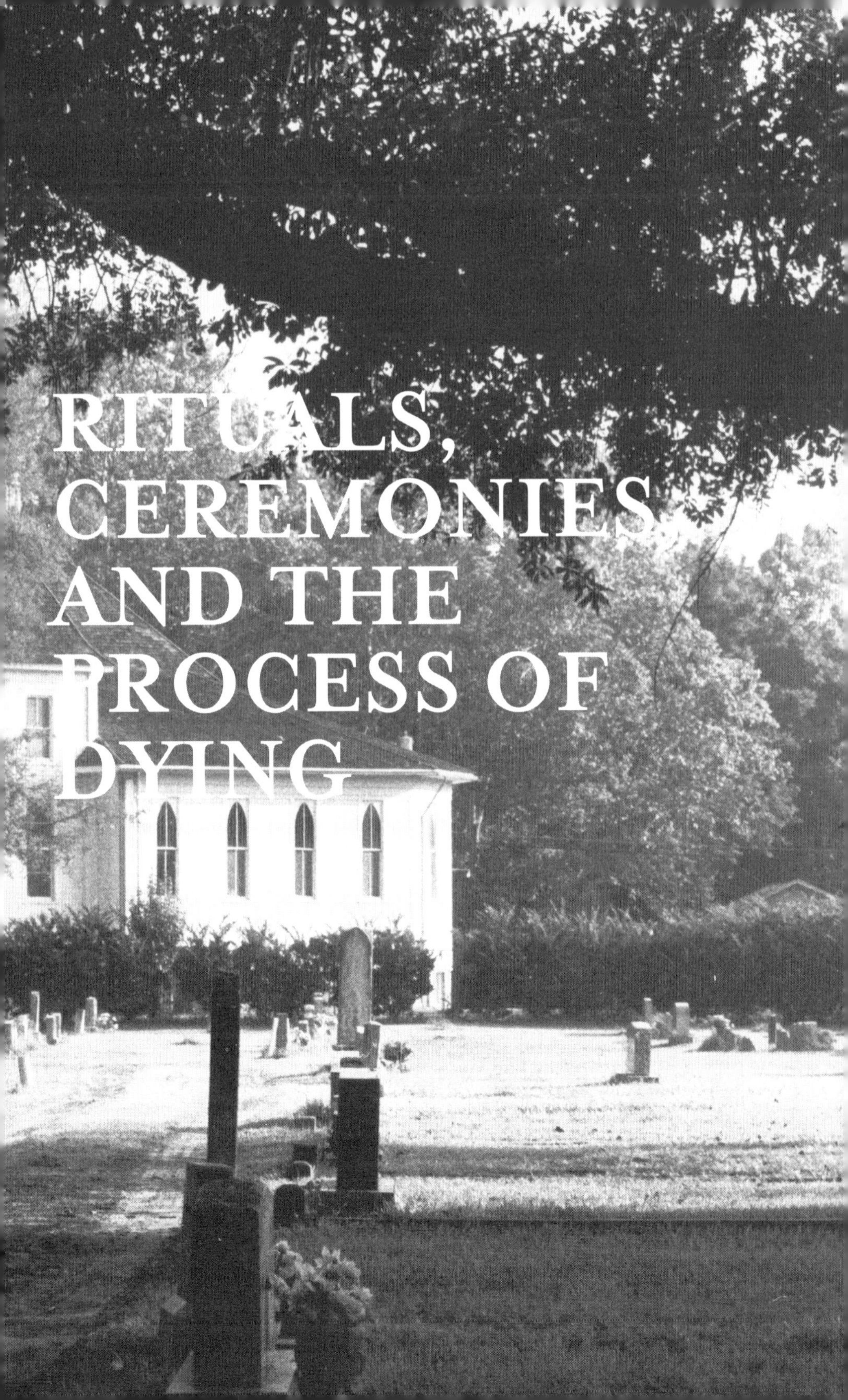

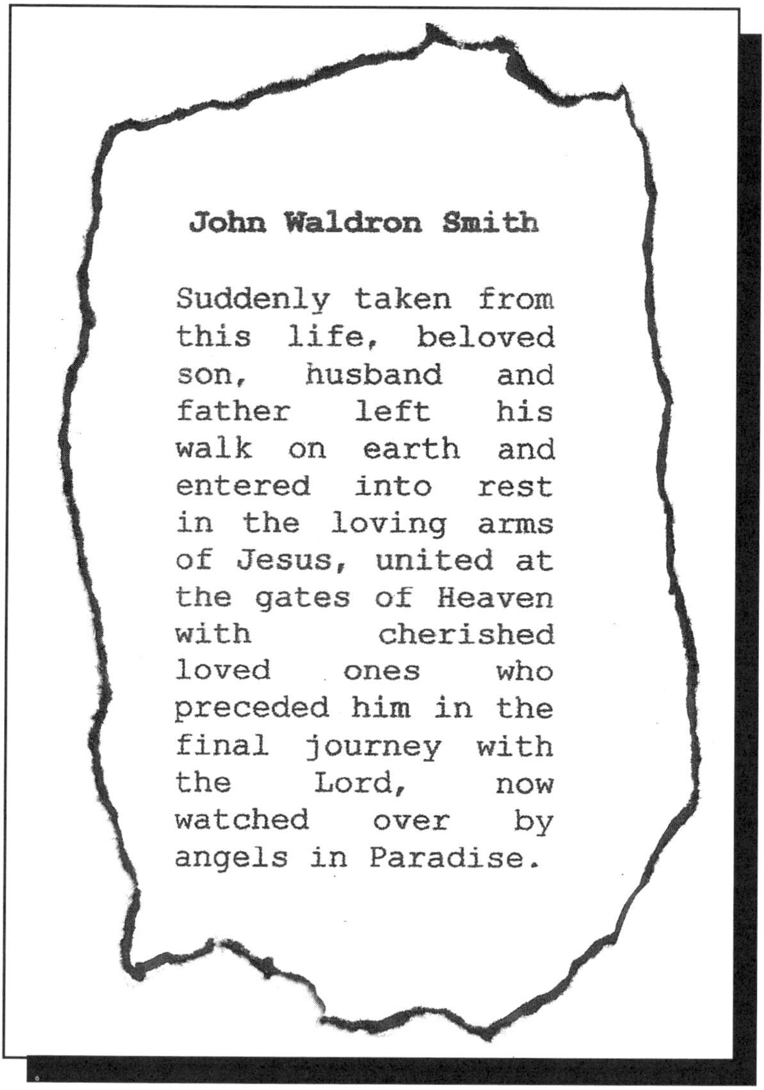
**John Waldron Smith**

Suddenly taken from this life, beloved son, husband and father left his walk on earth and entered into rest in the loving arms of Jesus, united at the gates of Heaven with cherished loved ones who preceded him in the final journey with the Lord, now watched over by angels in Paradise.

An extreme example of a euphemistic obituary

# MOST PEOPLE IN TEXAS DON'T DIE

**by Mildred Boren Sentell**

What was once a passing interest in newspaper obituaries has over the years become, for me, an abiding interest. I have observed that the obituaries, while reflecting passing tastes, more and more often concern younger and younger persons, many my age or even younger.

In almost all write ups of deaths, I find a reluctance—even a refusal—to employ the word "die" in referring to one's transition from this vale of tears to whatever state of being comes next. In the *Lubbock Avalanche Journal*, roughly two-thirds of deceased persons "pass away," "pass," or "pass on," or utilize some other means of transition; the remaining quarter to third of them (mostly Presbyterians and Catholics) may die. This is true in general for other newspapers around the state, unless one's demise occurs in San Antonio, where no one dies; everyone, according to the paper, passes on. Perhaps even better, if one is to avoid actually dying, would be to meet one's maker in Crane, Texas, where one Mr. Arnett, according to his obituary in *The Crane News*, "did not die; he just quit living."

Oddly enough, whichever the paper, the loved one is usually "preceded in death" by various family members. Whatever the means of transition, the ultimate destination is never in doubt, for invariably the loved one is assuredly to be in Heaven, joined by the pre-deceased, the Heavenly Father, and the Savior.

One might also have:

> "Departed this earth" or "Departed from this life"
> "Entered into rest" or "Entered into eternal life"
> "Left for Heaven" or "Went home to the waiting arms of Jesus"
> "Went to be with her Savior" or "Slipped away into his Savior's arms"
> "Been blessed to leave this life" or "Been suddenly taken from this life"

> "Made her transition" or "Graduated from this earth"
> "Been taken quickly and lovingly by the Angels into Paradise"
> "Been united in Heaven with those who preceded her in death"
> "Had our Heavenly Father take him by the hand and carry him home"
> "Was received by our Heavenly Father with arms extended"
> "Gained the victory she had strived for: to be in the presence of Jesus"
> "Gone on the best vacation of her life when the Lord took her to live in his Heavenly home."

Or perhaps:

> "The Angels arrived at the Health and Extended Care Center to take Agnes to her Heavenly Home"
> "Our precious loved one shed her broken wings and soared with the Angels into the arms of God"
> "She left this world of sorrow and pain to be with her Heavenly Father where she now has no pain" or
> "Her most outstanding legacy is the love of reading she instilled in all she knew. She especially loved reading God's Word, which was written so beautifully on her heart."

Heaven, besides being heavenly, is fancifully portrayed as offering all the pleasures enjoyed on earth by those who have reached that plateau. Most often they attend a virtual family reunion. One might be met at:

> "Heaven's Gate by our Lord and Savior Jesus Christ, his Daughter and Grandparents" (there seems to be some problem here with pronoun reference)
> "Because Christ does live, her daughters are confident of a heavenly reunion with their mother and father"

12A The Snyder (Tex.) Daily News Sun., Oct. 15, 2006

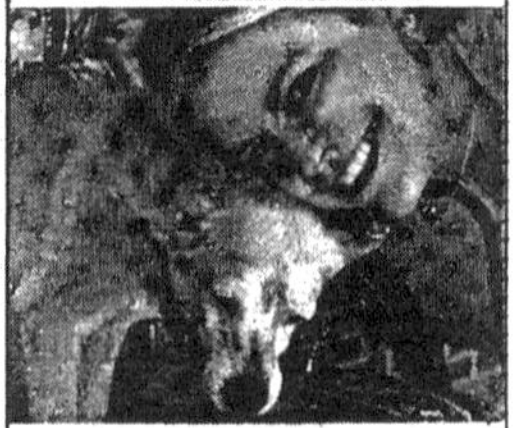

**Walter (Doug Dog) Davis**
**1985-2006**

Walter (Doug Dog) Davis went to his reward on Oct. 7th, 2006 while in the care of a great vet at an area clinic. He was still chasing cars only a few days prior.

He is survived by his human, Starla Davis Reese, her sister Stephanie Davis Parham, their parents, Randy and Debra Davis and a host of family cats and dog cousins.

His passion was running alongside traffic and he was active till old age finally took hold. He took great pleasure in putting his front feet on the edge of a box of new kittens, looking in at them and the mother cat, smiling broadly, wagging his tail, glad to welcome healthy new little ones. He never minded sharing his heated bed in the storeroom while they were small.

He watched the place well, nothing has been bothered here since he showed up as a barely grown pup one fall afternoon.

Burial was beside our driveway at the curb where he would stand and bark at the passing school buses. Gone, but not forgotten.

**An owner's homage to a beloved pet**

"Family members who await her arrival in heaven include her parents, her sister, brother and sister-in-law, brother-in-law, and nieces and nephew"

"Doug Dog Davis is survived by his human Starla, her sister, Stephanie, their parents, and a host of family cats and dog cousins."

There is something, also for every harmless Christian taste. We read that:

> "She lived the joy of the Lord on a daily basis. She is now dancing with Jesus in Heaven"
> "She is Making Heaven a brighter place with her dazzling smile and infectious laughter"
> "A cowboy to the end, he went riding and fishing once again in Heaven"
> "He will forever dance with the angels in Heaven"
> "Her love for Jesus is now rewarded by being in His presence and perhaps singing in the choir"
> "He is now playing ball with Jesus"
> "Doug Dog is chasing cars in Heaven and barking at the school bus" and
> "Jesus, the Master Carpenter, finished the mansion he was preparing for Bobby."

At times, metaphors abound:

> "One who will never be forgotten, he was one of those people who comes into our lives and leaves footprints on our hearts so that we are never, ever the same. 'To feel the love of people whom we love is a fire that feeds our life,' and he gave everyone plenty of fire to feed all his loved ones."
> "The pleasures of an azure sky, a blue jay on a wire, a nest of sparrows in the juniper, a smiling pansy in the garden, were reflections of a simple life of undaunted faith. She was strong as an oak tree and the winds that buffeted her branches left her unchanged and provided a home for us all. She was born on August 10, and had a birthday every year after that."
> "The sunshine in this world will be forever diminished with her passing."

There are also admonitions reminding all of the unexpected and final. We are reminded that ". . . before each of us is born we are assigned a time to die. For it is written that in order to live, one must die. The words 'well done good and faithful servant . . . come home' were the words that were whispered through the hearts of loved ones as our Eternal Father reached down to welcome Daddy home." Also, "It has been said 'Death is simply putting out a candle because morning has come.' We are thankful that Margaret is at peace."

The impulse toward generosity in the matter of character description of the deceased is long standing, and I have heard of people who were convinced that they were in the wrong funeral after hearing the eulogy given by an overly sympathetic speaker.

From the March 17, 1904, edition of *The Borden Citizen,* I read of the unfortunate death of one Andy Pylant. Headed "Neck Broken," the obituary reads:

> Probably the saddest death that we have ever been called on to chronicle occurred last Sunday morning about 15 miles south of this place.
>
> Mr. Andy Pylant had driven a bunch of horses up to the corral from the pasture and in the bunch was a one-eyed horse which obstinately refused to go in the pen, so Mr. Pylant decided to rope him and, unfortunately, when the horse reached the end of the rope, he turned with the blind side toward Mr. Pylant and ran against the horse he was riding, throwing both horses and breaking Mr. Pylant's neck. . . .
>
> No one seeing him last week in his perfect physical manhood would have dreamed that that was the last time he would have been seen walking the streets of this place. It was very fondly demonstrated that "no one knoweth the day nor the hour" he will be called hence to the mysteries of the "Great Beyond. . . ."

> The remains were brought to this place Monday evening for interment, and after a short funeral oration by Rev. H. C. Jolly, the lifeless form was tenderly laid to rest by his manly loving friends who, accepting the irrevocable decree of the Omnipotent, bade him God-speed on his trip to that "bourne from which no man returneth." The Citizen joins the host of mourners in extending sympathy to the unhappy family in their sad bereavement.

The *Roby News,* in April 4, 1906, contained the obituary of Mrs. J. C. Bridges, whose funeral was preached by Rev. J. L. Mills, a childhood friend of Mrs. Bridges and an intimate friend of all the family. After the mention of survivors and facts of her arrival in Fisher County, the paper wrote, "She had been a patient sufferer for a long time, she was a devoted wife, a loving mother, and a noble Christian woman, one whose influence helped to make the world better. She is now resting in that beautiful city where all is peace and happiness, waiting for her loved ones to follow her there."

The *Post City Post,* on April 18, 1937, observed the death of a "valued Pioneer Citizen," who "was apparently in no immediate danger when death came unexpectedly Monday afternoon about four. Friends had talked to him Wednesday afternoon on the streets as he went about his duties, and many did not know of his sudden illness." In addition to eight pallbearers, the paper listed twenty-two honorary pallbearers.

Occasionally, the paper finds it necessary to make a correction:

> "Virginia H. Krementz died in New Vernon, not Vero Beach, Fla. Dice, tennis balls, and playing cards were not placed in her coffin, but elsewhere." (Chester N.J. *Observer-Tribune*)
>
> "The first sentence of the cover story in today's 'Your' section should read, 'Preparing for a funeral is not a happy occasion.' The word 'not' was inadvertently dropped.

> *The Times Dispatch* regrets any discomfort it may have caused anyone suffering through the loss of a loved one." (*Richmond Virginia Times*)

The *San Antonio Express News* comments, "Deceased Couple Called Very Calm and Very Quiet." The usually shorter length of recent published obituaries may reflect the newspapers' growing practice of charging for the obituaries by length. In general, three line death notices, which give name, age, and place and time of funeral, will be free, but obituaries can cost in the thousands of dollars, depending on length and whether or not there is a picture of the deceased published. The *Snyder Daily News* will publish free a ten-inch obituary, including picture, if the subscriber uses a provided form. If the person uses his own words, the paper charges $6.25 per inch. An obituary for a dog costs that amount, no matter which form is used. The editor of the *SDN* considers the deaths of local people, former residents, and the relatives of local persons to be local news, thus the obituary is not a charged item.

The *Lubbock Avalanche Journal* publishes death notices free for people who live or previously lived in the *AJ* circulation area. These are published once and include the following information: name, date of death, age, town, time and place of services, and funeral home. The paper charges $4.50 a line for an obituary, no matter which form one uses, and also $27 for a small picture and $63 for a large picture. One lengthy list of sixty-seven survivors took six inches of column space and cost about $250. It included children and spouses, grandchildren and spouses, siblings and spouses, nieces and spouses, nephews and spouses, great-grandchildren and spouses, caretakers, and cousins. A full column will run about $1000.

A practice, formerly uncommon in West Texas, has lately been gaining acceptance: that of the memorial letter, usually addressing the dead person directly and written on certain anniversaries. A typical example reads, "Not a day goes by, Daddy, without us thinking about you and missing you. We can't believe it's been ten years; seems like yesterday. Thank you Daddy for all the wonderful memories, but most of all thank you for all the love you gave us. It is your love that will keep us from going until the day we're all together again. We love you and miss you, Mom and all."

Another reads: "Although you left seven years ago and we still grieve for you like it was yesterday, your love and faith stay with us always. Your sons, daughters, son-in-laws, daughter-in-laws, grandchildren, and great-grandchildren miss you and hold you close to our hearts always. Your husband who loves you has never forgotten you and will never forget you." Or perhaps a poem:

> No farewell words were spoken,
> No time to say goodbye,
> You were gone before we knew it,
> And only God knows why.
>
> God looked around his garden and found an empty place.
> He then looked down upon the earth and saw your tired face.
> He put His arms around you and lifted you to rest.
> God's garden must be beautiful; he always takes the Best.

I was visiting a friend recently, and she remarked, "I told Merton that if he got to Heaven before I did, not to expect me to write him any letters. I didn't expect that he would be subscribing to the *San Angelo Standard Times.*"

As a measure to prevent unnecessary pain to the survivors, many churches, newspapers, and funeral homes avoid any mention of a funeral, referring instead to a "celebration of life service," focusing on the life, admittedly now ended, of the individual. The newspaper obituary then will give time and place, and also a visiting time for calling on the family. Most also give the email address for sending condolences online. It is thus possible to sympathize with the bereaved without the discomfort of actually facing them. One funeral director told me that some people object to the term "funeral" because it sounds so final. Others say that funerals are barbaric holdovers of the past. Still others, as accurately, recognize that whatever else does happen next, a death has happened, and a funeral figuratively puts a period to this term of life.

And speaking of funerals and funeral homes (in what should probably be a footnote to my funeral home paper at WTHA several years ago), I must note the "unique" offerings available in Holbrook, NY, where the Harley-Davidson enthusiast can contract to be transported to his final resting place in the custom-made sidecar of a large—very large—black Harley. The funeral home owner says, "This is a unique, specialty item. When we use it, people are overwhelmed with it." The same business has a landscaped area with a central gazebo to be used for mourners' reflections, and also for the odd wedding photo, a community service the owner is glad to provide. He also provides a shop with memorial jewelry, including silver and gold thumbprints taken from the deceased, and crematory urns shaped to be used as a garden birdbath, a dissolvable container for internment in water (not to pollute), and a plush toy with an interior pocket for ashes, surrounded by a round, huggable body. The shop is on the way to the casket inventory, in order to soften the approach to the casket room.

Comforting in the extreme, is the acceptance by all that, whatever the vehicle for arriving there and while most people in Texas don't die, all, inexplicably, go to Heaven. I imagine that, after the joyful reunion with family, there is a stunned realization on the parts of many of the heavenly host that certain other individuals are there also. I've heard the expression "I'll see you in Hell," and I think that the shocked observer would, at times, far prefer that scene than to be forced to tolerate in heaven those who are likely equally amazed to see him there.

**Sue Friday**

# OAKHILL CEMETERY

by Sue M. Friday

We buried my mother, Thelma Alford McGeorge, in July of 2005, in Oakhill Cemetery outside of Hemphill in Sabine County. She was eighty-eight and had lived a long, mostly happy, very eventful life. She rests beside her mother in the same row as her father, a baby sister who died of diphtheria in 1913, both maternal grandparents, and several cousins, aunts and uncles. In the same cemetery are other people who knew her as a girl, and an ex-husband (my father). The body of Kit Smith, a young man shot in the back by outlaw relatives in 1883, is also there, but that is another story.

Oakhill Baptist Church and the small cemetery across a gravel lane are located about twelve miles south of Hemphill off Highway 87. Remote, totally surrounded by the Sabine National Forest, it is a quiet place. The old church is a one-room, hip-roofed structure with an adjoining newer fellowship hall. Tall cedar trees guard the chain-link gate of the cemetery. The gate is always unlocked. According to Weldon McDaniel's book, *Cemeteries of Sabine County, Texas, Volume 1,* the cemetery and church were sited in the early 1880s on high ground near a spring of good water. His records show that this is an ancestor cemetery. Of the slightly more than 400 graves, only five hold people born after 1950. Most were born in the mid- to late-1800s or early 1900s.

My early memories of Oakhill are from my childhood in the 1950s. A city girl most of the time, I spent summers at my grandparents' farm outside of Hemphill in order to get out of the polio epidemics in Shreveport. At some point during the summer a "cemetery working" would be scheduled. Families with people buried at Oakhill were expected to take care of their own graves. This meant hoeing out the grass, picking up spent yard flowers left behind in fruit jars, repairing the fence, and perhaps planting a flowering bush. On the scheduled day we kids were loaded in the back of the pickup along with the hide seat straight chairs from the porch, a fried chicken lunch packed in a pasteboard box lined with a tablecloth, and the needed saws, rakes, and hoes. The adults started early to be through before the heat of the day. We kids had a great time playing chase, hiding, and telling ghost stories. I remember being told to stay off the graves, that it was disrespectful . . . and anyway, they might fall in—a delicious imaginative thrill that fueled our play for days afterwards.

From the perspective of passing years, the warning was a good one, probably given from experience. The early coffins were constructed of wood and once they rotted, the graves did sink in. To protect from this, some graves, like those of my great-grandparents, Leander and Marthy Conner, had a cement cap poured over the mound of earth. When the dirt fell in, no one could tell.

The last person to be buried the old way was a neighbor, Mr. Bill Ener. His body was prepared at home, dressed, and laid in a pine coffin lined with a quilt. The men of the community made the coffin, the women the quilt. The coffin was placed on wooden chairs in the front room, the same room where we sat when we visited through the years. I peeked at him only once. He didn't look much different than in life—very old and very thin.

My grandfather sat up with Mr. Bill's body through the night. A great one for yarns, he had once told us one about two men sitting up with their friend during the night. They roasted sweet potatoes in the fireplace to sustain them, but one fell asleep. The other took the potatoes, arranged them along the crossed arms of the corpse and shook his friend awake. "Look there! Elmer got our taters!" he said. The other man looked and ran out the door. The first one laughed at his joke and settled back. After a while he couldn't stop glancing toward the coffin. There seemed to be a slight smile on the face of the dead man. The hairs on the back of his neck stood up. A minute or two later he also ran out the door, leaving the hot potatoes in the cold arms of the corpse.

By the time my grandparents, Adron and Ada Alford, passed away in 1970, visitation and the funerals were held at Starr Funeral Home, as the funeral home was air conditioned. When my mother reached the age of eighty, she decided to tell me what she wanted, as she said, "If I die." I was to go see Squeaky at Starr funeral home. She had placed a marker reserving her site at Oakhill years before. When the time came, I did make arrangements through John "Squeaky" Starr. He helped us by going to a closet and pulling down a dusty cardboard box with the records of the arrangements from my grandparents' funerals. I was able to choose for Mother by seeing what she had chosen for her mother and father. "I loved your mother," Squeaky said when we sat down, and then he told me several funny stories about her. I felt myself relax as he talked, knowing that as with all our people who had gone before, she would be in good hands.

Traditionally, the casket is left open for visitation and the funeral, but Mother had not done well the last few years of her life, and it showed. "Don't worry," Cousin Gwen said, "Squeaky will make her beautiful." Gwen, of Mother's generation, was right. Mother looked stylish, elegant and much younger than her age. She would have loved it, and because we knew how she always liked to look her best, we were comforted. She was dressed in a burgundy pants suit and wore a strand of pearls she adored that had come from my husband's mother (turned so that the safety pin clasp didn't show). Her nurse's cape from the '30s was displayed and then placed in the casket for the burial. A staff member at Starr told me that something from life is often placed inside the casket: a stuffed animal, a note, sometimes a can of beer.

At my grandfather's funeral service, M. J. Rice sang "In the Garden." I remember that M. J. almost didn't get through it, as "Uncle Adron" had been an important part of his life. For Mother's service we also chose the old hymns, "In the Garden," "I'll Fly Away," "Amazing Grace." Of course, now they are recorded and piped in through speakers. The service was conducted by Brother Bob Gwinn of Camp Springs Baptist Church. It was personal and rousing, promising in detail the glories of life after death. "Where did you get the real preacher?" I was asked afterwards by a Church of God relative.

The sheriff's department provided an escort to Oakhill and Mother was carried to the place she had marked by grandsons, sons-in-law, and Dale Ener, grandson of Mr. Bill Ener. After that service we all went to the home of eighty-five-year-old Cousin Zuda for food she and other cousins provided. About forty of us stood around stuffing ourselves with BBQ and banana pudding, telling stories on Mother and saying how she would have approved of the day.

Six generations of our family now lie under the soil of Sabine County. Mother will be the last, as my sister and I have decided on cremation. At the same time, both of us felt that Mother's service was something we wanted our grown children to be part of and remember as a link to our family history. Our children acknowledged this link, and although it seems strange to describe a funeral as satisfying, Mother's was just that. Scattered from the Carolinas to Houston, we no longer work our graves at Oakhill, but contribute to the cemetery association which sees to the upkeep. Even without that personal involvement, Oakhill will always be our home cemetery. Mother rests in a good place.

Grand reunion at Oakhill Baptist Church, September 30, 1950. The author is the little girl in the center

A. C. Sanders

## A MOST UNUSUAL UPBRINGING

by A. C. Sanders

Most men stumble into their life's role. A chance encounter sparks a flame, a career pursued; a birthright endows one a profession. Some drift from trade to trade until something sticks. Others simply drift. My grandfather, Bab, labored as a ranch hand, then a butcher, until finding a life's calling when he landed a job at a furniture store sometime around 1920. The owner operated a funeral parlor in the back of the store. Eventually, Bab became one of the first licensed morticians in the Lubbock area.

Until his mind became fogged with dementia, my father often recounted with nostalgia those days at the furniture store. As a boy, he was assigned the daily duty of dusting the furniture displays. Often a call came in from a ranch or small community out on the Staked Plains requesting the services of an undertaker. Bab loaded his equipment into a Model T Ford, Dad hopped into the passenger seat, and off they went across the prairie, there being few roads to their destinations. They traversed one property to another. At each fence line, Dad jumped out, opened the gate, then closed it after the old Ford passed through. Flats and breakdowns were commonplace, and ruts suddenly transformed to axle-deep loblolly should a thunderstorm strike. A forty-to-sixty-mile journey occupied most of a day.

Upon their arrival at the ranch, neighbors already gathering, the men helped Bab lay the body out on the dining-room table. If there was not one available, he hauled in a portable embalming table which unfolded much like a massage table used today for home visits. Dad helped Bab wash and embalm the body. Women convened in the kitchen to prepare and spread out food. Men retired out back to build a coffin. Bab and Dad dressed the body, if it were a man; women dressed and fixed the hair of a woman. The men helped put the body into the coffin, then moved it into the parlor for viewing by friends, family, and neighbors. (In the latter part of the nineteenth century, the term *casket* replaced *coffin;* the new nomenclature stems from a French word referring to a special box that holds precious items, like a jewelry box.)

Folks converged from miles around. That evening everyone feasted on potluck. Depending on the religious persuasion, a wake was sounded with much singing, praying and storytelling. An old fear from antiquity, before the age of embalming, professed that a deceased might not actually be dead, and thus could be buried alive. The celebration and noise making was an effort to "wake the dead" prior to burial the next day. All attempts failing, they assumed it safe to proceed with the funeral.

Women slept in the house. Men bedded down in the barn, and pulled shifts "keeping the vigil." This tradition served two purposes—one spiritual, one practical. Religious lore alleged that Satan would slip in under cover of darkness and steal the soul of the deceased. However, he was powerless to achieve this in the presence of a Christian guardian, or after a proper burial was completed. Around-the-clock vigil against insurgency by the devil insured the spirit of a deceased was launched in the right direction.

A more practical reason for the vigil was to protect the body from desecration by predators, human and animal. Often the deceased was dressed in finery, appointed with jewelry and other family heirlooms, until after the funeral. In some cases these artifacts were buried with the body. Also, in isolated areas of the country, especially if embalming was not performed, animals might come around and feed on, or maul the deceased. Keeping the vigil provided both spiritual and earthly security over the dearly departed.

Next morning began with a huge breakfast served up by the women. Platters filled with eggs, bacon, slabs of ham, and biscuits were passed around—perhaps even grits or potatoes ladled with gravy. Liberally garnished with the delicacies of homemade jellies, jams, or applesauce, the meal was washed down with hot coffee.

The body was loaded onto a buckboard wagon or truck for a final trip to the church, if nearby, or to the cemetery. Family and friends processed on horseback, wagon, and automobile. Burial took place in a community cemetery, or a family plot on the ranch. After the graveside service was completed, the men lowered the coffin into the ground and completed the burial, witnessed by all. Everyone headed back to the house where the life lost was celebrated with a covered dish meal, visiting, storytelling, singing, and perhaps some dancing. While the party was in full swing, Bab and Dad packed up the Model T and bounced across the savanna of the Llano Estacado toward Lubbock.

In 1938, Dad married my mother, a musician and teacher. The funeral business was in its infancy, and the Depression ravaged the country. They lived their first two years together at the funeral home with the rest of the Sanders family. My grandfather never hesitated to roust all hands on deck in emergencies. Mom was promptly drafted to play piano for services conducted in the chapel.

Today, one of her favorite tales is set in that era, when one of the local gangsters was killed in a shootout with the law. Funeral homes seldom pick and choose their customers. This violently dispatched soul was one of several Yancey brothers, each of whom could kill at the drop of a hat—the entire clan notoriously rotten. No preacher in Lubbock stepped forward to preside over the

**The Sanders Funeral Home**

funeral. Bab called his ace in the hole, older brother Liff Sanders, a Church of Christ preacher who rode the circuit in West Texas on horseback at the turn of the century. Liff preached the Gospel in school houses, churches, court houses, saloons, or wherever folks gathered in a community. He ministered to some unsavory characters, and often packed heat when he served the Lord. Liff was fearless. He did not back down from the Yancey boys.

After a couple of hymns, Liff stepped to the rostrum to offer the homily. In silence his gaze penetrated each face of that renegade family before him. Then he pointed a finger over the pulpit at each one and proclaimed in a loud, ominous voice, "The Lord giveth, and the Lord taketh away! He who lives by the sword will, by God Almighty, die by the sword." After a pause to let those words soak in, Liff pointed to the open casket before him and continued, "You boys take a hard look in this casket. If you heathens don't clean up your ways, each one of you will end up just like this rascal brother of yours." The Yanceys began to squirm in their seats and growl to one another.

Mom says she was considering refuge under the piano bench. As she looked around, Bab, my father, and his brothers were beginning to hug the walls, trying to make themselves scarce. The Yanceys withstood the brow beating, and the burial completed without gunplay. But afterward, Bab was heard to mutter he would damn sure consider the righteousness of any future deceased before inviting Brother Liff to officiate another funeral.

Dad doubled over with laughter each time he told one particular tale on his father. A family sat across the desk from my grandfather, Bab, one spring day in 1931. The patriarch of their clan had died suddenly at a business meeting in Lubbock the day before. While sitting at the conference table, this notorious wheeler-dealer, devoid of ethics, stopped in mid-sentence, clutched his chest, and pitched forward. Rushing him to the hospital had been a mere formality. Ol' man Lockhart had died before his head hit the table. Now the family was making funeral arrangements.

"Papa wasn't a religious man, so there won't be no church funeral," the older son announced.

They decided to hold a small memorial service the next day in the funeral home chapel. Afterward the family would return to their ranch on the Texas/New Mexico border in Baily County. The following morning Bab would drive over to the county cemetery with the casket and the family for a brief graveside service. Bab called the Baily County Clerk's office to arrange for the grave to be dug, and verify the 10:00 a.m. time of service and burial.

At dawn two days later, Bab left Lubbock in the loaded hearse, allowing enough time to arrive early and check things out, just in case something might go wrong. He wanted to make sure a gravedigger was on hand to close the grave after the service. He stopped in the town of Muleshoe and got directions to the small cemetery out by the Lockhart spread, then headed on out. As he pulled into the cemetery, he saw a huge pile of dirt next to the grave site. Bab stepped from the hearse and approached the mound of freshly dug dirt where an old fellow leaned on his shovel, a pick casually tossed to one side.

"Howdy!" the old man muttered as Bab peered into the gaping hole.

"Hi. How deep did you dig this damn thing?"

The gravedigger shifted his feet, thumbed his sweat-stained hat back on his head, turned and spat a stream of tobacco juice into the hole. "Twelve foot!"

"Hell, it's only supposed to be six feet. Why so deep?"

"Folks in this county want to make sure that mean sunuvabitch can't climb out."

With the advent of the motorized hearse in the 1920s, funeral homes met the needs of communities for ambulance service by double-using the hearse as an ambulance. By the 1950s, many funeral homes purchased specialized vehicles for medical transport. This remained the prevalent mode of emergency and ambulance transportation service until the late 1960s and early '70s. Present day Emergency Medical Services evolved as a relatively new phenomenon.

In 1929, Bab and my grandmother, Lena, founded their own establishment, Sanders Funeral Home. It is operated today as a family business by my cousins. My father was a licensed mortician, as were his younger brothers. I worked at the funeral home throughout high school and college, and logged time as an apprentice embalmer. I functioned as ambulance driver and attendant on thousands of medical transports, aided the preparation of dead, and assisted with hundreds of funerals of almost every religious persuasion. I have witnessed changes in the funeral tradition over time and the consolidation of many family owned funeral homes into internationally owned conglomerates. This is regrettable, in my opinion.

Modern houses do not include a parlor—that room in which babies are baptized, daughters courted, gossip exchanged over tea, engagements announced, weddings celebrated, and the dead waked. The age of convenience ushered most familial functions from the environment of home. The hospital serves for birthing, and a country club for announcement, wedding, and anniversary parties. A nursing home provides a venue for dying, and a funeral parlor for viewing and waking the dead. Daughters are courted in the backseat of a Buick. No longer is there time for casual, genial conversation over tea, but perhaps we might meet at a nearby watering hole for a raucous happy hour.

However, on rare occasions, in the 1950s, we prepared the body at the funeral home and then drove it out to the family home where it lay in state until funeral time. This was usually in a rural setting, so friends and neighbors would not have to drive into town to view, wake, and celebrate. Often, the vigil was still kept, men taking shifts staving off the devil by their mere presence. We provided a pot of coffee.

My grandparents lived above the funeral home until they died. Because someone had to pull duty twenty-four hours a day, all our family celebrations took place at the funeral home. There the Sanders clan observed Christmas Eve together. We cousins grew up never realizing the strangeness of our unique tradition until I was in the first grade. Returning to school after holidays, my teacher asked each student to stand and tell the class where he, or she, spent

**A hearse, circa 1950s**

Christmas and how our family celebrated the occasion. I stood up and announced the Sanders family celebrated Christmas Eve at my grandparents'. The teacher asked where they lived. I replied, "At the funeral home." She offered condolence for their demise. "No, they're not dead. They live there." Whereupon she dragged my smart ass down to the principal's office explaining, this Sanders boy needed serious counseling and he displayed a very dark humor.

Upon hearing my recount of holiday cheer, the principal threw her head back and howled with laughter. "Yes, I'm sure he did spend Christmas at the funeral home. The Sanders boys buried my late husband last year. His grandmother, Lena, is a friend of mine, and she does indeed live there, upstairs."

On occasion in this business, fate tosses celebrity your way. In February 1959, I was privileged to experience that week in which we buried Buddy Holly. Though this made me an object of intrigue and curiosity at Lubbock High School for a few days, the historical ramifications of that event were not apparent to me until many years later. Had I been more aware, I would have made notes for posterity. Yes, wisdom is often wasted on the old.

While working as a teenager, I overheard my Uncle Gordon actually talk a family out of purchasing an expensive bronze casket which had been in stock for nearly two years. After they left, I asked why he had not sold them the white elephant they wanted. His reply still smolders in my memory. "I know they cannot afford that funeral. Right now, they are looking through emotional eyes. Six months from now, grief passed, reality sets in, they'll still be making payments on a funeral long over. They would become bitter towards us for having sold it to them. Besides, it wasn't the right thing to do."

My younger sister, Cindy, lived with our grandmother Lena at the funeral home while attending summer school at Texas Tech in 1968. Recently, she related an experience I had never heard. Our uncles were special characters who teased and joked, but when plying their skills in the grim profession, one saw beneath the surface hijinks an empathy and compassion for those in their care. Cindy was honored to witness that ministry one day that summer.

They had a full house, bodies in every family room plus the chapel. One was that of a young woman tragically killed in a boating accident. Cindy was recruited to greet families and visitors at the door and escort them to the proper viewing room. She was standing back by the offices with our uncles Gordon, Cecil, and Lloyd when the front door burst open, almost flying off its hinges. A young sailor in uniform stumbled in, cried out in anguish and collapsed, weeping, slamming the marble floor with his fist. She uttered, "My God, what happened to him?"

Gordon said, "A year of fear, exhaustion, and now this grief has crushed him."

Cecil explained, "We've had to delay the funeral for him. The girl was his older sister, and they were particularly close. It took the Navy two days to find him on a ship in the Gulf of Tonkin, off

Vietnam. He has spent the last twenty-four hours traveling to get here in time for the service. He's spent."

Lloyd knelt over the young man, stroked him, then helped him to the men's room to collect himself. Our three uncles formed an unobtrusive perimeter around the young sailor and his family, protecting privacy, quietly lending support. Cindy told me that experience was an epiphany for her. She witnessed up close the nature of the business, the importance of the service provided by our family—indeed, a true calling, a ministry of sorts.

In 1963, Jessica Mitford published her expose of the funeral business *The American Way of Death,* marking the beginnings of regulations and "reforms" to protect the public from charlatan undertakers. Yes there were, and are, those unscrupulous bastards who fleece people at their most vulnerable time. Prior to this upheaval, people purchased a casket, the price of which included complete services. Whatever the family needed, we made every effort to provide. Now shopping a funeral requires an à la carte menu of services from which an unknowing public must pick and choose. In my view the reformed system lends much more vulnerability to compromise than before.

Modern intelligentsia decided funeral rituals were pagan and passé, really—a waste of good money better spent on the living. You see, dead is dead, and the dead don't care anyway. As a young man with a cynical streak, I, too had a hard time justifying all the hoopla. But with age, maturity, and perhaps a modicum of wisdom, I have modified that position and value the place of tradition in our families and society. The dead embodies that tradition.

It first hit home when, accompanied by my wife, I made a pilgrimage to the Vietnam Wall. I saw names emblazoned there, those I had known, some with whom I was present when they died. It was real. They are alive today inside me and the others who knew them and served with them. The Wall is a place for me to go reconnect with them, reflect and meditate their being, and through them, my being.

I see it when my own sons visit graves of family members known and never known. I see them visibly moved by what is contained beneath that earth—a part of who they are. For decades the grave of my great-grandfather was known to be somewhere on the old family ranch in Jack County, Texas, but no family member alive had ever been there. It was said my grandfather visited it once, drawn to it as though by some cosmic force. I felt this need, a burr under my saddle that could not be relieved until I found that grave. On Christmas 2002, my wife, older son, and I found it. We drove two dirt roads and scrambled over two barbed wire fences to get there, a solitary place on the open range where I belonged. I scratched an itch that day. I found a little piece of myself.

**The Sanders Funeral Home**

Naw, the dead don't need funerals or grave markers. God will take care of their needs however He sees fit. We, the living, need them desperately—a holy place in time to go back, pay homage, celebrate the past and find ourselves. A grave does not contain the life of one deceased, only weathered bones. The life entombed beneath that gravestone is our own, our past. From this place we reconcile our present, and see more vividly our future.

This past October, a cousin on my mother's side of the family died suddenly in Lubbock. It fell upon me to guide his daughters through the funeral process. My father's generation is dead, and the next couple of generations now operate the family funeral home. They learned their profession well. I leaned on them during those days, and they did not let me down. The "Sanders boys" still follow their calling to a special ministry—one that makes me proud.

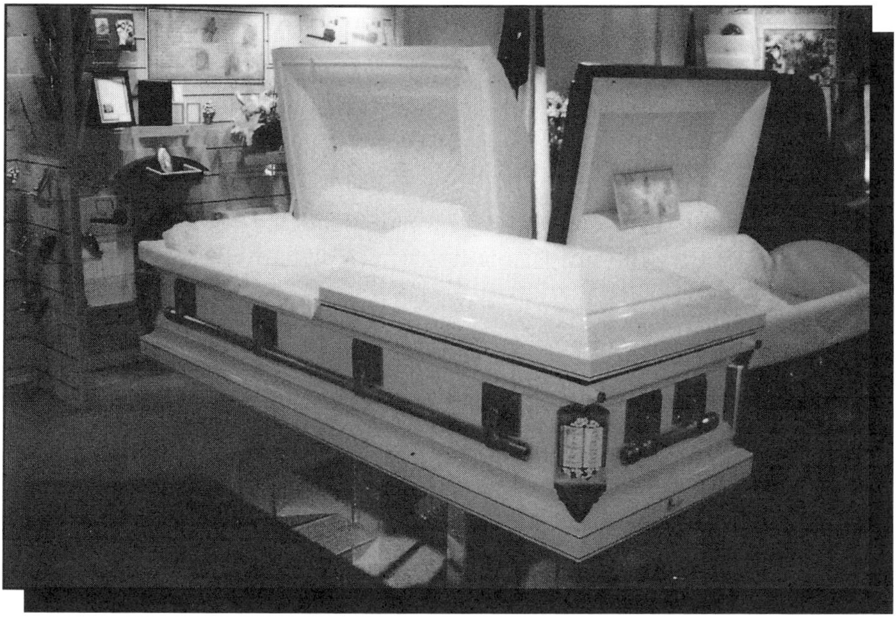

A showroom of contemporary casket choices

# FUNEREAL HUMOR

by Kenneth W. Davis

Folk humor like most other traditional forms of humor depends heavily on incongruity. The unexpected at the wrong place and time often provides cause for laughter. Certainly, this principle is true regarding happenings at such solemn events as funerals and graveside services, or, to use the more uptown phrases: memorials, remembrance worships, or celebrations of life.

An example of humor in the midst of sorrow is a story told often in my misspent youth in Old Bell County. During the mid-1930s the Depression forced many small farmers into bankruptcy. Some went on relief while others moved to small towns to try to find jobs that would pay at least enough for the feeding of their families. One such farmer, a man of considerable accomplishments in farming and in begetting children—some with his wife and others in chance encounters—lost the farm where he and his wife and seven children (all under the age of twelve) had enjoyed a good enough life. The family moved into town where the man of the house soon had a prosperous barbeque stand going and was making more money than ever before in his life. He and his wife were blessed with two more children, and with another woman or two he fathered perhaps three other children. All seemed to be going well for this man and his family—legitimate or otherwise. But one afternoon he fell over dead while basting a couple of goats he was custom-barbecuing for a rancher's daughter's wedding feast.

The grieving widow called a neighbor to help with finishing the barbeque and with making arrangements for her husband's funeral. The friend was a devout deep-water Baptist who knew well all the preachers in a twenty-five-mile radius. He asked a middle-aged graduate of Southwestern Baptist Theological Seminary to conduct the service which, to accommodate the expected large crowd, was held in an open air tabernacle often used in summer night revival services because there were no air-conditioning systems in the church buildings. Although the deceased was not a church attendee and did have a reputation for heroic womanizing as well as for drinking bootlegged liquor, his splendid barbeque gave him a stout measure of social acceptability. Barbeque is important.

The funeral began with a spirited rendition by a red-robed choir of "There Is a Balm in Gilead," followed by "Just Over in the Glory Land." Then the minister began. He exhorted the audience to grieve for the loss of a civic leader whose business benefited the economy as well as the stomachs of the town, whose devotion to his family was noble, whose compassion for the poor was venerable, and whose love for Jesus was admirable. At this point, the grieving widow punched the oldest child, a twelve-year-old boy, in the side and said in a whisper that was heard all over the tabernacle, "Go up there and see if that is your paw in that box!"

Many grown men and almost all of the women at the service fought valiantly to keep from laughing loudly. Few loud guffaws occurred, but there was an abundance of snickering. This event—a true one; my parents were in the audience of mourners—has the key element of incongruity. The disparity between the minister's statements and the truth about the man's character is humorous enough, but given the added element often identified as situational humor this difference between appearance and reality provoked mirth. And, as all who will remember from their youth, in long church services anything even mildly unusual became uproariously funny.

Another funeral story is one the late Dr. Dudley Strain, longtime pastor of the Lubbock, Texas, First Christian Church delighted in telling from his days as a ministerial student when he was pastor of a small rural church in Indiana. A 102-year-old veteran of the Grand Army of the Republic (the Yankee army!) died and the then just Brother Strain was asked to do the graveside service, which was to include full military honors. The deceased had many children, grandchildren, and great-grandchildren. After Brother Strain made a few suitable remarks and read appropriate scriptures, the family was asked to stand for the firing of a salute by a haggard little cluster of Civil War veterans, all of whom were a bit unsteady on their feet. The captain of this group, in a frail, squeaky voice cried out, "Ready, Aim, Fire." Not everyone in this rifle toting honor guard heard the word "Fire," so they didn't pull their triggers until they heard other guns firing. The brief staccato of shots—or the heat—caused the grieving widow to faint and fall to the ground. A small great-grandson about six years old screamed, "Oh, God, they shot grandma!"

Comic incidents seem to be more common at gravesides than in church buildings. Dr. Michael Passmore, current pastor of Lubbock's First Christian Church, recalls a graveside service at a rocky, brushy cemetery where snakes made their homes. At one service, Dr. Passmore looked down and saw a grass snake moving between the undertaker's large feet toward the grave over which the yet-to-be buried coffin rested. The man screamed several unprintable words and ran toward a nearby tree to try to climb out of harm's way. Dr. Passmore added that in a country cemetery near Abilene, Texas, rattlesnakes are common and pose real threats to mourners. Grass snakes are hardly real dangers, but, of course, snakes *can* cause people to hurt themselves.

Dr. Passmore also tells of an incident when a large horsefly flew into an open casket at a graveside service. The undertaker tried in vain to shoo this fly away. Finally, someone took a funeral home fan and swatted it firmly. The sound of the fan striking the corpse was memorable.

Another incident fraught with incongruity involved a mechanical breakdown. The not often used but splendid Cadillac funeral car of a Clovis, New Mexico, mortuary had a brief mechanical failure while transporting a leading dowager from nearby Muleshoe, Texas, to a barren country cemetery. The entire procession stopped and, of course, highway traffic in all four lanes stopped out of courtesy. Several of us got out of our cars to see what the delay was. I was not in the funeral procession, but didn't want to sit and sweat in a hot car on a late July afternoon, so I went with several other men to see what was wrong and perhaps offer help. As we neared the defunct hearse, we overhead a conversation in one of the elongated limousines for family: "Well, it's just like the selfish old witch: she never was on time for anything in her life . . . she always had to make a grand entrance thirty minutes late. Well, she is going to be late leaving just like she was late getting anywhere."

Ministers have real difficulties sometimes in trying to compose a meaningful set of comments for either a funeral or a graveside service. James Peel, youth minister of Lubbock's First Christian Church, shared a brief anecdote about planning a service for an elderly matron he had never met. He interviewed several of the lady's grandchildren thinking they would surely have incidents from the life of their grandmother that would be appropriate to share in the funeral message. Mr. Peel said that every one of the grandchildren agreed that their late grandmother was a mean-spirited, shrewish, arrogant, selfish, egotistical wretch. I don't know what Peel finally decided to say at this service, which was an early one in his ministerial career. I trust that from some source, comforting words for the family and others present were provided.

A somewhat similar story is from Texas and Southern lore about funeral services. I first heard the story in Bell County. In the small town of Holland just after the beginning of the twentieth century a reprobate scoundrel, drunkard, gambler, and suspected cattle thief died apparently of lead poisoning administered by an irate husband. A circuit rider who was passing through town on his way to Salado was pressed into doing the memorial. Many people attended, mostly to be sure that the rascal was really dead. He had, after all, been known to lie about everything else while on earth. The circuit rider was at a loss to say anything, so after a brief, somewhat generic prayer about the difficulties humans have and a stout plea for God's everlasting mercies, he turned to the audience and asked if any one of the deceased's friends would like to offer remembrances. There were no volunteers. The silence was awe-inspiring.

Finally, from the back of the sanctuary came the strong voice of a young cowboy who, like the circuit rider, was just a wayfaring stranger on his way to greener pastures for the winter in the Brush Country about which J. Frank Dobie wrote with such enthusiasm. The cowboy said, "Well, if there ain't nobody goin' to say somethin' about the dead man, I can say a few words about Texas. Yee, haw!" As is the case with many supposed real events, this one was supported with a formulaic opening statement such as, "My great uncle Tom's first wife's cousin heard about the cowboy at the funeral of that old rip who died in Holland a spell back. . . ." This is what is called an appeal to authority or provenance statement. I don't know if the incident really happened. In the years I spent in graduate school in Tennessee I heard several variants of the same sort of story. Perhaps as Dobie is supposed to have said, "If it isn't true, it ought to be."

A final story about dying lacks the humor of the preceding ones I've recorded, but it does have the element of incongruity in it. Dr. Michael Passmore tells of the time he was at the deathbed of a long-time faithful church member who in a frail voice asked for a prayer. Following the prayer, the heart monitor's line went flat, indicating the cessation of life. Nurses came immediately, checked the machine as well as the man's pulse, and were disconnecting the monitor when the man spoke up in a rather clear voice and said he had seen a great light. Then, he really did leave this plateau for whatever lies beyond. The nurses were all but terrified. The incongruous or unexpected always elicits strong responses: sometimes these responses are comic and sometimes they provoke fear or even consternation. Regardless of the precise nature of the responses, they tell us about some key folkloric elements in our broad spectrum of human concerns.

Herb Sanders

# A FAMILY SECRET

by Herbert H. Sanders

One of the most vivid memories of my young years is the Sunday meals at my grandmother and grandfather's house. All of the girls were fantastic cooks and all wanted to show off their talents. The house smelled like Thanksgiving every Sunday. After the meal was over and the dishes were washed, it was time for visiting and the kids were excused to play in the yard until the noise level got so loud it was interfering with the talk in the house. That was usually a signal that it was time to go. All pots and pans and dishes had to be gathered and picked up by their owner. Goodbyes were said and plans were made for next Sunday.

On the way home Dad sometimes took Mother home, and then he and I would go into the black area of Oak Cliff to see an old black lady. She was nearly always sitting in a swing on the front porch seeming to be waiting for us. Her name was Flo and I was in love with her. She laughed all of the time, and she was so big that she laughed all over. She always got out of the swing and gave Dad and me a big hug.

There were goodies always available and Flo smelled just like what she had been cooking. When it was time to go, she always had a bag of something for Mother. Sometimes Dad would hand her an envelope as we were leaving and she would give him another hug. I wondered what was in that envelope, but I was too shy to ask.

Some years later, one Sunday morning we were dressed for church but did not go to our church. I realized we were in the neighborhood of Flo's house. We went by her house and did not stop. We went around the corner and stopped behind a lot of cars in front of a small church. When we reached the door, two black men shook hands with Mother and Dad and then led us down the aisle to front seats. After we were seated, Mother explained to me that Flo had died and this was her funeral service.

I had been to one funeral not too long before (PaPa, Dad's dad). This one was nothing like his. There was singing and dancing, and they called it a celebration. I loved every minute of it and thought it was so happy, like Flo. The preacher met us after the celebration and took my hand and shook it just as he did Mother and Dad's. He told me Flo had talked a lot about me and how she was proud of me. On the way home it came to me that Flo was no longer with us. She was gone like PaPa and the little dog I had forever that got hit by a fire truck.

A few days after the funeral when Dad got home he looked me up and asked if I had anything to do after dinner. I told him I had already done homework and had no other plans. He said, "Stick around then. I have to tell you a story." My mind was running away. What have I done now? After dinner he came into my room and sat at my desk. He told me to get comfortable because this was a long story.

When he was nine years old his mother was diagnosed with cancer. PaPa was going to need help because Grandmother could not handle the chores she was used to doing. The two older sisters were in school in Virginia and he did not want to take them out and cause them to miss a semester. He had talked to Aunt Betty and she had agreed to let him hire a black couple from her.

This was a good arrangement because Flo, the lady, had cared for Grandmother until she had gone off to school. Jessie, her husband, was a top hand on the farm and could relieve PaPa of some of his work so he could be with Grandmother. PaPa thought this was such a good idea he hired another black man to help Jessie and he had even more free time.

As time went by Grandmother became weaker and weaker. PaPa spent most of his time with Grandmother. He wanted to take her to the Methodist hospital in Oak Cliff but she said she'd had five children in this bed (two girls died, one at two and one at five) and she'd die in this bed. PaPa gave up and hired a nurse to stay with her. This didn't work either. Flo was jealous of the nurse's time with Grandmother and it was a running battle of who would wait on her. Dad said he heard Flo tell PaPa that she took care of this little girl from the time she was born until she was a young lady and she was not going to give that up now. The nurse had to go.

Some sharecroppers had moved in down the road and Jessie told PaPa they were less than nice people. In addition, things were disappearing around the farm since they moved in. He said that he was positive that we still had ten bags of oats but now there were only eight. Also, there was corn on the floor in front of the bin as if someone was not too careful when they were helping themselves to the corn. Jessie said he had started making rounds at different times at night, and he thought he saw someone twice but they were too far away to recognize who it was.

One night, PaPa had been to Lancaster trying to buy some more land that abutted his and it was after dark when he got home. It was a moonless night so it was extra dark, but he thought he saw a movement in the direction of the barn. He always had his old .40 caliber single action revolver with him and he took it out and went around the other side of the house and, stooping low, made his way to the opposite side from where he saw the movement. He opened the side door just enough to squeeze in and then crawled to where he could see the doors at the other end. Sure enough the door opened all the way and he could see the outline of a man's body.

PaPa stepped out into the barn. "Stand where you are, whoever you are. I have a gun and I will shoot." The person turned as if to make a run for it and PaPa fired. The person fell and PaPa started approaching him slowly. When he was half there he heard a very familiar voice say, "Mr. Joe, think you killed me." PaPa ran to the person on the ground because he knew the man on the ground was Jessie. He had for sure killed Jessie, because he was dead before he got him to the house.

The house was quiet except for Flo's low moaning. She did not cry. She only let out a low mournful moan as she rocked back and forth. Grandmother was not told what had happened. She was as low as she had been since she first became ill. PaPa had gone for the deputy and it would be a while before he returned. When he did come, the deputy looked at the wound and then went to the barn and looked where PaPa had shot from and where Jessie had fallen. They came back into the house and Dad heard him tell PaPa that it was a damn fool thing he did but he knew it was an accident, so he was going to write it up as an accidental shooting. The deputy left and a few plans were made for the "celebration."

It was decided the funeral would be held in the house. Jessie would be taken to a mortician in Lancaster, the black pastor would be notified, and burial would be in the section of the Taylor-Deem plot that was reserved for black people since the days of slavery. The cemetery was on PaPa's land; that made a little convenience for the family. All costs would be covered by Mr. Joe Sanders. The funeral would be held in the black tradition, at 12:00 noon Sunday.

The day after the funeral PaPa made a rare speech to everyone involved in running the farm. He said he was going to be gone for a few days and he expected the place to carry on as if he was there. The inside would be Flo's responsibility and Hash, the new man, would cover chores outside. With that he picked up his case and walked out.

PaPa was back in four days. He said nothing about what his trip was for. All he would say is that they would all know in due time. Dad did notice that he had some new clothes and a new hat. All attempts to trick him into telling what he did while he was gone failed.

Grandmother was steadily getting worse. The doctor from Lancaster came once a week but he let everyone know that there was nothing he could do. She finally was comatose and stayed that way for a day then died on Dad's birthday. It was a sad time but everyone felt easier because her suffering was over. The funeral was at the house and the burial was at the family cemetery. She was buried beside her two daughters in the plot reserved for the Sanders family.

That night Dad found out where PaPa had been on his trip and what he had done. He started by asking all to sit down and be quiet until he was through. He said, "I went to Dallas. The first thing I did was hire a lawyer that my banker in Lancaster recommended. The second thing was to seek out the best real estate company to cover the whole USA. I intend to sell this farm and I am not going to give it away. Another item, I went shopping for some real estate myself. Flo, I bought a nice little bungalow, and when this place sells I will move you into it furnished, and you can live there until you die, rent-free. I will pay for all the maintenance and utilities and you will be out not one dime. In addition to all that, I will furnish you with money every two weeks for your own pleasures. My new lawyer has made my will and you will be taken care of even after I die."

Now my Dad ended the story by looking at me and saying, "Now you know what was in that envelope that you and I carried to Flo every two weeks. The house belongs to me now that my Dad is dead and I intend to sell it and use the money to bring the Taylor-Deem Cemetery up to ship-shape." He went ahead with his plans. The area is beautiful: huge blackjack oak and native pecan with a deep-gorge running creek. It is close to a college campus and there is evidence the students use it for picnics at times. No vandalism is evident.

My eldest son and eldest grandson take our tools and visit the place once or twice a year. The target of our curiosity is the headstones. There are quite a few that can still be read, but the largest number are not readable. The oldest we have found is a young girl that died in 1846. The newest found is Aunt Betty Crabtree. She was my Grandmother's oldest sister who died in 1945.

**The Walls, site of Texas executions since 1924, during a rare snowfall in 1947.**
*City of Huntsville Walker County Treasures photo*

# DEATH BEHIND THE WALLS: RITUALS, FOLKTALES, AND TRUE STORIES

by Ruth Massingill

## Welcome to the Execution Capital of the World

Huntsville, a tiny dot on the map, marks the location of an East Texas town of 35,000 residents. Motorists traveling seventy miles an hour on Interstate 45 could easily miss the exit sign about an hour north of Houston, but mention Huntsville to anyone in the state and there will almost assuredly be instant recognition. Go fartherafield—New York, Canada, England, or France—and many have heard of Huntsville.

Since 1924, death sentences for the State of Texas have been carried out in this East Texas town where incarceration and education are the twin pillars of the local economy. Mostly, the populace prefers not to be reminded that their town is sometimes called the execution capital of the world. In fact, the death ritual occurs so frequently—usually several times a month—that local citizens scarcely notice "routine" executions. Only when national or foreign media roll into town for a high-profile case does attention focus on the Huntsville Walls unit, site of more than 400 executions in the past twenty-five years alone. Although the prisoners' families may mourn their passing, few in Huntsville grieve for the killers who meet their fate there. For the most part, Huntsville's citizens, like Texans in general, unwaveringly support the death penalty despite recurring hints of wrongful convictions and corruption in the criminal justice system.

On a global scale, the United States incarcerates more people than any other country in the world, housing more than two million prisoners—one fifth of the world's inmates[1]—at an annual cost in excess of $57 billion.[2] This prison population crosses every cultural border known to humankind. Many people, regardless of social strata, are touched by the criminal justice system, either directly or indirectly. Crime and punishment have become highly charged emotional issues successfully used for political gain by world leaders and by small-town politicians alike. For these reasons, Huntsville can be said to have broad social significance as a community that lives daily amid issues of international concern.

Beneath these outward political concerns, a wealth of lurid folk legends surrounds the death tradition; native East Texans have grown up hearing such stories. The urban legends are born of misinformation and superstition, but plenty of bizarre stories actually occurred. The best sources for these gruesome vignettes are the public information officers (PIOs) for the Texas Department of Criminal Justice and the veteran Texas reporters who have covered the TDCJ beat for years. These eyewitness tales are as varied as the human experience, ranging from poignant to macabre. Ultimately, each one is, as they say in East Texas, serious as a heart attack, because they all end in death, for both the convicted and their victims.

## Living—and Dying—Behind the Walls

The nerve center for the death tradition in Huntsville lies behind red brick walls only two blocks from the downtown square but a world away from the slow-paced, conservative lifestyle of this small pineywoods town. The compound of prison and support services occupies about ten square blocks of prime downtown real estate. Shaded by ancient oaks, the two-story fortress constructed in 1848 and known simply as the "Walls" is at the center of the complex. Barbed wire tops the thirty-two-foot-high walls, scanned by armed guards in the corner towers. A hodgepodge of brick structures has been added over the years. Administration buildings, warehouses once used to gin cotton for prison garments, and living quarters for high-ranking corrections officers encircle the prison. Perhaps it is telling that few residences in old Huntsville neighborhoods are constructed of red brick—for many, red is the color of prison. The deep orange-red of the buildings in the prison complex is the hallmark of "Corsicana

Reds," bricks made of native clay, fired in kilns in the East Texas town of Corsicana, and thereafter making them cheap and readily available.

Ironically, the first Texas inmate to be executed by electrocution in 1924, Charles Reynolds, was from Red River County, in the red-dirt country north of Corsicana. Three hundred and sixty inmates followed Reynolds to the Texas electric chair, nicknamed "Old Sparky," until the U.S. Supreme Court declared capital punishment "cruel and unusual" in 1972. A year later, the Texas Penal Code was revised to allow assessment of the death penalty again, and Texas resumed executions in 1982, using the "more humane" method of lethal injection.[3]

Even in tight budget years, prisons are a growth industry in Texas. On average, the State of Texas houses about 150,000 prisoners, with more than sixty percent in and around Huntsville. The number of inmates in the city varies between 9,000 and 15,000; it is a much-worn joke that every third or fourth citizen is an inmate. Death row for men is at the Polunsky unit near Livingston, about forty miles due east. Women on death row are housed at the Mountain View unit in Gatesville, in the Hill Country northeast of Austin. The society of the condemned is primarily a male culture; of the approximately 360 prisoners on death row, fewer than a dozen are women.

## The Rituals of Death by Execution

In the ritualized death of capital punishment, the last events of the condemned's life take on great significance and are often grist for sensationalized news coverage. The PIOs agree that each prisoner handles the last minutes of his or her life differently and that no two executions are quite the same. Some of the condemned opt for black humor; they make jokes, even play pranks. "Some of them get in the holding cell that is adjacent to the death chamber and they act like comedians—they stand up and do one-liners—tell lawyer jokes," says former PIO Larry Fitzgerald. "Some of them are very introspective, very quiet, very reflective; some are very prayerful."[4]

*Last Meals Make Headlines*

An ongoing frustration for the prison public information officers is the media's—and the public's—overweening interest in sensational topics, to the detriment of more substantial stories. The last meal of the condemned, for example, has long been the target of morbid public curiosity and therefore the focus of numerous media stories.

A popular misconception is that prisoners can order anything they wish for their last meal, but the PIOs quickly debunk that myth. No truffles or lobsters—the last meal has to be something that can be concocted from ingredients on hand in the prison kitchen, although there are stories of occasional exceptions, such as PIO Larry Fitzgerald purchasing fresh cherries to fulfill a prisoner's craving. However, prisoners who hope to delay their executions by ordering exotic cuisine are destined to be disappointed. "Facing lethal injection, death row inmates make requests ranging from the strange (a jar of dill pickles) to the ethereal ('justice, equality and world peace')," wrote *Houston Chronicle* reporter Rachel Graves in an extensive story on last meals of executed prisoners. "But in the end, prison officials say, most simply want a cheeseburger."[5]

It is not unusual for the last meal to be uneaten. Brian Price, who prepared 171 final meals for prisoners in Huntsville, reports that Karla Faye Tucker, the first woman to be executed in Texas since the 1800s, asked for fruit and a salad with ranch dressing as her last meal in 1998, but returned her plate untouched.[6]

The last meal ritual in Texas, according to Graves, dates to the early part of the twentieth century, when prisoners requested something such as cake they could share with the handful of others on death row. Since then, the last meal has become a personal statement whereby an inmate makes a political comment, provides a media "sound bite," or just makes the inevitable more palatable with a final portion of comfort food. A list of death row meals for most of the killers executed since 1982 was the most popular feature on the official TDCJ website for years, but was removed in 2004 during a reorganization of the site.

"We had a ton of calls about that," recalls PIO Michelle Lyons. "We took it down because we had complaints—people said it was in poor taste, we shouldn't have it, we were making a spectacle. We had it there in the first place because people always wanted to know what the last meal was."[7]

However, the website that publishes a national chronicle of condemned killers' last meals, www.deadmaneating.com, is still kept current by its founder, Mike Randleman, of Santa Monica, California. The site features a crude drawing of a hanging stick figure and provides plenty of fodder to fuel morbid curiosity. "Food and death are two of the most emotionally charged things in our lives," Randleman said when explaining his creation.[8] The site lists the "last ten diners" and those with the "next reservations" in addition to selling dead man-branded merchandise, ranging from T-shirts to thongs, and from mouse pads to mugs.

*Last Words Are Powerful*

The last words of the condemned, like the last meal, are traditionally reported by the media and are posted verbatim on the TDCJ website. The privilege to utter a last dying speech to assembled witnesses is a First Amendment right. In Texas, the warden is required to ask the prisoner if he or she has any last words, and the convicted must be allowed to give the entire statement—with no durational or editorial restrictions.[9] Final statements run the gamut from tearful to unrepentant to obscure. Inmates typically direct doleful goodbyes to family members, especially their mothers. "Tell Mama I love her and tell the kids I love them, too. I'll see you all," concluded Kia Johnson (June 11, 2003).

Many convicts are converted while on death row, taking what long-time *Huntsville Item* publisher Don Reid called the "Jesus route," and express faith in the hereafter. Reginald Reeves's final words had the tone of a benediction: "I know your spirit and God dwells within us and we are all one big family of humanity; we must all learn to love and live together. I will see you on the other side. Thank you for your hospitality" (May 9, 2002).

As often as the condemned admit their guilt and remorse, there are at least as many who proclaim innocence until the end. "If you think I did this, you need to think again," said William Chappell.

"All I was asking for was a DNA and I could not get it. . . . You are murdering me and I feel sorry for you" (November 20, 2002). Some go to their death angry with their accusers, whom they blaspheme with their last breath. Edward Ellis said, "I just want everyone to know that the prosecutor and Bill Scott are sorry sons of bitches" (March 3, 1992).

Many inmates are functionally illiterate, and their final words are somewhat cryptic, such as this statement by James Ronald: "As the ocean always returns to itself, love always returns to itself. So does consciousness, always returns to itself. And I do so with love on my lips. May God bless all mankind" (December 15, 1998). The distinction of the shortest statement might go to Warren Bridge, who succinctly said, "I'll see you" (November 22, 1994). Charlie Livingston used his last words to point out, "You all brought me here to be executed, not to make a speech" (November 21, 1997).

Most final statements are three to four minutes long, but a few inmates have stretched out the last moments of their lives with voluminous discourses. *Houston Chronicle* reporter Kathy Walt recalled an inmate who had the "gift of gab": "He loved to talk. I mean, he talked up a blue streak to the point that I had to quit visiting him because I couldn't get anything else done." This particular execution was not one of the thirty-eight Walt witnessed as a death row reporter, but the talkative inmate created his own legend, which she still remembers. "He almost filibustered his execution past midnight he talked so much. He actually stopped and asked for a drink of water to moisten his mouth, and they gave him some and he ticked off names of reporters over the years he'd talked to; he talked about wardens and fellow inmates on death row."[10]

The power of last-breath statements is considerable, according to Kevin O'Neill, writing in the *Arizona State Law Journal:* "Because they emanate from a person who stands on the brink of extermination, these utterances are more likely to influence public opinion than any billboard, banner, or editorial."[11] On the other hand, some inmates are ready, even eager, for the escape of death: "There was a biker [who] was almost too excited about the execution," Lyons remembers. "He was used to being out on the road, and he could not stand being kept in a cell. So, when he was on the gurney, he was happy and he was singing the words to Robert Earl Keen's 'The Road Goes on Forever and the Party Never Ends.' It was just definitely memorable."[12]

## A Ritualized Countdown to Death

A high-profile execution takes on many of the trappings of macabre entertainment; all of the elements of high drama are concentrated in the death ritual: fear, loss, sorrow, courage, and vindication, climaxing in the moment when the ultimate price is paid. If the condemned has no public visibility, the execution is reported—if the media notes it at all—in a brief news story. But if the killer's story has captured the public interest, reporters swarm to Huntsville and the media spotlight shines brightly on the small town, where a line of more than a dozen vehicles at the downtown stoplight is usually considered a traffic jam. Once the lethal injection has done its work, the satellite trucks and convoys of reporters move on and residents resume life as usual.

After the inmate's appeals are exhausted and the fateful date is set, the execution is usually orderly and methodical, moving like clockwork from one step to the next until the ritual is complete. Most executions attract little if any attention beyond that of the families of the victims and the condemned. However, high public interest, which translates to high media interest, can complicate the PIO's job and sometimes can derail the systematic process.

One such high-profile case involved the execution of a black man from Houston who was arrested in 1981 and later convicted for the robbery and shooting of a customer outside an area supermarket. Gary Graham was twenty when he was arrested, and his conviction rested on the testimony of an eyewitness who said she saw Graham reach into the victim's pockets and then shoot him as they scuffled. During Graham's trial, testimony revealed that he had been charged in ten robberies and was a suspect in two shootings, ten car thefts, and eight other robberies.[13]

Over the course of the nineteen years Graham spent on death row, his case became internationally known and reporters from around the world came to Huntsville for interviews. Media reports questioned the veracity of the lone witness and explored the world of violence and neglect in which Graham grew up. As national celebrities and organizations such as Amnesty International took up Graham's cause, media interest grew exponentially. The Hollywood-like climate of the media coverage became even more pronounced when Graham's twenty-one-year-old son was arrested for murder and robbery. (Gary Lee Hawkins did not join his father on death row but was found guilty and assessed a life sentence.) With the years of accumulated sensationalism, in the last day of Graham's life Huntsville became the focus for a "media circus" from the PIOs' standpoint.

*The Final Fortnight*

Here's how the countdown to the six p.m. execution usually progresses and how it varied for Gary Graham in June 2000:

*Day 14*—Time to order the last meal. No alcohol or cigarettes are permitted, but the prison chef tries to accommodate all reasonable requests. A criminal justice professor at Sam Houston State University suggests there is a practical consideration for the last meal: "If you can provide creature comforts, you're going to have a more malleable individual to strap down and to execute," says James Marquart.[14] Graham declines a last meal, explaining that he does not wish to accept food from those who intend to kill him.

*Day 12*—Time to select attire and name witnesses. Most inmates are indifferent to their dress for their last day on earth, electing to die in their "prison whites"; they give more attention to naming the last people they will see. The inmate can name up to five people to witness his execution, but many die without family or friends present.

Graham is dressed in a white "hospital-style" paper robe so he cannot use his clothing to hang himself, according to Fitzgerald. For witnesses, Graham asks that Jesse Jackson, a member of Amnesty International, the Reverend Al Sharpton, and Texas governor George W. Bush attend his execution.

*Day 10*—Most inmates receive little public support. But members of the New Black Panthers and the Nation of Islam take to the streets in Houston to protest Graham's scheduled execution.[15]

*Day 7*—At this point, legal efforts on behalf of the convict are usually over, but in Graham's case his lawyers continue to file appeal after appeal to the state's pardons and parole board until hours before the execution. The attorneys also field interviews from all the major news networks; the media feeding frenzy is in full cry. The case becomes a major issue in Bush's presidential campaign. Media reports point out that Graham will be the 135th person to be executed under Bush's watch as governor. Some articles begin to talk about "Texacutions," and hecklers disrupt several campaign events. Bush responds that his job is to uphold the laws of the state.[16]

Mindful of the growing media interest, the PIOs prepare for the onslaught. Based on experience gleaned during previous high-profile executions, such as that of pickax murderer Karla Faye Tucker, the PIOs prepare a media compound to corral the reporters. Fitzgerald says the key to successful media relations is to see that each reporter gets the same information: "[Members of the] media are a lot like lemmings; if you put up a compound and rope it off and say, 'You stay in here and we'll come out and address you and you'll get everything everyone else gets,' they'll stay there. If you don't, they'll just run everywhere."[17] Anticipating an influx of TV reporters, the public information office even constructs camera platforms for the news crews.

*24 hours*—Most convicts are transferred to the holding cell at the Walls on the day of their execution, but Graham's high media profile prompts transfer a day early for security purposes. Graham promises to resist transfer and urges his supporters to protest what he terms his legal "lynching and assassination."[18]

Fitzgerald issues a media statement that Graham briefly resisted the transfer but was subdued by guards and placed in shackles. "He always said from the outset he would resist; [I didn't expect] a change of heart," Fitzgerald says.[19]

*12 hours*—Witnesses and media begin to arrive. Media witnesses for Graham's execution will be AP reporter Mike Graczyk, *Huntsville Item* reporter Michelle Lyons, UPI representative Wayne Sorge, *Houston Chronicle* reporter Salatheia Bryant, and Lloyd Gite, of Fox 26 News. Many members of the media circus arrive well before the day of the scheduled execution.

*7 hours*—Trays of sandwiches are laid out for the guards and chaplains. The PIOs try to avoid any indication that this is a festive occasion; in a much-regretted slip of the tongue, Fitzgerald once referred to the snack plates as "party platters" with unfavorable public relations repercussions.

*5 hours*—The PIO makes one last visit. Fitzgerald leaves his office and walks across the street to the Walls to visit the inmate. "I [talk] to him about what his final statement will be, what he can expect in the way of witnesses who will be coming in, which members of the media will be there," Fitzgerald says.[20]

*4 hours*—The PIO reports to the media on the prisoner's "demeanor." Fitzgerald addresses the media compound, which in Graham's case is filled with print and broadcast reporters from across the world. He reports that Graham met with his spiritual adviser and paced in his cell adjacent to the death chamber.[21]

*2 hours*—The last meal is delivered to the holding cell. The prison chaplain often sits with the inmate while he eats. Graham refuses all food, asking only for coffee.

*1 hour*—Protesters gather outside the Walls. Usually, this is a small group; sometimes the sole protester is Dennis Longmire, a criminal justice professor at nearby Sam Houston State University who estimates he has been present on the protest corner for at least ninety percent of the executions during the past two decades. While passionate about his beliefs, Longmire does not support confrontational politics. "I don't challenge the prison system for being murderers, and sometimes advocacy groups will be there on the corner with bullhorns chanting . . . challenging the correctional officers. To me, that's counterproductive."[22]

While he opposes capital punishment, Longmire is sympathetic to townspeople who work at TDCJ, observing, "I've seen correc-

**While the prison system provides "bread and butter" for about one-fifth of the residents, community leaders must cope with controversy, public criticism, and international media coverage.** ***Ruta Reproductions photo***

tional officers get on their knees, cross themselves, and say a prayer. Then they get back up and do their duty. So I know some of them don't agree with what's going on, but they're just trying to make a living and feed their families."[23]

On Graham's execution day, about two hundred anti-death penalty advocates march, wave signs, and chant, "Let Gary Graham live." Death penalty advocates also show up, including a handful of Ku Klux Klan members bearing Confederate flags. About two hundred law enforcement officers are also on hand to ensure peaceful protests. Fitzgerald recalls that Jesse Jackson wanted to speak to the crowd from the podium, but Fitzgerald denied the request. "My dilemma was if I had let him do that, then I would've had to give the podium to the KKK too, and I did not want someone in full KKK drag standing in front of a state seal."[24]

Some inmates hold out hope until the end that a reprieve will stop the execution process, and occasionally the much-awaited stay has materialized. In Graham's case, the six p.m. execution time is delayed due to a last-minute appeal to the U.S. Supreme Court and a civil suit against the Texas Board of Pardons and Paroles. The high court declines to hear the case, and Fitzgerald reports to the media that the board has denied a reprieve or a pardon, paving the way for the execution to take place.[25]

*30 minutes*—Witnesses are escorted to the viewing area in the death chamber. Since 1996, close relatives and friends of the victim as well as family members of the convicted have been allowed to witness executions. Witnesses for the victim and for the inmate have separate viewing rooms. The PIO serves as an escort for the media representatives, who accompany either the victim's or the inmate's witnesses. Correctional officers search everyone who enters the prison, a standard security procedure.

*10 minutes*—Time to leave the holding cell and take the "last walk." A five-man tie-down team straps the inmate to the steel gurney that will be his deathbed. Graham has stated repeatedly that he

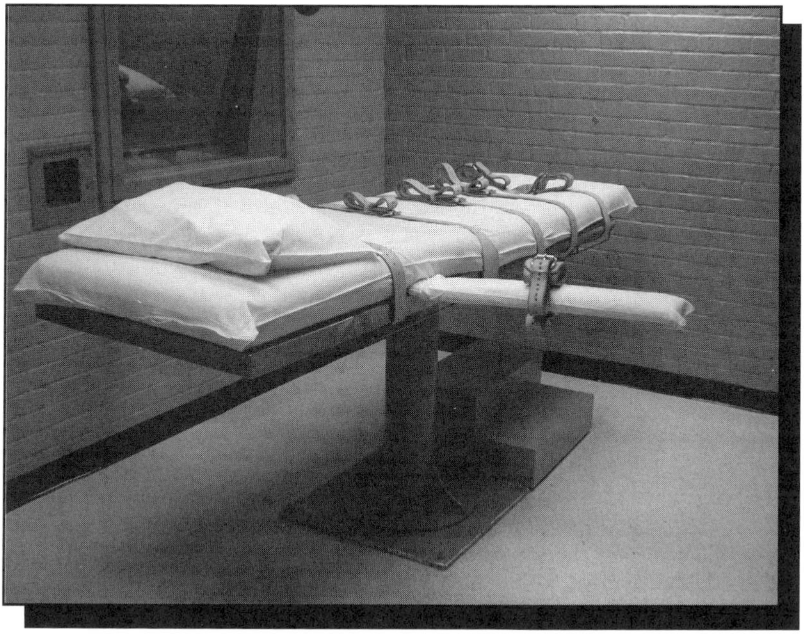

**The gurney where the lethal injection is made.** ***Texas Department of Criminal Justice photos***

will resist at every point. Fitzgerald has assured the media, "We have an extraction team at the ready. . . . They'll be ready for it."[26] Despite his struggles, Graham, like the hundreds of condemned who came before him, is secured to his deathbed with the standard eight leather straps, plus additional restraints.

*5 minutes*—Time for the final statement. With saline solution already flowing into their arms and a microphone dangling overhead, prisoners have an opportunity to speak their last words. If an offender prefers to write rather than speak a final statement, the PIO transcribes it and hands it out to the media after the execution.

Graham's rambling final statement is much longer than usual—1,268 words. He affirms his innocence and thanks his many supporters, including the Reverend Al Sharpton and Jesse Jackson, as well as international figures such as Bianca Jagger, who is also a witness to the execution. Struggling to the last, Graham says, "I'm being lynched. The death penalty is a holocaust for black Americans."[27]

*1 minute*—The warden signals the execution to begin. The presiding warden for Graham is Jim Willett, who was the senior warden during forty executions that year alone. When Willett began as the "Death House Warden" in 1998, he removed his glasses as the signal for executions to begin, but later got an electronic device when he realized prisoners knew about the glasses ploy.[28] Once Willett gives the go-ahead, a cocktail of drugs sedates the body, collapses the lungs, and stops the heart in short order. A medical examiner declares the official time of death. For Graham, death comes at 8:49 p.m., almost three hours behind schedule.[29]

*Afterward*—Witnesses exit and the warden draws a white sheet over the dead face. If the body is unclaimed, it is buried by the state in Joe Byrd Cemetery, the prisoners' graveyard sited on a knoll nicknamed Peckerwood Hill, and marked with a simple headstone. The twenty-two-acre prison cemetery is just east of the SHSU campus. The most infamous prisoner ever to be buried there was Satanta, a Kiowa Indian chief. Convicted of killing seven white settlers in 1871 during the Salt Creek Massacre, his death sentence was commuted to life, but unable to tolerate confinement, he died in 1878 by diving headfirst onto a brick wall from a second-story

**Simple headstones in "Peckerwood Cemetery" mark the final resting place for executed prisoners with no one to collect their bodies.**
***TDCJ Media Services photo, courtesy of the Texas Prison Museum***

window in the Walls. Satanta was buried in Peckerwood, but for eighty-five years his tribe tried to have his body returned to Oklahoma. Finally, in 1963, the tribe received legislative approval, and his remains were reburied in Fort Sill, Oklahoma.[30]

Graham does not lie with the abandoned; his family claims the body and buries him in his hometown of Houston. After the execution the PIO provides the media a sheet containing the offender's last statement and an execution recording, which gives the minute-by-minute account of each step of the execution: (1) Taken from holding cell; (2) Strapped to gurney; (3) Solution flowing; (4) Last statement; (5) Lethal dose began; (6) Lethal dose completed; (7) Pronounced dead.[31] Fitzgerald, who has witnessed close to two hundred executions, deals with the unique pressure of his position by not taking the job home. "It's just my job to be there as a witness and report what I see," Fitzgerald says. "There were some executions that stand out in my mind and I'll never forget. However, a majority of them are just a blur, and I have trouble the next day even remembering the guy's name." He has no difficulty remembering this inmate. "Actually, Graham and I got along very well."[32]

## URBAN LEGENDS TAKE ON A LIFE OF THEIR OWN

Some legends persist through generations even though there has never been a shred of evidence to support the stories. Both the public as well as the news media are familiar with a variety of folktales regarding prisoners and executions.

### *"The Light Blinks When the Switch Is Thrown"*

One of the most popular and enduring of these is the legend of the lights. When *Huntsville Item* reporter Don Reid was in the death chamber waiting to view his first execution in 1938, he asked the assistant warden if the prison's lights would dim when the executioner "threw the switch" on the electric chair. The warden gently set him straight: "The Death House has its own set of generators. That only happens in the movies—the lights of the town going dim and the townspeople hiding under their blankets so they won't know and all that tripe."[33]

More than sixty years later, the PIOs still get that same question. "Did the lights really flicker? Well, that's not so," Fitzgerald patiently explains. "It is my understanding that it is against the law to use a public utility to execute. Anyway, we had our own generator—our own setup—we did it internally."[34]

After Old Sparky was retired in 1964, the myths continued. Former death row reporter Kathy Walt says that many envision the inmate being sedated or forced onto the gurney where the lethal injection takes place. Although there is a tie-down team at hand, prisoners seldom "kick up a ruckus," according to Walt. During the three dozen executions she covered, there were no such scenes. "I always attributed that to the prison staff and to the counseling, particularly from the chaplain, who got them ready for their fate."[35]

### *"Death Is Cheaper than Life"*

Execution as a cost-saving measure is the basis of yet another misconception, Lyons explains. "A lot of people say we should execute them because it is a lot more expensive if we keep them alive all that

**Former "Death House Warden" Jim Willett says that everyone who visits the Texas Prison Museum where he is the director wants to see Old Sparky, the final seat for 361 condemned prisoners between 1924 and 1972. *Texas Prison Museum photo***

time. That is not true—it's more expensive to put someone on death row because most of these inmates are indigent."[36] A number of studies support this contention: One of the more recent, by the Death Penalty Information Center, found that the cost of a death penalty case in Texas averages about $2.3 million.[37] Fitzgerald adds, "Most of the people who wind up on death row are indigent, so the taxpayers are paying for the initial trial on both sides of the aisle. Then in Texas if you get a capital death sentence, the appeal is automatic, so then [taxpayers] are paying for the attorney general's office as well as for appellate attorneys to walk it through the state as well as the federal appellate process."[38] By contrast, the current estimated cost per day to house an offender in Texas is $61.58, according to the TDCJ website's "Death Row Facts."[39]

Many taxpayers probably don't realize that the most expensive "amenity" prisoners receive is medical care. With the aging prison population, this expense promises to accelerate, but it represents one of those complex stories reporters seldom tackle. The costs vary dramatically depending on the age of the offender. According to a 1999 report by the Criminal Justice Policy Council, health care for "elderly" offenders (fifty-five and older) costs the state $14.80 per day, while younger offenders require only $4.93 per day.[40] Interestingly, food and security costs are about the same—roughly $2 a day per offender.[41] Prison produces premature aging—offenders generally have the health problems of people ten years older in the free world.[42] Prisons are problematic for diseases such as HIV/AIDS and hepatitis. "I can't tell you how many clients we've lost to disease," says Jim Marcus of the Texas Defender Service, which represents death row prisoners. "At least five of our clients have died before they could execute them."[43]

*"Prisons Are Country Clubs"*

Because the world inside a prison is outside the experience of most Texans, perceptions of life behind the walls are often colored by images presented in the popular media, hearsay, or pure misinformation. Of course, the State of Texas has long been the focus for larger-than-life personalities, tall tales, and Wild West images for some Americans, and certainly for people in other countries. Perhaps the most widespread misconception—for foreigners and state residents alike—is the "country club myth," the idea that prisoners work little if at all and live in air-conditioned comfort with cable TV and Internet access. The actual circumstances are a country mile from that image.

Death row offenders are housed in single-person cells measuring sixty square feet without air-conditioning. In Texas summers, when daytime temperatures often climb past 100 degrees, the prisons are a miserable place to be.

Robert Pruett, who is on death row for killing a male correctional officer at the McConnell unit, describes his world:

> We are locked in [our] cells for 23 hours a day, with one hour of recreation per day. Anytime we leave our cells, we must be restrained with handcuffs and escorted by two officers. All visits are noncontact, and recreation occurs in a single-man cage, alone. All physical contact is strictly prohibited . . . We aren't allowed televisions, microwaves, access to swimming pools, or any other absurd things like that, as the media would have the general public believe.
>
> The environment is geared toward sensory deprivation. The scenery never changes for us: cold steel bars, imposing white walls, dirty concrete floors, and whatever view we have from our four-foot-by-three-inch windows. Our options for action each day are limited to recreating, writing, reading, creating art, listening to the radio, and talking with each other through our doors.
>
> We're lulled into a routine that repeats itself for months and even years at a time. Our every action soon becomes mechanical, and our behavior becomes more reflective of a robot than of a human being. I sometimes get my days mixed up; life becomes a blur, creativity diminishes, depression can creep in, some fall prey to psychotic behavior, and others attempt suicide.[44]

Ordinary citizens, however, don't see these scenes inside the walls; public opinion is often based on hearsay and perceptions largely formed from movies and television. "There are two types of people when it comes to prisons—those who think we are not beating the prisoners enough and those who think we are coddling them," Fitzgerald says wryly.[45]

## Bizarre but True Last-Breath Stories

The public appetite for the odd and bizarre doesn't end with last meal stories. A couple of the more unusual true execution stories involve an errant glass eye and a missing handcuff key. Fitzgerald recalls an execution of a nameless prisoner from San Antonio who surprised his executioners after his death:

> He committed a crime in which he took a banker and his wife hostage at their home in Alamo Heights and the plan was to get the husband, who was a bank officer, to go down and get the money out of the bank to free his wife. Well, it went awry and he wound up killing the woman and of course he got the death penalty for it. . . . He was probably legally blind or very close to it; he wore very thick glasses. When we put him on the gurney for some reason we didn't have his glasses on him. He was being pronounced dead by the physician, and the guard checked his pulse and looked in his eyes with a flashlight, but no one told them this guy had a glass eye. It popped out and the guard grabbed it before it hit the ground and kind of stuffed it back in.[46]

Lyons tells the bizarre execution story she has heard most frequently:

> One of the strangest was the execution of Panchai Wilkerson. He is the inmate who spit out a handcuff key—yes, he was taking his last breath and he popped this key out of his mouth and caught everybody off guard. Nobody had any idea he had a key in his mouth. The first question is, "Could he have escaped?" No, he couldn't have. Inmates that are transported have two sets of handcuffs and he had a key to one of them, but he didn't have a key to the other set. So, he could not have escaped, but we never found out where he had gotten the key or how he hid it all that time.[47]

Facts are truly stranger than fiction when it comes to execution stories. "There are always bizarre things, situations you would never have thought of," Lyons continues. "We had a situation where a man was about to be executed for killing a ten-year-old girl, and the girl's mother, who was his girlfriend at the time, wanted to witness the execution, but she was serving time in Gatesville for killing the girl's biological father. It's just a huge ordeal; you can't make this stuff up." [48]

Although death row prisoners have few possessions, entrepreneurship thrives until the end. By Texas law, inmates are not allowed to profit from their notoriety, but many try to do so, especially death row prisoners. Personal items offered for sale range from fingernail clippings, offered by "railroad killer" Angel Maturino Resendiz, to items of clothing. Murder memorabilia listings sometimes turn up on eBay, the international auction site sometimes called the world's largest garage sale. Lyons remembers a death row inmate who tried to auction off a witness spot for his execution. The PI officers had the listing pulled from the web site. The witness slots are the property of the condemned, but they have no monetary value. "You can put whomever you like to witness your execution, but you're not allowed to take money for it," Lyons says.[49]

## Death Takes Its Toll on Storytellers

Although some view the death ritual as a vestige of Texas's frontier mentality, seasoned death row reporters recall when executions were by far less sedate than they are now. "Well, in the early days there was—party is not the right word—but there was an atmosphere of 'this is a big event and a lot of people came to town for it,' " remembers Kathy Walt, who spent ten years in Huntsville covering death row, first for the *Huntsville Item* and then for the *Houston Chronicle*. "That's when they did executions at midnight." Students from the nearby college sometimes added to the revelry, congregating outside the Walls to drink beer and "cheer the execution on," Walt recalls.[50]

Because executions have taken place so often in Texas since they were reinstated in 1976, they have lost much of their news appeal. Walt notes, "When the death penalty was started up again, all those details became a fascination—this is what he said, this is what he ate—now, the stories that run in the paper are three or four paragraphs; it's not front-page news anymore."[51] The majority of the men on Texas's death row are black or Hispanic, many with impoverished and illiterate backgrounds. The horror of their crimes may bring them to the public's attention for a short time, but usually by the time of their scheduled executions only the convicts' and victims' families are still involved with the story. Usually, their executions are barely noted by the media or by the citizens of Huntsville.

Kelly Prew of the *Huntsville Item* was reluctant to accept the assignment to cover her first execution. "I felt completely out of the loop. I was in the room and no one knew who I was and I just felt like I was watching a train wreck happen . . . I had a lot of anxiety about it. I swore I would never do it again."[52] After that first experience, Prew reconsidered and agreed to continue to cover executions, but decided she would take time to get to know the condemned prisoners beforehand.

Death row reporters who get to know inmates during years of interviews and then attend their executions must find ways to deal with their own emotions. Walt, a seasoned reporter who never flinched from asking tough questions and was not easily swayed by prisoners' claims of innocence, took a pragmatic approach during her years of death row coverage, but she admits it was not always easy to keep her emotions in check. "It was more difficult to watch an inmate be executed if it was one I had interviewed on many occasions and had gotten to know. Over the years it became a very depressing issue to deal with."[53]

In his compelling book, *Have a Seat, Please,* Don Reid, *Huntsville Item* reporter, editor, and publisher, chronicled thirty-five years of covering the prison system, during which he witnessed 189 executions. Reid interviewed most of the men who were put to death and was instrumental in obtaining stays for several, but his book makes it clear he was always haunted by the execution experiences, even when he was convinced of the prisoner's guilt.

"As time passed, I became in effect a functionary of the Ritual of Death," Reid wrote. "Prison officials quickly learned I had a soothing effect on men who were ready to go down. So prison officials welcomed me into the official family, partly to make their job easier. . . . [They] don't like to see a man create a wild scene by fighting his way step by step to the chair."[54] Reid continued, "Finally, I began to see my visits to Death Row as a form of duty because I could help the inmates with my presence. And with that, I simply grew accustomed to the job. Accustomed but not calloused, for the time never came that I did not leave the Death Chamber shaken and to some degree haunted."[55]

Only a few news people have witnessed more executions than Reid. One of them is Mike Graczyk, the Associated Press reporter from Houston who has been present for more than two hundred executions since 1984.[56] Although he refuses to discuss his personal stance on the death penalty, Graczyk takes care to interview the victim's relatives after the execution. "The biggest complaint I hear from victims' rights advocates or family members of the murder victims is: 'I wish he would have died the same way my loved one died. It's too quick, too clean, and too sterile.' "[57]

Carla Faye Tucker, the pickax murderer who became a born-again Christian in the fifteen years between her arrest and execution, drew sympathy from many quarters, ranging from former PIO Larry Fitzgerald, who describes her as a "very spiritual person,"[58] to anti-death penalty activist Dennis Longmire, who says, "Everybody associated with [Karla Faye] acknowledged she was not the monster who was convicted."[59]

Despite latent sympathy for some condemned women, the executions go forward. When appeals from a host of supporters failed, Frances Newton was put to death in September 2005, the first African-American woman to be executed in Texas since the Civil War. Coincidentally, her court-appointed attorney was Ron Mock, who lost numerous capital cases and was notorious for falling asleep in court while defending Gary Graham.[60]

Reporters also must separate their own principles from their jobs as media witnesses to executions. Janet Parker Dial, who personally is against the death penalty, clearly remembers the first execution she covered for the *Item*. "I kept having these Walter Mitty kinds of thoughts: 'I'll just stand up, say this is wrong and stop the execution,'" Dial recalls fantasizing. She did not sleep the night before the execution, and because the sentence was carried out at midnight did not sleep on execution night, either. Instead of trying to stop the death ritual, she focused on practicalities: "I reminded myself not to lock my knees and to take deep breaths."[61]

The bizarre civility of the execution process gives reporters new to the beat pause. Special etiquette questions arise: Are the rules of comportment similar to those for attending a funeral? What does one wear to an execution? In the Old South tradition of falling back on convention under difficult circumstances, most witnesses attending executions adopt somber attitudes. Dial wryly recalls her dilemma over what to wear to her first execution: "I usually dressed casually at work, but that didn't seem appropriate, so I went shopping and bought a dark green dress."[62] Some create rituals for the occasion; Walt remembers a reporter who always purchased a new outfit—not necessarily in a dark color—to wear to an execution.[63] Humor—dark or otherwise—is frowned upon, but the surreal nature of the situation is unsettling. "It is a cold, clinical setting; it looks like an emergency room with the prisoner strapped to the gurney. The witnesses stand around and make polite conversation while someone dies," Dial says.[64]

Reporters from other parts of the country sometimes misinterpret this stiff upper lip attitude as callousness and view Texas as part of the Old West's "life is cheap" mentality. Even in the twenty-first century, Huntsville, like most small Texas towns, is essentially a closed society that treats outsiders politely but holds them at arm's length. National reporters sometimes complain that the PIOs block them from attending executions. Denis Johnson, a *Rolling Stone* reporter who spent several weeks in Huntsville trying to view one of the five executions scheduled for May 2000, categorized Texas as "grandly and profoundly Southern, reclusively and myopically Southern."[65]

Eric Thompson has been covering executions for KPFT, the Houston affiliate of Pacifica Radio, since 2003, and he sees the contrast between the PIOs' public face and the actual situation as bizarre. "In the back of my mind, I can't help but be interested in how people are so methodical [when] someone is going to be dying and their paperwork makes them complicit in this death. But they always seem to block it out and are almost oddly smiling, cheerful, like 'It's just another day here and thanks to all the visitors for coming out to the Walls.' "[66]

Paradoxically, the brutality of executions is the focus of a growing body of criminology research that suggests that execution publicity may actually increase violent crime. SHSU Criminal Justice professor Longmire explains that this "brutalization research looks not only at the process of execution, but also at how widely it is publicized. It traces violent crime rates after the execution for a series of weeks and correlates with the volume of media coverage." The result, Longmire says, is a short-term but significant increase in violent crime.[67]

## The Last Word

More prominent than the sixty-seven-foot statute of Sam Houston standing guard at the edge of town, more enduring than the 130-year-old state university known for its criminal justice program, execution rituals, urban legends, and bizarre tales are inextricably tied to public perceptions about Huntsville.

Black humor and Southern civility become coping mechanisms in situations too bizarre to be fictional. Political agendas and individual egos often distort or redirect decisions. Prisoners present their own worldviews, appropriately phrased for their purposes. Which perceptions reflect reality? Which are wishful thinking or even deliberate manipulation? It is often left to the PIOs to provide explanations and to cope with long-standing traditions and ingrained stereotypes. And, like anyone caught between conflicting opinions, the PIOs absorb some of the barbs meant for others. Reporters also struggle to set aside their own prejudices and personal beliefs so they can meld facts and impressions to tell the "real" story.

This relationship of dependence and aversion has been in place in Huntsville for so many decades the insiders find it commonplace. They are taken by surprise when outsiders are perturbed or horrified by the prison culture and death rituals carried out in the town. However, the otherworldliness of life and death in prison will assuredly continue to be a popular media theme; it makes for great stories. Unfortunately, the stories lend themselves to sensationalized treatments, which are easier and more popular than the messy, complex, ambiguous "truths." For everyone involved, the greatest danger may lie in becoming both accustomed to and calloused by the realities of life—and death—in Prison City.[68]

## ENDNOTES

1. "How the Rockefeller Drug Laws Harm Society." January 2004 position paper, Available at: http://www.interfaithimpactny.org/positionpapers/womenprison.htm.
2. Marc Mauer. "Comparative International Rates of Incarceration: An Examination of Causes and Trends." Presented to the U.S. Commission on Civil Rights, June 20, 2003.
3. "Death Row Facts." TDCJ website, Available at: http://www.tdcj.state.tx.us/stat/drowfacts.htm.
4. Larry Fitzgerald (former TDCJ public information manager). Interview by Ruth Massingill, Huntsville, Texas, April 7, 2003.
5. Rachel Graves. "Ordinary or Odd, Last Meal Can Tell Inmate's Story." *Houston Chronicle*, April 6, 2003. 33A.
6. Ibid.
7. Michelle Lyons (TDCJ public information officer). Interview by Ruth Massingill, Huntsville, Texas, March 29, 2005.
8. Graves.
9. Kevin Francis O'Neill. "Muzzling Death Row Inmates: Applying the First Amendment to Regulations That Restrict a Condemned Prisoner's Last Words." *Arizona State Law Journal 2* (winter 2001). Available at: http://www.web.lexis-nexis.com/universe/document?_m=8ddfe74ccb00a5417f0841ffd8d91b2&_doc.
10. Kathy Walt (spokesperson for Texas governor Rick Perry and former *Houston Chronicle* reporter). Interview by Ruth Massingill, Huntsville, Texas, December 13, 2003.
11. O'Neill. 7.
12. Lyons interview, 2003.
13. Gary Graham. "Executed Offenders." Offender Information, TDCJ Death Row Information website. Available at: http://www.tdcj.state.tx.us/stat/000696.jpg.
14. Graves.
15. Salatheia Bryant. "Graham Executed after Struggle." CNN.com Transcripts, June 23, 2000. Available at: http://archives.cnn.com/2000/LOCAL/southwest/06/23/hci.graham.execution/index.html.

16. "Countdown to Gary Graham's Execution in Texas." CNN.com Transcripts, June 22, 2000, Available at: http://transcripts.cnn.com/TRANSCRIPTS/0006/22/bn.05.html
17. Fitzgerald interview, 2003.
18. Bryant.
19. Ibid.
20. Fitzgerald interview, 2003.
21. Bryant.
22. Dennis Longmire (criminal justice professor and anti-capital punishment activist). Interview by Melody Davison, Huntsville, Texas, June 21, 2005.
23. Ibid.
24. Larry Fitzgerald (former TDCJ public information manager). Interview by Ruth Massingill, Austin, Texas, March 17, 2005.
25. "The Execution." PBS, Frontline, Available at: http://www.pbs.org/wgbh/pages/frontline/shows/execution/.
26. Bryant.
27. Gary Graham. "Executed Offenders." Last Statement, TDCJ Death Row Information website. Available at: http://www.tdcj.state.tx.us/stat/grahamgarylast.htm.
28. Sara Rimer. "In the Busiest Death Chamber, Duty Carries Its Own Burdens." *New York Times,* December 17, 2000. Available at: http://www.deathpenaltyinfo.org/article.php?scid=17&did=354.
29. Kate Randall. "In Cold Blood: The State Murder of Gary Graham." World Socialist website, June 23, 2000. Available at: http://www.wsws.org/articles/2000/jun2000/grah-j23.shtml.
30. "Prison Driving Tour." A publication of the Huntsville Convention and Visitors Bureau Huntsville/Walker County Chamber of Commerce, distributed March 2005.
31. Michelle Lyons (TDCJ public information officer). Interview by Tina Baiter, Huntsville, Texas, May 19, 2005.
32. Fitzgerald interview, 2003.
33. Don Reid. *Have a Seat, Please.* Huntsville: Texas Review Press, 2001. 25.
34. Fitzgerald interview, 2003.
35. Walt interview, 2003.
36. Lyons interview, 2003.
37. G. Sasser, et al. "Facts and Issues—Criminal Justice: Capital Punishment." League of Women Voters of Texas Education Fund, 2002.
38. Fitzgerald interview, 2005.
39. "Death Row Facts." TDCJ website. Available at: http://www.tdcj.state.tx.us/stat/drowfacts.htm.
40. Tony Fabelo. "Elderly Offenders in Texas Prisons." Criminal Justice Policy Council Report, 1999.

41. Scott Nowell. "Lite Sentences: TDCJ Cuts the Calories for Convicts, Leaving Them and Guards Grumbling." *Houston Press,* October 23, 2003; "Prison System Will Get Attention." Editorial, *Austin American-Statesman,* January 2, 2005.
42. Fabelo.
43. Jim Marcus (administrator and attorney, the Texas Defender Service). Interview by Ruth Massingill, Houston, Texas, August 15, 2005.
44. Robert Pruett. Texas Death Row, Livingston, Texas, 2003.
45. Fitzgerald interview, 2003.
46. Ibid.
47. Lyons interview, 2003.
48. Ibid.
49. Lyons interview, 2005.
50. Walt interview, 2003.
51. Ibid.
52. Kelly Prew (*Huntsville Item* reporter). Interview by Tina Baiter, Huntsville, Texas, March 10, 2005.
53. Walt interview, 2003.
54. Reid, 31–32.
55. Ibid., 32.
56. Rachel Graves. "*Houston Chronicle* Reporter Thinks, 'Stop, You're Killing Him.'" *Houston Chronicle,* July 4, 2003. Available at: http://texasmoratorium.org/article.
57. Stefano Esposito. "Kennewick Murderer's Execution Draws Closer." *Tri-City Herald,* September 2, 1998. Available at: http://www.tri-cityherald.com/news/oldnews/1998/0902.html.
58. Fitzgerald interview, 2003.
59. Longmire interview, 2005.
60. "From Death Row: Texas Set to Execute First African-American Woman since Civil War." *Democracy Now,* August 25, 2005. Available at: http://www.indybay.org/news/2005/08/1762183.php.
61. Dial interview, 2004.
62. Ibid.
63. Walt interview, 2003.
64. Dial interview, 2004.
65. Denis Johnson. "Five Executions and a Barbeque." *Rolling Stone,* August 17, 2005. 53.
66. Thompson interview, 2005.
67. Longmire interview, 2005.
68. See, generally, *Prison City: Life with the Death Penalty in Huntsville, Texas,* Ruth Massingill and Ardyth Broadrick Sohn (Peter Lang, 2007), especially Chapters 3 and 4. The author would like to thank Peter Lang Publishing for generously giving permission to use material that first appeared in *Prison City.*

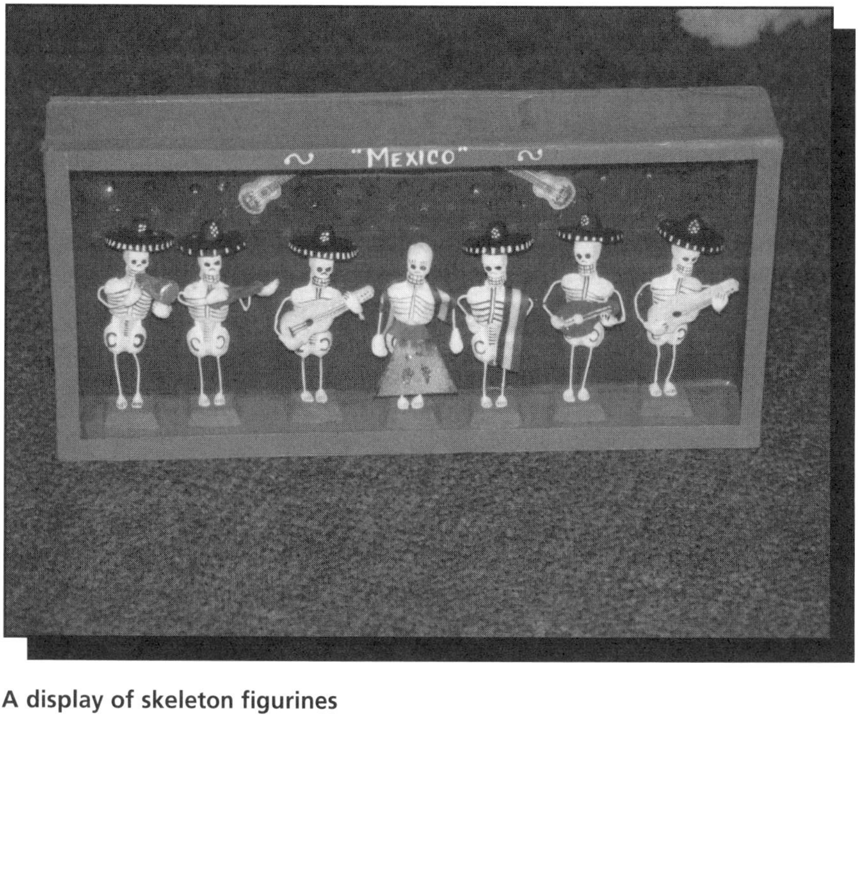


A display of skeleton figurines

# ORIGINS AND CELEBRATIONS OF *EL DÍA DE LOS MUERTOS*

by J. Rhett Rushing

Harvest time. The crops are in and the fields are torn and broken from giving their all. What has been nurtured and tended since the first warming winds of spring is now cold and dead and spent. Ghosts roam here as the line between the living and the dead is blurred and any door separating them stands ajar. This is the liminal time of transition and uncertainty. This is *Samhain*.

In Northern European history when the ancient Celts farmed and struggled—before the Christians and even before the Romans—*Samhain* was the end of the harvest time when farmers gave thanks for the bounty and prepared for the long winter to come. It was a time of celebration, but equally a time of caution. The normal rules and behaviors were suspended and time seemed to stand still.

For agricultural peoples the world over, the fall equinox signaled the end of the year, the onset of the Harvest Moon (when many farmers worked by full moonlight to gather crops before the weather turned bad), and the beginning of winter. The symbolic "death" of the crops was celebrated with feasting, with the ritual burning of the "Wicker Man" made of stalks and stems left over from the harvest, and the scattering of ashes over the fields to ensure fertility in the coming seasons.

It was time of remembering the human dead as well, including the offering of foods and prayers. And since the dead were free to wander the earth, the living stayed close to their homes. If anyone had to be out at night, they were careful to wear a mask so as to confuse the ghosts who might be seeking them. In Ireland, travelers carried small lanterns carved from turnips to light their way, and those turnips were frequently carved with spooky faces as well.

Roman conquest did little to alter *Samhain* celebrations, but the coming of Christianity and organized Catholicism made a mark still in evidence today. For a thousand years all across Christendom, the church worked to supplant "pagan" rituals with Christian characters and themes, and by the conquest of the New World, Roman Catholicism had turned the harvest festival from harrowing to holy.

In an attempt to de-emphasize the spooky and liminal aspects of the season, it was decided that a day of celebration for all the hallowed saints would satisfy the farmers' need for a celebration while shepherding it into a religious event. For the most part this was a successful conversion, but it did not address the people's need to "blow off steam" after the hard work of harvesting. *Samhain* had allowed for a period of ritualized misbehavior and a suspension of the normal rules governing daily life. Simply retooling the feast did not cure the social restlessness, and being as creative as only humans can be, the night before All Hallows Day became the target for eeriness and mischief—All Hallows Eve, or Halloween.

Coming to the New World, Catholic conquerors again encountered harvest festivals where agricultural populations celebrated with feasting and a time of reverence for the dead returning to share the harvest. For untold centuries, Toltecs, Mayans, and Aztecs typically dedicated an entire month to the dead, and enjoyed a corn harvest fully intended to be shared among the living and the deceased. Again incorporating indigenous practices under the blanket of Catholic belief, All Saints Day took root in New Spain as a day of veneration and remembrance for those gone on. Initially, November the first was dedicated to recognized Catholic saints, but since children could die in a state of grace, the "little saints" were included as well. November the second (All Souls Day, or as it is known in Mexico and the American Southwest, *El Día de los Muertos*) developed as a formal time for remembering deceased adults.

**Food *ofrendas* commonly left for the dead**

There are no formal guidelines for celebrating *El Día de los Muertos,* but there are several hallmarks of the holiday. Altars, whether constructed in the home or in larger, shared spaces, are often decorated with images of the deceased and filled with *ofrendas,* or offerings. These offerings frequently include *pan de muerto,* bread baked only during this season, in the shapes of the *Virgen de Guadalupe* or other religious figures, skulls, skeletons, or little animals if intended for *los angelitos* (deceased children). Other offerings include candies, sugar skulls, candles, toys, favorite foods, beer or tequila, and marigolds by the score.

Oftentimes, cartoon-like skeleton figurines known as *calaveras* are placed on the altar. These serve as humorous reminders of our shared humanity. Stripped of all pomp and pride down to bare bones, these clown-like figures sing and dance and remind us that no matter how important we feel ourselves to be in life, we are all equal in death.

**A colorful skeleton figurine to be left at an altar**

Perhaps the most traditional of *El Día de los Muertos* activities is the visit to the graveyard. Families will often eat breakfast and visit the church to light a candle before packing rakes, hoes, flowers, paint, tools, and a selection of foods. Outside the gates of the cemetery vendors crowd the streets selling marigolds, *milagros,* religious images, foods of all sorts, candles, and every sort of flower vase and picture frame.

Arriving at the *campo santo* (cemetery) the family will pull weeds, align grave decorations, repaint faded items, water grass or flowers, sprinkle water over bare earth, and sweep and generally clean up the gravesite in honor of the deceased. Afterwards, a cloth or blanket may be spread over the grave and the family will enjoy a meal.

**A display of altar items at UTSA's Institute of Texan Cultures**

In some locations and among some families, visits to the grave take place the night before All Souls Day so that family and friends can drop by and spend the night "remembering" the deceased with songs and stories, food and drink. The living are brought together, the dead are remembered, and the family is whole. As with most Tejano celebrations, the ultimate goal of each gathering is to reinforce and reestablish family unity. It may be easier to understand this social function in terms of memory, for as long as one is remembered by the family, one still has "life" in the family. *El Día de los Muertos* is entirely about life and death and remembering.

Grayson County Courthouse

# FROM THE GALLOWS: A CONFESSION AND APOLOGY

by Jerry B. Lincecum

One of Dr. Samuel Johnson's more acerbic comments has often been quoted or paraphrased: "Depend upon it, sir, when a man knows he is to be hanged in a fortnight, it concentrates his mind wonderfully." Grayson County had its first legal hanging in Sherman on Friday, April 8, 1869, and a statement from the gallows by one of the men who was executed seems to confirm Dr. Johnson's theory. In the fiftieth-anniversary edition of the old *Sherman Courier*, on August 15, 1917, a lengthy account of the first legal hanging is given.

Before reviewing the document, however, let's briefly consider the literary and folk tradition it fits into. In 1871, a London bookseller named Charles Hindley published a "large and curious assortment" of miscellaneous writings that he collectively entitled "Curiosities of Street Literature." A major portion of this collection consisted of "gallows literature" of the streets. These accounts of public executions, dying speeches, and confessions range from the execution of Sir John Oldcastle in 1417 to the trial and execution of F. Hinson, who was hanged at the Old Bailey in 1869. Hindley writes that "Execution Ballads" for notable murders could command "a most enormous sale," as the reports of two 1849 cases achieved estimated sales of some two-and-a-half million.

Thus, it is hardly surprising that at almost the same time Hindley published his book, a newspaper in Sherman, Texas, would give extended coverage to a public hanging. Moreover, the *Courier's* account leads one to suspect that the confession and apology delivered from the gallows by one of the prisoners was composed with the assistance of a minister or other well-educated person. Certainly his diction and syntax do not match those of folk speech in North Texas at this time.

The *Courier* account begins: "During the Civil War and in the days of reconstruction immediately following, North Texas was overrun with bad characters from the North and East, and a reign of terror, as it were, prevailed for a number of years. The early settlers of Texas were practically all God's noblemen, and before the civil war there were indeed few thieves and robbers in Texas. (I hear no irony in this remarkable statement.)

"These men, (William O.) Blackmore and (John) Thompson, were staying in the southern part of Grayson County, pretending to farm, but in reality lying in wait to steal and rob. One day in the early part of 1869 they were in McKinney, the county seat of Collin County, and saw a stranger exchange a quantity of gold for greenbacks (currency).

"The traveler left for the north and these men followed him, overtaking and murdering him at night in Grayson County, south of Van Alstyne. When the body of the man was found, the whole community was called together and each required to give an account of himself, and all were able to give a satisfactory account except these two men. (Note: The above procedure is said to be an old English custom employed in the detection of criminals.)

"Suspicion pointed to the men and an investigation followed. They were duly tried in the courthouse of this county and hanged at the southeast corner of the old courthouse in Sherman. C. B. Dorchester of this city, as a boy, witnessed the hanging." (In another account, W. H. Chisholm is listed also as one of the small boys who witnessed the executions.)

"The sheriff of the county at that time was Jacob Gumm, who lived near Van Alstyne. At the time of the execution Gumm was at home sick and the men were hung by John Hunter, his first deputy. Dr. J. B. Stinson was county physician, and in his official capacity pronounced the men dead.

"I. T. Akers, father of Burt and Walter Akers of this city, was also one of Gumm's deputies, and he guarded Blackmore and Thompson from the day of their sentence until they were hanged. There being no cell or secure place in the old jail, the men were chained to the floor and armed guards watched them night and day."

Each of the two young men was allowed to make a statement prior to being hanged. The *Courier* article carried what appears to be the complete public statement of each man. Blackmore's last words probably set a Grayson County record in length, and one suspects that he had considerable assistance in composing it. A quick count of the words recorded shows a total of approximately 790 words spoken. The following are a few excerpts:

"I confess I was concerned in the murder of a man for which I am about to die by the law of the land. I am heartily sorry, and I know it is just that I should die. Before I die I want to say a few words to the young men of my country as a warning to them. In my childhood my parents taught me my duty to God and man. They didn't even allow me to play marbles on Sunday. I was a good boy up to my fifteenth year, when I went into the Confederate army.

"Unfortunately for me, I went into a company of very wicked men. They were my companions, and step by step, I imitated their example, my conscience often checking me until I committed the crime which brought me here. It was not in my heart to be a murderer, but I have been made almost to believe there was no hereafter. I have been led astray by bad men.

"I have been in prison about eight weeks, loaded down with chains, but, thank God, they will be removed today. Oh, that every man felt as I do! There would be no use of shackles or prisons, but all nations would be at peace with God.

"The sheriff has been kind to me and the guards also. I have never called for anything that was necessary but what I got it. I was doing well until this came up, farming in Collin County. A man from Mississippi by the name of Thompson came to where I was living, and I took him in as a partner.

"He was a man of fine appearance. He proposed to me several depredations, and at last I consented to go with him. . . . I was afraid of myself when he told me of the daring deeds he had committed. I tried to persuade him to leave, but he would not heed.

"He persuaded me not to work for a living—that there was an easier way to get it. Oh, that I had never seen him! Young men, if you keep wicked, profane, drinking, gambling company, you will certainly rush to ruin too. God has forgiven me and I have a hope of soon being at rest. I have no unkind feeling toward anyone, and in my heart I forgive all who have been unkind to me.

"I trust you will not feel vengeful towards me when I am gone. I have some friends who have already gone to the beautiful home of the angels, and I trust through the boundless mercy of God that I shall join them. My precious mother still lives. I know this sad news will break her heart, but may God sustain and comfort her. And now, my friends, my time is come, and I wave you the kindest farewell."

In reading this account, one can understand why "gallows literature" was popular in the eighteenth and nineteenth centuries. In our own time the widespread coverage of the O. J. Simpson trial and, more recently, the prospect of his publishing a book that might include a confession are certainly related to our ancestors' morbid interests. There are several things left out of the article that it would be interesting to know: (1) Did Blackmore speak extemporaneously? (2) Did someone write his speech for him, a preacher perhaps? (3) Did Blackmore deliver it while standing on the scaffold just before the trap was sprung? (4) How many people witnessed the hanging? Unfortunately, the answers will likely never be known.

## Sources Consulted


Giornale Nuovo (Of things near and far): "Gallows literature." http://www.spamula.net/blog/2006/03/gallows_literature_1.html (accessed Jan. 24, 2008).

R. C. Vaughn. "First legal hanging in the county." *The life and times of Grayson County*, Texas. Sherman, TX: Big Barn Press, 2006. 27–29.

Weldon O. Williams. *A journey through history: Chronological listing of public officials*, Grayson County, Texas, 1846–2000.

SUPERSTITIONS,
STRANGE
STORIES,

AND VOICES
FROM THE
"OTHER SIDE"

Charlie Oden at a reunion of the T&NO (SP) Railroad

# THE SPIRIT THAT WALKED TOWARD HORNSBY'S BEND

**by Charlie Oden**

There are a number of accounts of this story. All agree with the overall story and differ in some of the details.

And this story is a part of me. The 1920s came and went before air conditioning. The month of August each year was so hot that our family would sit in the yard at night seeking some relief from the heat. Usually about nine p.m., a cooling breeze would stir, and we could go to bed. Sitting outside was a time for telling stories. Dad, who was born in 1881, and Mom, who was born in 1884, would tell exciting tales, like Uncle Billy shooting his old gray mule, or about where Sam Bass and his gang hid their loot.

Another favorite yarn was this Wilbarger story. It is a spooky story. It took place no more than thirty miles from our house, and I closely identified with it. It is an entertaining tale that has attracted writers for over 175 years, including J. Frank Dobie. I have searched a number of these versions to find additional information to add to the story that Dad and Mom told. Now, on to our story.

The event happened in Stephen F. Austin's second colony of about 900 families. The action was at Pecan Springs and at Hornsby's Bend. Pecan Springs is located in Austin between East 51st Street and Rogge Lane, and is almost on Springdale Road. That would be about two good whoops and a holler east of Austin's Robert Mueller Municipal Airport. About three miles or so southeast of there on Highway 969 (Webberville Road), there is a pullover on the highway. This is the location of the Rueben Hornsby property. Visible from the pullover is a padlocked gate to the burying ground of the Rueben Hornsby family; part of this land the Hornsby family lived on.

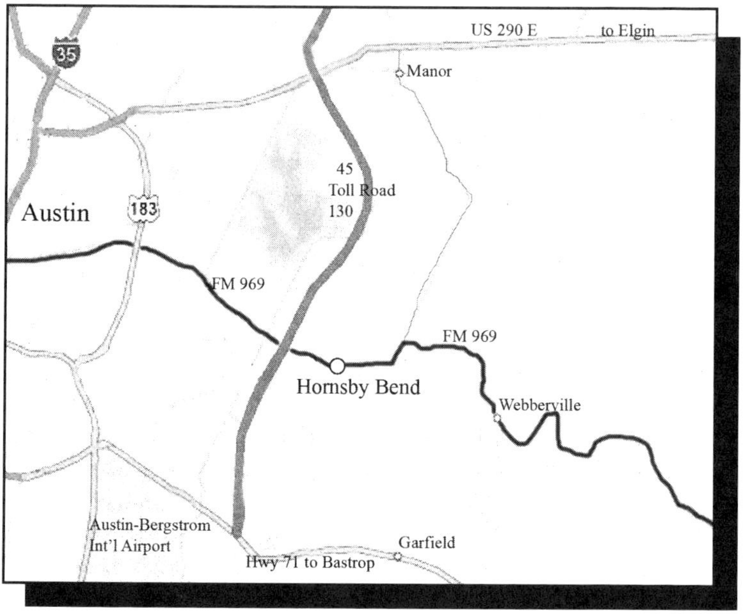


**A map showing the general location of Hornsby's Bend**

Josiah Pugh Wilbarger and his wife moved to Texas from Missouri in 1827. Well educated for his time, he taught school at Matagorda and LaGrange. He settled in a bend of the Colorado River about ten miles above Bastrop. At the time Texas was a part of Mexico, and Mexican law governed the colonists. In 1832, the Mexican government granted him a headright,[1] 4,428 acres of Texas terra firma.[2]

Naturally, there was a demand for his surveying services. In August of 1833, Wilbarger was returning home with a surveying party. That morning, they had seen a lone Indian and had chased him, but he had gotten away. They stopped for their noon meal at Pecan Springs. With Wilbarger were men named Strother and Christian, colonists prospecting for headrights, as well as Haynie and Standifer, two men down from Missouri, to see about moving to Texas, the current land of opportunity.

A party of Indians had been watching them for several days. One of the things Indians had learned about the White Eyes was that, when surveyors were working, there soon would be White settlers who would take even more of their land, land the Indians depended on to support their families. Their land gave them wild game for their meat, their clothing, shelter, tools, and utensils. From the land they got pecans, berries, wild plums, greens, onions, honey (from bee trees), and herbs for medicines.

Their reasoning was simple: the more surveyors you kill, the longer it will be before your source of support, the land, will be taken from you, forcing you to go elsewhere to find a living. Make sense? To them it did. And this particular party planned and executed a successful attack against these encroachers of European stock.

When Josiah and party stopped, Christian, Strother, and Wilbarger unsaddled their horses and hobbled them so that the horses might more easily rest and graze during the stop. Haynie and Standifer, the men from Missouri, loosened the cinches on the saddles on their horses and staked them close at hand in grass and near water. The Indians attacked when the White men were settled into their meal.

At the first shot, the men leaped for cover behind trees and began returning fire. The attackers mortally wounded Strother almost immediately. One shot broke Christian's thigh; another smashed his powder horn. An arrow went through the calf of one of Wilbarger's legs. Another shot struck his thigh. Nevertheless, he ran to Christian's side and set him against a tree. He primed Christian's weapon (it was already loaded), and jumped for his own tree. A second arrow in the other leg caused him to fall. Haynie and Standifer both fired their muzzle-loading weapons.

When Haynie and Standifer saw the other three men down, they knew that if they did not get the heck out of there, there would very soon be five men down. They ran to their horses, tightened the cinches, leaped into the saddles, and began their flight. Wilbarger saw them and managed to get to his feet and run toward the horses, thinking to get up behind one of the riders, but he fell before reaching them. Some accounts say that Wilbarger fell because he was shot in the back of the head, the ball exiting under the chin. Some accounts ignore this fourth wound. Both Haynie and Standifer saw Wilbarger fall, so they spurred their horses and rode hell for leather for the Hornsby place. Looking back, they saw Indians swarming around their victims. How many Indians did the five men kill or wound? We don't have any information as to the casualties the Indians suffered, if any.

The victors cut the throats of Strother and Christian, scalped them, and stripped their bodies. Wilbarger was conscious, but couldn't move. When they got to Wilbarger, they apparently decided that he was dead, because they didn't cut his throat. They did, however, strip him (they missed one sock) and scalp him. But not the whole scalp at once, as one would think. No. Each of the victors who had a part in killing him (as they thought) was entitled to a share of the scalp. Each took a piece of the scalp about the size of a silver dollar.[3] Wilbarger later reported that though he felt no pain from the scalping, the peeling of each piece of scalp sounded like a peal of thunder.

Now think about this: Wilbarger's previous wounds were in the legs and thigh. Yet he was paralyzed when he was scalped. A shot in the neck that exited under the chin could have grazed the spine and damaged a nerve in such a way that he was temporarily paralyzed and unable to feel pain during the scalping. Further, there would have been a neck wound. The accounts I have read focus on the head wound and make no mention of as serious a thing as a shot through the neck.

Change channels to Standifer and Haynie. They reached Hornsby's Bend, their horses all a lather, and reported the attack. A rider was sent down river to the Wilbarger settlement to summon help and to notify Josiah's wife. The Hornsby family, aided by Haynie and Standifer, barricaded the place to protect against an Indian attack.

Now change channels back to Wilbarger. He regained consciousness about mid-afternoon. Blood was oozing from his head wound, clotting more and more; flies were swarming about his head and neck. He managed to pull himself to the nearby spring to drink. He lay in the spring a long time to cool himself, and dropped off to sleep. On waking he felt frozen. He dragged himself from the water. He saw a few snails and ate them. At sometime during this part of his ordeal he covered his wound with his wet sock. He fell asleep again, waking about nightfall. He then was able to take stock of his situation. He was severely wounded. He was unable to walk. He was without food. He was about three or a little more miles from the safety of the Hornsby's place. Indians might be close by. He decided to start toward Hornsby's. He dragged his naked body about a half-mile before he gave out. He pulled himself to a tree and rested against it. He lapsed into a coma.

While in the coma he had a remarkable vision of his sister Margaret who was living 700 miles away in Missouri. In this vision Margaret told him, "Brother Josiah, you are too weak to go any farther by yourself. Stay here, and help will come tomorrow by the setting of the sun." She spoke other words of comfort and then walked toward Hornsby's Bend. Josiah called after her, entreating her to remain with him, but the Spirit continued walking toward Hornsby's Bend. The stars that night were big and bright, deep in the heart of Texas.

Let me let you in on a little secret. Margaret had died just the previous day. Telephone communication was yet to be invented. It took weeks for a letter to reach its destination. Note, too, that Josiah recounted his vision of Margaret long before a letter arrived notifying him that sister Margaret was dead in Missouri.

Change channels back to Rueben and Sarah Hornsby's house. Sarah Hornsby was awakened about midnight by a vivid and terrible dream. She saw Josiah leaning against a tree, naked except for a sock covering his head, wounded and bleeding, but alive. She awakened Reuben and told the dream to him. He suggested that the dream was caused by overwrought nerves, but she insisted that this vision was true. Reuben awakened Standifer and Haynie. They told again that they had seen Wilbarger fall and had seen the Indians scalping him. There was no doubt in their minds that Wilbarger was dead. After everyone had gone back to sleep, Sarah had the identical dream. (Some accounts say there were three dreams.)

Sometimes women get tired of men telling them that they are wrong. This was one of those times. Sarah was convinced that her dream vision was real. By about three a.m., she had the household up and about, eating breakfast and preparing for the search for Wilbarger. The help they had sent for arrived along with

Mrs. Wilbarger, and by daylight the search party was ready to move. Sarah sent with them three bed sheets and a Mexican gourd of milk. Two of the sheets were to wrap the bodies of Strother and Christian for their burial; the third sheet and the milk were for Josiah.

The men of the party rode along expecting attack from Indians at any moment. The search for Wilbarger went on through the day. Then, late in the afternoon, a bloody body stood up before one of the searchers. The man thought it was one of the Indians and called out, "Here they are, boys!" leveling his rifle at the same time. Josiah cried out, "Don't shoot! It's me, Wilbarger."

His rescuers wrapped Josiah in a sheet and placed him in the saddle of William Hornsby, Reuben's sixteen-year-old son, who supported Josiah during the several miles journey back to the bend. Mrs. Hornsby nursed her man at the Hornsby's for about thirty days before taking him home. His was a very large head wound. It never healed. She had her silk wedding dress packed in her trunk. She fashioned the silk material into soft caps that Josiah wore from then on. When he went outside, he wore a soft fur cap. The head wound became his main problem for the rest of his life. He was able to return to surveying, and he taught children in his community. He died from an infection in the wound on April 11, 1844, when he was forty-five years old.

In 1932, the remains of Mr. and Mrs. Josiah Pugh Wilbarger were reburied in the State Cemetery in Austin. The red granite monument erected on the old Manor Road marking the site of Pecan Springs has been removed. There is another monument marking the Hornsby home site.

Many years after the Spirit appeared, a lady named Eva Hill LaSueur Karling wrote this story in a forty-one-verse poem titled "The Spirit that Walked at Hornsby's Bend." Its last three stanzas read:

> This story is still related
> By descendents in reverent awe,
> Of that strange night and the Spirit
> Which their ancestors heard and saw.

Today the old spring still gushes
And flows in a trickling rill,
And the old oak bends and listens,
Brooding o'er the mystery still.

And the blue hills stand a-dreaming
Of that strange and mystic sight
And the pensive quiet prairie
And the Spirit that walked that night.

[A version of this story previously appeared in the *Cotton Patch Rag*, a Houston Folklore Society publication.]

## Endnotes

1. Roy A. Clifford. "Wilbarger, Josiah Pugh." *Handbook of Texas Online.* http://www.tshaonline.org/handbook/online/articles/WW/fwi8.html.
2. "Texas 1821–1833." *Texas Almanac* (2004–2005). *Dallas Morning News.* 36.
3. Indians had a practice called "counting coups" for rewarding actions of bravery in the presence of the enemy. The sharing of the scalp may have been a form of counting coups.

An enigmatic feline

# A GRAVE MISTAKE

by Jennifer O. Curtis

It's been said the only sure things in life are death and taxes. However, I came to question that proverbial wisdom when raising my family in Houston, Texas. Our sense of family always included animals, and there have been many through the years. One cat, in particular, is memorable for his ability to have the last word—even from beyond the grave.

I first saw him clutched to my daughter's chest. "He's a stray," she said. I looked at the young tom draped carelessly over her arm; the cat blinked and snuggled closer to her. The kids named him Mr. Peabody, reflecting a certain dignity and aloofness he had. I didn't realize it at the time that this was the pet that would be the constant in a changing household. He became the children's confidant and counselor, silent witness to their outpourings of frustration as they grew up, his fur bedraggled with their tears.

He was also a con artist with the children and my husband, allowing them the privilege of petting him while gazing adoringly into their faces and purring loudly and contentedly at their slightest croon.

But with me, he declared war.

It was snarl at second sight. He would walk by, look at me and HSST. He never heard of the old saying, "Don't bite the hand that feeds you." Usually a silent stare declared his hunger, but if that didn't work, a nip at the heels herded me along. If he was ravenous, he would rub against my legs while gazing up sweetly, and then bite my legs.

As a rule, our animals knew enough to stay out of the kitchen when I was busy preparing a meal for the eight of us in the family. Not Mr. Peabody. He'd slip into the kitchen, sit silently behind me, and carefully lay his tail behind my heels. If I stepped back, he would erupt with a screech, bat his ears back and stalk the kitchen, slapping his tail from side to side. If I screeched when I stepped back, juggling whatever I was holding, his HSST would be accompanied by a backward glance and smirk that seemed to say, "Gotcha."

It didn't take much provocation for his historic HSST to erupt. My presence was enough. Just letting him out the door at his request was cause for a backward glance, snarl, and HSST. The cat didn't wait to grow old to get crotchety—he was born bad-tempered, except for when he was around the children or my husband, or when he wanted to be fed.

He kept himself remarkably clean, considering the amount of fighting he was engaged in. His skin shown pink through the snowy fur of his tummy; the black, brown, and gray motley markings capping his head and back glistened with his careful, constant grooming. His purr rattled unevenly to the depth of his contented sighs.

As self-appointed guardian of the family, he accompanied the children on their bike rides, escorted the ex-bikers adorned in their prom gowns, and resided over the wedding parties. With age, his fur lost its glisten and seemed to grow in clumps. He would sit, swaying from side to side, almost sightless and hard of hearing. His HSST and paw swing were less vigorous if I screeched as I stumbled over him, but he still smirked over his shoulder and slapped his tail from side to side as if he were saying, "Gotcha."

The vet told us we had a choice. We bought him a little time, but the day came when he took his last breath in my arms. We aren't pet cemetery folk, nor do we place beloved companions in garbage cans. We picked a corner of the yard to bury him, away from people traffic and tree roots. A gully washer rain began as my husband picked up the shovel. Half an hour later, he staggered into the house, gasping for breath.

"Those tree roots are longer than I thought, and that gumbo is terrible. . . . It's so dark I can't see a thing. . . . I hope I'm digging deep enough." Lightening flared as he went out to finish the job.

After the storm, I went to make a phone call, but the line was dead. I told the family that the storm had knocked out the phone. One of the kids casually asked if we had buried the cat in the corner where the phone lines were. Couldn't be, I thought. Then I remembered my husband's exhausted face and comments about how hard those tree roots were to chop through—the tree roots that really shouldn't have been there. Might be . . .

It was. The next morning revealed the chopped phone lines at Mr. Peabody's grave. The phone company was a little incredulous when we explained how the problem had come about, and because it was the weekend, we were without a phone for three days.

I pictured that cat shaking with laughter as we dug him up and reburied him. That cat couldn't have been buried with quiet decorum. Deep grief, thunder and lightning, severed phone lines, laughter and remembrances escorted this swaggering kitty on his final journey. As we laid him to rest, I thought I heard "HSST . . . Gotcha!"

**A page from *Odd Texas*, a book of trivia cartoon-like illustrations by Jack Harper and John Newbern, published in 1936**

# LARGER THAN LIFE, EVEN IN DEATH

by Robert J. (Jack) Duncan

In one respect, death is a lot like a Hollywood film: at the end, everything presumably fades to black just before the credits roll. Throughout history, many Texans have been larger than life, even in death. Occasionally, one finds an unusual inscription on a tombstone, runs across a newspaper article about a fatal "freak" accident, or while waiting in the barbershop for a haircut, hears someone discussing a person who "cheated" death, or an odd event or final request having to do with death or burial. This article examines several such diverse vignettes.

Many people have firm ideas about what is to be done to their bodies after death. In *Texas, My Texas,* James Ward Lee mentions the death, in 1923, of an old man named Isham Summers in Red River County. Summers had been a prosperous bottomland farmer. He wanted the preparations for his burial to be carried out by friends and family, as was the custom in the South in the nineteenth and early twentieth centuries. He had appended this note to his handwritten will: "I have at all times a suit, shirt, and underclothes nice enough to be buried in. Do not buy anything. I do not want an undertaker at any time. I want a coffin made of heart lumber and I want the carpenter well paid for making it. Take my body to the cemetery in a spring hack."[1]

Some of the characters and events in Larry McMurtry's novel *Lonesome Dove* have approximate counterparts in real-world history. The Hat Creek Cattle Company, a partnership business owned by aging former Texas Rangers Captains Woodrow F. Call and Augustus McCrae (Gus) in the novel, parallels the real partnership of cattlemen Charles Goodnight and Oliver Loving. As Gus lies on his deathbed, Call promises to return Gus's body from Montana to Texas for burial. He has the cadaver packed in salt and charcoal to preserve it during the long trek. In real life, it was thirty-one-year-old Goodnight who, in 1868, returned the corpse of his fifty-five-year-old partner, Oliver Loving, packed in charcoal, from Fort Sumner, New Mexico, to Weatherford, Texas, for a Masonic burial.[2]

Likewise, the black cowboy Josh Deets in *Lonesome Dove* seems to be at least partially modeled on the real person Bose Ikard, who worked for Charles Goodnight. The inscription that Call carves on Deets's wooden grave marker[3] is closely patterned after Ikard's tombstone in Weatherford's Greenwood Cemetery, into which Goodnight had the following testimonial cut:

BOSE IKARD
1859–1928

> "Served with me four years on Goodnight-Loving trail, never shirked a duty or disobeyed an order, rode with me in many stampedes, participated in three engagements with Comanches, splendid behavior."—C. Goodnight[4]

If Ikard needed a letter of recommendation to present to Saint Peter, it would be hard to imagine a more favorable—or more forceful—one than this, which is written in stone. Too bad you can't take it with you.

Josiah Pugh Wilbarger was scalped by Comanches and left for dead in 1833. He was found the next day, naked and covered with blood, but alive. He lived for eleven years. He wore knitted caps to cover his bare skull, over which skin did not completely grow.[5] In 1845, Wilbarger bumped his head on a low doorway in his own cotton gin, and that accident led to his death at his home near Bastrop.

A book called *Odd Texas* tells of a cowboy decapitated near Frio, Texas, in 1880. As the mounted cowboy was roping a steer, his rope became tangled around his neck. Unfortunately, he had one end of the rope tied to his saddle horn. Also unfortunately, his attempt to lasso the steer was successful. With the steer pulling one direction, and his pony pulling the other, the rope pulled tight and—well, you get the picture.[6]

In 1927, the Texas State Bankers Association announced that it would pay a reward of $5,000 to anyone who killed a bank robber while he was in the process of robbing a bank. The intent of the reward should have been hard to miss when the next line in the announcement said, "but not one cent for a hundred live ones."[7] Not surprisingly, the reward led to numerous fake bank robberies that were fabricated for the sole purpose of collecting the reward and that resulted in murder.

In one such episode, two Anglo men "hired" four Mexican laborers and took them to Stanton. The Mexicans could understand little English. The two Anglos took the Mexicans to a building (a bank) in Stanton and told them to stand outside. The Anglo men drove away. Soon a fire mysteriously sprung up in a church across town, drawing most of the small town's residents. While that was going on, the two Anglos came back and shot at the Mexicans. They killed two and seriously injured a third.[8] The Texas State Bankers Association quietly withdrew their "dead robber" reward in 1929.

"Uncle" Gus Wilson, a lifelong bachelor in Collin County—who lived almost all of his life in the same log house—appreciated hard work. Through hard work and good investments, Uncle Gus became wealthy. He would occasionally eat supper with one of his tenant sharecropper families. If Gus thought the family was deserving, he might leave the signed deed to the farm under his dinner plate, as a sort of gigantic tip.

In the 1920s, when Gus's brother died, Gus apparently accepted his own mortality. He went to McKinney and ordered his tombstone. He had a sculpture of his dog, Joe, carved on top of the gravestone, along with the inscription, "Joe and I are going home." Under his own name, he requested that these numbers be cut into the stone: 1845–193. He had the stone delivered and installed in the family cemetery near his cabin. When Gus died in 1935, at the age of 90, the stonecutter came out and added the final digit. With all the precision of an insurance company's mortality tables, Gus had looked at his situation objectively and decided that it was very unlikely that he would live into the 1940s.[9]

On Saturday, October 12, 1928, elephants were being walked from railroad boxcars to the Corsicana circus grounds. H. D. (Curley) Pritchett, who earlier had been an elephant handler, helped unload the elephants that day. Black Diamond, a nine-ton bull Indian elephant, was devoted to Pritchett, his former handler. As the elephants were being led through the streets of Corsicana, hundreds of people watched. Suddenly, Black Diamond became enraged.

Eva Donohoo, a fifty-one-year-old woman, was standing between two parked cars near the intersection of W. First Avenue and 13th Street. Without warning, the elephant knocked Pritchett out of the way, then hit Donohoo in the face with his tusks, and knocked her down. The next day's *Dallas Morning News* says, "The beast then reached in with its trunk, dragged the woman from between the automobiles and flung her to the ground, stepping on her and jabbing at her with his tusks."[10] W. M. Cannon, who had been talking with Donohoo, and another man challenged Black Diamond and got her away from the elephant twice, but each time Black Diamond grasped her again with his trunk. Finally, the elephant was calmed somewhat and chained to other elephants. Donohoo was taken to the local hospital by ambulance, but her skull had been crushed, and she died a few minutes later.

Two other people had been injured in the attack, and the cars that Donohoo had been standing beside had been wrecked. Four days later Black Diamond was destroyed by more than 150 rifle shots. It turns out that when Pritchett was Black Diamond's handler, more than a year earlier, Donohoo, in the presence of Black Diamond, had hired Pritchett to work on her plantation. He took the job, and the elephant saw Pritchett leave with Donohoo. Evidently, Black Diamond was not only devoted to Pritchett, but also insanely jealous of his attention.

Eva Speed Donohoo's tombstone in Corsicana's Oakwood Cemetery states that she was "killed by [an] Al G. Barnes Circus elephant."[11]

Ben Hawley was a McKinney resident until his death several years ago. Often I would see him walking the streets of McKinney; during his last several months, he traveled them using a walker. It always worried me that Ben walked several feet from the curb, well into the street. It was not hard to imagine his being struck by a car driven by a newcomer unfamiliar with that habit of Ben Hawley's.

Ben often visited the public library, especially on extremely cold days. Some of his peers were there just to escape the bad weather, but Ben would sit there for hours, reading as he enjoyed the warmth.

After Ben Hawley died, one day I was in the local shoeshine parlor waiting for a shine, and the conversation turned to Hawley. Scott Turrentine, whose family owns a local funeral home, was getting a shine. He mentioned Ben. I told him that I had been surprised to read in Ben's obituary a few months earlier, that his remains were being shipped to California for burial. The story that Scott related that day was a revelation.

"Yes, we had Ben's funeral in Frisco, and then we shipped his body to the West Coast, just as he had directed," he said. Scott went on to say that when war hero Audie Murphy triumphantly returned to Collin County from World War II, and before he went to California to become a movie star, there was a period of time when he just lounged around McKinney, probably trying to adjust to his newfound celebrity. He hung around the square and the downtown area in general. He and Ben got to be buddies at that time. After Audie moved to California, on several occasions Ben rode the train west to visit him. On one of those trips, Ben visited Forest Lawn Cemetery in Hollywood. Suddenly he had an inspiration: he would be buried with the movie stars. So, Ben bought his Hollywood cemetery lot before returning to McKinney. And now Ben sleeps among the stars.[12]

There is a beautiful, poignant, heartbreaking story in Larry L. King's *True Facts, Tall Tales, and Pure Fiction*. There is nothing fictional about the story that comprises the chapter entitled "Happy

Birthday to a Fine Boy,"[13] except that a few names were changed. In 1900, a twenty-six-year-old Texas farmer, "Charlie Hasp," discovered his wife Ida and his good friend and neighbor Morris King engaged in sex, possibly a rape. Larry King, Morris's grandson, says:

> He made them both dress, told a weeping and trembling Ida to stay in the bedroom and herded Morris out of the house at gunpoint.
>
> "Morris, I've got to kill you," he said. "For you have wronged me."
>
> "Oh, God!" Morris said. "Can I have a minute to pray?"
>
> "Yes. But be quick."
>
> Morris dropped to his knees in the sandy loam and asked the Lord to receive his soul and to be merciful to him, a sinner.
>
> When he said "Amen," the young farmer shot him in the back of the head at point-blank range.[14]

So, as a result of the "Unwritten Law," Larry King's father, the eldest son of Morris, had to become the man of the family—a large family—at the age of twelve. Another result was that Larry King never had an opportunity to know his paternal grandfather; he missed knowing him by twenty-nine years.

When a husband killed another man under such circumstances, the so-called "Unwritten Law" meant that a jury could conclude that it was justifiable homicide. A famous such case, in 1911, initiated the Boyce-Sneed Feud. When Lorena (Lena) Sneed—Mrs. John Beal Sneed—admitted to her husband that she was infatuated by Al Boyce, Jr., Sneed had her committed to Arlington Heights Sanitarium in Fort Worth. A few weeks later, Boyce helped Lena escape. They "eloped" to Canada. John Sneed shot and killed Boyce's father, alleging that he "had assisted his son in breaking up Sneed's home."[15] During the trial in Fort Worth, "four men were killed outside the courthouse, and women fought with hatpins in the courthouse halls *and even in the courtroom*" (emphasis mine).[16]

The jury failed to reach a verdict, and the judge declared a mistrial, effectively acquitting Sneed. When reporters quizzed the jury foreman about how the jury could acquit, he responded with: "The best answer is because this is Texas. We believe in Texas a man has the right and the obligation to safeguard the honor of his home, even if he must kill the person responsible."[17] John and Lena Sneed reunited. They eventually struck it rich in the East Texas oilfields, moved to Dallas, and lived a life of luxury for more than three decades. Both died in the 1960s.

Versions of the so-called "Unwritten Law" actually *were* written into law in three states: Utah, New Mexico, and Texas. (The Texas statute was Texas Penal Code Annotated, sec. 1220 [1861].)

In a ghoulish murder case, eight-year-old Timothy O'Bryan of Houston died after eating trick-or-treat candy that had been poisoned with cyanide on Halloween night, 1974. His father said that the candy had been given to the little boy by "a 'hairy-handed' weirdo at one of the houses they had visited together."[18] But police found evidence that the father, Ronald Clark O'Bryan, had himself bought the cyanide and poisoned his own son to collect the proceeds from a life insurance policy he had taken out on the boy. Ronald was convicted, and the judge set his execution for midnight on Halloween, 1982. "In fact, O'Bryan won several stays, but when he was finally killed, shortly after midnight on 31 March 1984, Texans all over the state showed up in bars wearing Halloween costumes."[19]

John O. West, researching folk grave decoration along the Rio Grande in the 1980s, met and photographed a survivor of premature burial. Pablo Pacheco, as a young man, contracted influenza during the 1918 epidemic. Earlier he had told his family repeatedly that he wanted to be buried at home. Fortunately, he was buried (in his own backyard) wrapped in a blanket rather than in a nailed-shut coffin. Three days later, Pablo awoke from a coma and dug himself out![20] Later, he built an elaborate monument to his very personal miracle.[21]

## ENDNOTES


1. James Ward Lee. "Old-Time Buryings." *Texas My Texas,* UNT Press: Denton, 1993. 87.
2. J. Evetts Haley. *Charles Goodnight, Cowman and Plainsman.* Houghton Mifflin: Boston and New York, 1936. 182–184.
3. Larry McMurtry. *Lonesome Dove.* Simon & Schuster: New York, 1985. 723.
4. Bill Harvey. *Texas Cemeteries.* UT Press: Austin, 2003. 260.
5. J. Frank Dobie. "The Dream that Saved Wilbarger." *Tales of Old-Time Texas.* Little, Brown and Company: Boston and Toronto, 1928. 34–41.
6. Jack Harper and John Newbern. *Odd Texas.* Banks Upshaw and Company: Dallas, 1936. 51.
7. A. C. Greene. *The Santa Claus Bank Robbery.* UNT Press: Denton, 1999 (revised edition). 28. Additional information about the reward is on pp. 29, 128–129, and 144–145.
8. Ibid. 128–129.
9. Robert J. Duncan. "Pioneer Angel." *McKinney Living,* vol. 10, no. 1 (Spring 1999). 10–12. Also see Kent Biffle's "Uncle Gus Loved Sharing His Wealth." *Dallas Morning News,* July 16, 2000. 43A.
10. "Mad Elephant Kills Woman, Injures Man." *Dallas Morning News,* October 13, 1929, part 1, page 1. See also an article by Mrs. Fred P. Hodge (who was Eva Donohoo's niece), "Black Diamond." *Navarro County Scroll,* vol. XIV, 1969 (probably on or around October 12, the 40th anniversary of the tragedy), available online at http://www.rootsweb.com/~txnavarr/biographies/b/black_diamond.htm. Mrs. Hodge says that Black Diamond did not step on Eva Donohoo.
11. Bill Harvey. 92–93.
12. Robert J. Duncan. "A Warm Glow for Ben Hawley." *McKinney Living,* vol. 17, no. 6 (August 2006). 46–48.
13. Larry L. King. *True Facts, Tall Tales, and Pure Fiction.* UT Press: Austin, 1997. 71–85.
14. Ibid. 73.
15. Thomas H. Thompson. "Boyce-Sneed Feud." *The Handbook of Texas Online,* s.v. http://www.tshaonline.org/handbook/online/articles/BB/jcb2.html. [For additional information, see numerous articles published in the *Dallas Morning News* between January 15, 1912, and February 8, 1912.]
16. Thomas H. Thompson.
17. Ibid. The jury foreman's name was James D. Crane.
18. Bill Ellis. "Death by Folklore: Ostension, Contemporary Legend, and Murder." *Western Folklore,* vol. 48, no. 3 (July 1989). 215.

19. Ibid. For more on this case see Sylvia Grider's "The Razor Blades in the Apples Syndrome" in *Perspectives on Contemporary Legend,* Paul Smith, Ed., University of Sheffield: CECTAL, 1984. 128-140.
20. John O. West. "Folk Grave Decoration Along the Rio Grande." *Folk Art in Texas,* Francis Edward Abernethy, Ed., PTFS XLV, SMU Press: Dallas, 1985. 51.
21. Ibid. A photograph of Pablo Pacheco on the steps of his monument is on p. 46.

A portrait of Rachel Sullivan Dougherty

# MESSAGES FROM THE SPIRITUAL WORLD

by Mary Margaret Dougherty Campbell

Current society has a fascination with the paranormal. Flipping through the TV channels, one is not surprised to find shows about ghost hunters, mediums, haunted houses, and haunted battlegrounds. Some people even go to great lengths to contact the dead, spirits in the "other world." They sit in the dark around a Ouija Board hoping to get a message spelled out, or they attend a séance holding hands with fellow communication seekers hoping to hear a familiar voice, or they seek out mediums who claim to bridge the real world and the spiritual world, again hoping for some sort of contact. While these people actively seek communication with the dead, others have the communication simply happen to them.

My grandfather Francis Xavier Dougherty was 75% Irish and 100% Catholic. Catholics, in particular Irish Catholics, seem to have a propensity for communication with the spiritual world. My grandfather's niece Rachel Bluntzer Hebert wrote a book of biographical sketches of the San Patricio Irish entitled *The Forgotten Colony: San Patricio de Hibernia,* in which she devotes one chapter to legends and lore, including "ghost stories." In the book's foreword, she begs the question, "How can one write about the Irish and not include tales of the supernatural which abound in this region?"[1] An explanation comes from a Church official: "A Vatican theologian Fr. Gino Concetti stated in the Vatican newspaper *Osservatore Romano,* 'According to modern catechism, God allows our dear departed persons who live in an ultra-terrestrial dimension to send messages to guide us in certain difficult moments of our lives.' "[2] Through research into such communication in the Dougherty-Sullivan family, I categorize the "messages" into four types of communication: voices, dreams, actions, and visions.

Family stories involving voices from the dead span four generations, beginning with my great-grandmother Rachel Sullivan Dougherty, whose story is recounted in *The Forgotten Colony.*

According to the account titled "Voices in the Night," one September night the widow Dougherty lay in bed trying to sleep but feeling uneasy, restless. Even praying the rosary for a second time that night did not quiet her "feeling of apprehension, a waiting for something to happen."[3] At midnight, "A voice from the far corner of the room cried, 'Rach! Rach!' " She immediately recognized it. It was her dead sister, Millie. The voice seemed to come nearer with each word, and when as if it hung above the foot of the bed, it appealed to her urgently, "Phene is in trouble. She needs you." Phene was her sister, Josephine Sullivan, who was at the time in Beeville taking care of Millie's fragile daughter Ida Wood. Rachel "was as sure that she had heard Millie's voice as she ever was of anything in her life." She "sat bolt upright in bed and said, 'Mill! Mill!' but there was no answer."[4]

Even though it was midnight on the night of the year's first norther, the frail widow drove her buggy as fast as she could to Beeville. Some time after 3:00 a.m., Rachel arrived at the home where Phene held vigil at Ida's bedside. Phene said, "O Rach, I'm glad you're here. I knew you were coming." When Rachel asked how she knew, Phene told her that at midnight "Ida was restless and spent. I was standing by her bed when suddenly I heard a voice cry—your voice—cry 'Mill! Mill!' It seemed to come from the foot of the stairs." Even Ida heard the voice, as Phene recounted to Rachel: "Ida sat up in bed and said, 'I heard Aunt Rachel calling Mother.' "[5] Rachel then explained hearing Millie's voice at Round Lake at the same time Phene and Ida heard Rachel's response in Beeville.[6] So, Millie had summoned Rachel to go to Phene and Ida.

One cousin, who wishes to be known simply as "One of the Beeville Cousins" (whom I will refer to as "Our Beeville Cousin"), also recounts this story, with a few variations. For example, in her version, Rachel's response to Millie's appeal for help was "I'll come, Phene." Either way, both versions depict the departed Millie's communicating with her sisters. This version emphasizes the distance and what it took for Rachel to make the journey. "Aunt Rachel set out alone for Beeville, some thirty miles away, a journey

**Dougherty house at Round Lake, San Patricio, circa 2003**

calling for considerable courage."[7] Having at least these two versions of the story in the family emphasizes the fact that, as is typical of oral tradition and lore, every teller has his or her own version of the same basic story. Historical record dates Ida Wood's death on June 21, 1906.[8] Setting the story in September during the year's first norther makes a better story than a sultry night in June.

Rachel and her husband Robert Dougherty had a large family, traditional among Irish Catholics. Of their seven children, two were school teachers who never married but returned to the family home on Round Lake at San Patricio to be with their aging, widowed mother. The women continued their mother's tradition of maintaining a haven for children, lost souls, and anyone who needed love and care. Three of their nephews, Jimmy Dougherty, Dudley Dougherty, and Bobby Nogueira were soldiers stationed in Europe during World War II. Another family story involving voices comes from Geraldine D'Unger McGloin, who spent many summers as a child at Round Lake with Aunt Mamie and Aunt Lida. She recalls gathering in the living room every night, saying the rosary for all the soldiers, particularly the three nephews. Of the three, Jimmy had spent the most time at Round Lake growing up and even called Aunt Mamie "Mummy." Geraldine says, "We all lived in a chronic anxiety about his welfare." One bright, sunny day, Geraldine went into the house through the front door, turned to her left, and went into the front bedroom, where she saw Aunt Mamie standing. "She looked kind of shaken, and she had her hands up to her head. I don't recall whether I asked her if anything was wrong or not, but I instinctively knew that something was." Aunt Mamie said to Geraldine, "I just heard Jimmy's voice from over there," indicating a corner of the room by a large wardrobe, "and he said, 'Mummy, I'm home.' " Geraldine, being a child not knowing how to respond, says she "was completely perplexed. The only thing I did know was that she was very, very upset." So, Geraldine gently maneuvered Aunt Mamie over to a cedar chest at the foot of the bed, where she got her to sit, gave her a little pat, and left. Unsure of the time frame, Geraldine recalls that soon after Aunt Mamie heard Jimmy's voice, the notice came that he was missing in action, followed not long after by the news of his death. He had been killed in the Battle of the Bulge. According to Geraldine, "The implication was that he was home in Heaven."[9]

More recent stories involving voices come from my uncle Bob Dougherty and his daughter Mary Catherine Dougherty Brown. Uncle Bob recounts that for a number of years, no matter where he is living, he has heard voices in the night calling his name. Sometimes he hears a woman's voice, other times a man's. He will hear "Bob" in "a nice voice" that sounds real to him. " 'Course it would wake me up and then be gone. Every time it did it, it'd scare me to death, and I'd start saying 'Hail Marys' and 'Our Fathers' and would fall back to sleep eventually." The voices always sound familiar, but he has never been quite certain of their identity. The woman's voice resembles Aunt Mamie's, or that of his maternal Aunt Catherine. He says the man's voice has a Mexican accent and could belong to any one of many people he has known. He asserts, "[The voice] wakes you up, you know. You're *wide* awake immediately when they say your name."[10]

Mary Catherine, on the other hand, knows exactly who spoke to her: her mother, Verna Lee. Moments after Verna Lee had been pronounced dead, the hospital staff asked the family and friends gathered in the room to step out for a moment. Mary Catherine bent down to pick up something off the floor and went down on her knees. Her mother told her to "Get up!" She didn't want any spectacles at her death bed! A few nights later, Mary Catherine heard her mother call her name about 3:00 a.m. She recalls, "I could hear her voice. She said my full name," which only Dougherty family members use.[11]

For the first three days after Verna Lee died, she tried to talk to me, too, but I did not realize what was happening. In life, she called me "M" and I kept hearing her voice saying "M" over and over in my head for those days between the hour she died and the day of the funeral. A couple of weeks later, when I was having lunch with her sons Robert and Pat, they started talking about their mother's communication with them and their siblings. As I listened, it dawned on me: "Oh my Gosh! Aunt Bernie tried to talk to me, too, but I was too stupid to know what was going on and didn't pay attention!" Honestly, I had just thought hearing her voice in my head was part of my grieving process. I still wonder what she was trying to tell me.

The way Verna Lee Dougherty communicated with her son Pat was in a dream, which is another means by which we have communication with the dead. Pat told me that his mother came to him in a dream and told him he needed to start exercising. I asked what he did about it. He said, "I started exercising. I figured she knew something I didn't, so I'd better do what she said." Minding his mother even after she died.

Pat's brother Robert studied in the seminary and talks of many dreams in which he has had visits from people, many of whom he never knew when they were alive. According to Robert, these people come seeking prayers. He explains, "They are poor souls needing prayer. Once you die off this earth, you can't pray for yourself; you have to pray for others. That's why they come to us. They're needing prayer." This is what is known in the Catholic Faith as intercessory prayers. "Sometimes," he continues, "people come and bring others with them for you to pray for." When Robert first began having the dream visits, as they are called, he had "more contact" because he did not know why they had come to him and would try to question them, converse with them. When he has such a dream visit now, he starts praying immediately and loses contact with his visitor(s).

From his study in the seminary, Robert learned that seminarians experience dream visits from prayer-seeking souls frequently because they make a special point of praying "for the poor souls in Purgatory." One specific visit Robert recounts occurred years before he entered the seminary, though. Robert says that our cousin Joe W. Reynolds visited him for prayers for quite a while after he died. Then one night, Joe W. came into Robert's dream to thank him for his intercession. Joe W. "came to me. He was outside of his kitchen door, and he had his hat off, and he gave me a real, real loud grito—the happiest he'd ever been, so I assumed he was in Heaven, [that] he was happy and thanking me." (A *grito* is a loud holler in Spanish that expresses happiness or enthusiasm.) Robert also had a particular dream visit from our grandmother Nonnie Dougherty, who sought prayers for her brother Manch Harrod who had recently died. According to Robert, prayer seekers come "not to the holiest but most compassionate people."[12]

The previous story about Rachel Dougherty's hearing her dead sister's voice telling her that their sister Phene needed her also involves a dream. When Rachel went into the bedroom where her niece Ida lay dying, Ida told Rachel about a dream she had had that night. In the dream, Ida was a child climbing a tree at Round Lake while her mother Millie and Aunt Rachel picked wild grapes. Ida fell out of the tree, and Rachel screamed and ran to her. Ida said, "The look on your face frightened me for a moment. You were pale and trembling. 'Mill—Mill' you cried. Mother came. And when I saw her, I was no longer afraid. There was a smile on her face as she took me into her arms." Before dawn that morning, Ida died.[13]

Another dream visit put many family members' hearts and minds at ease in 2004. Cousin Catherine D'Unger was found unconscious at the foot of her winding staircase, her head having struck hard on the Saltillo tile. As she lay in a coma in a Corpus Christi hospital, we all feared the worst as we tried to determine what might have caused Catherine's fall. She was a private investigator, and some among the family suspected foul play. Additionally, she had drifted from the Faith, and some worried for her soul. As she was being wheeled into surgery, Monsignor Mike Howell rushed to her side to give her an Apostolic Blessing, which he told Catherine's sister Geraldine absolved Catherine of all her earthly sins. However, only Geraldine knew about the blessing and could not tell the rest of us, for she suffered a stroke on the day of her sister's death. Two nights later, Our Beeville Cousin had a dream visit from Catherine, who called her by name and told her to "wake up . . . It's me, Catherine. I'm OK." The next morning, Our Beeville Cousin called Claude D'Unger, Catherine's brother; Rachel Whisenant, her daughter; and me, among others I'm sure, to share the good news that Catherine was okay. That curt, to-the-point message sounded to me like it came straight out of Catherine's mouth. Like the other family members, I did not doubt for a split second that the experience was not real. It was not until years later that Geraldine told me about the Apostolic Blessing. Apparently, Catherine "turned up in a dream to each of four good friends, in each looking vitally young and happy and assuring them that she was fine," as Our Beeville Cousin relates.[14]

This same cousin has had dream visits from other family members, as well. In one dream, her father, who had been dead four years, came to her home as she decorated the Christmas tree. Her three sons, her husband, and her mother all sat in the room, but no one else could see her father. Instead of the white-haired seventy-year-old man they had buried, her father now appeared to her as "the young father [she] remembered from . . . childhood." She recalls that in the dream "He stood there with what seemed to me to be such a warmth of happiness radiating about him . . . 'This is the way folk in Heaven look,' " she realized. He walked over to and sat down in what had been his favorite chair in her home before he died, and fondly watched his grandsons. She continues, "My mother rose and said she believed it was time to go home. . . . As she went to leave by the same back porch door Dad had entered, he rose smoothly and followed her. As he reached the door, he turned and these words came to my mind: 'I'll never be very far from Mama' and he closed the door." This dream "kept [her] comforted and sane through many hard times." Years later, when her youngest son was twenty-nine, she received a call that he "was missing in the Rio Grande—he had been swept out of sight around a bend while swimming." As she explains, "It was every mother's worst nightmare. He went missing on a Sunday and wasn't found until Thursday." However, that Wednesday night, she knew he was okay because she had an experience in which she saw her son "laughing—loud, hearty, joyous laughter—laughing in Heaven." Since then, her son has visited her in dreams from time to time.[15]

I, too, have had dream visits. Like Robert, I did not understand them. They either made me happy or made me wake up crying, depending on who showed up in the dream. Either way, such dreams always made me feel uneasy at best. Now, though, I am more aware of their significance. Recently, my grandmother Nonnie came into my dream. I was overjoyed to see her. When she took both of my hands in hers, I could *feel* her touch. I told her how much I love her and miss her. She told me she loves me, too. At that point, someone else came into the dream. Knowing she would leave because someone else was there, I said, "Please don't go," but she did, anyway. In just a moment, the other person left, and she came back, which thrilled me. When I asked her about my dad, she pursed her lips in a way only Nonnie can and shook her head. In the first part of the dream, her purpose was to comfort me; in the second, she sought prayers for my dad.

Geraldine and Catherine's mother, Justine Bluntzer D'Unger, told Geraldine once that she knew her parents Vincent and Kate Dougherty Bluntzer are "on the other side. They always help me from the other side." Geraldine says that her mother "sat in her house by herself for years and went through some very tough times, always comforted by that thought." Her mother's philosophy was, "These people cared for me in life and they comfort me from the other side." According to Geraldine, "She told me that just like I'm sitting here talking to you, with no sensationalism, nothing. She didn't say, 'I see them' or 'I hear them.' She just felt it."[16] Such a feeling is not quite like a dream visit, but the belief that someone out there still cares and is helping us through hard times echoes Fr. Gino Concetti's statement. Considering the various dream experiences noted here, visitors come to comfort us or seek prayers from us.

Occasionally, the communication takes a more physical form. Something that happens in the physical world can be a type of communication from someone "on the other side." Our Beeville Cousin had one such experience this year on Memorial Day. Traditionally on Memorial Day, she takes small flags and puts them in the ground at her father's grave, his twin's grave, Jimmy and Dudley Dougherty's graves, and graves of other veterans she has known because, as she says, "Irish keep family graves in good shape." For a while, vandals destroyed some of the graves in the Catholic cemetery in Beeville, Dudley Dougherty's gravestone's having been one overturned. Our Beeville Cousin had written a lengthy letter to the editor of the local paper extolling Dudley's service to his country and community during his life time. This particular Memorial Day morning, it was about six o'clock with not a breath of air moving. After setting the flags, she drove back around to look at them before leaving the cemetery. When she "got by Dudley's plot, the flag snapped and fluttered and blew for two minutes." She said, "It was the nicest, dearest thing. It was Dudley saying hello."[17]

Another action in the same cemetery happened to Mary Catherine, who recalls that when she had paid off her mother's cemetery plot and the headstone was in place, she "went to the gravesite" to see how everything looked. She recalls of the day, "There was no wind anywhere. We both liked wind chimes, and there was a wind chime way, way up in the tree" that day. "That's the last time I've heard from Mama . . . she didn't leave until we buried her."[18]

Not only has Nonnie come to me in a dream visit, she also made sure something physical happened. She had some acreage in South Live Oak County on which she had built a weekend home. When we sold the place seven years after her death, my sister Kries and I went to that house before the real estate closing to pick up a few things and say goodbye, so to speak. I decided to take, among other things, a large, heavy, ornate floor lamp that had a thick milkglass-type shade. Kries carried it out of the bedroom, down the hall, through the living room, down the sidewalk, and through the yard gate before setting it down at the back end of my SUV. We planned to slide it in from the back, so I climbed into the back seat to retrieve the shade end.

When Kries picked up the lamp to put it in, the heavy shade toppled off, hit the dirt, and broke into lots of white pieces. She was devastated, but for some strange reason, an abnormal calm came over me. She bent down to pick up the pieces and cut her finger. I told her to go to the kitchen sink to wash off the blood while I went to the bathroom for a band aid. When I opened the top drawer in the bathroom, I started laughing. We had opened every drawer, every closet, every cabinet in every room but the bathroom, which we had not entered at all that morning until I went for the band aid. I hollered at Kries: "I know why you cut your finger!"

By this time Kries had entered the bathroom to see me holding a small glass tray that Nonnie had put her hair pins and other personal items on every night, a tray I remember her having all of my life, and from the looks of it, it may have even belonged to her own mother. I explained to Kries, "Nonnie made you drop that shade and cut your finger to get me back in here to get this tray. She saw we were leaving it behind and wanted me to have it."

A few months later, I was looking in boxes in the attic for some old photographs and came across a small dish with a lid and a matching toiletry bottle that had belonged to Nonnie. I took them out and set them on a marble table in my bedroom. Every day I looked at the two pieces, and one day as I looked at them, I realized, "That tray matches these pieces!" So, I took the tray from the closet and completed the set on the table. Don't even *try* to tell me my grandmother didn't send me into that bathroom.

The fourth type of communication is visions. The oldest story of this type we have is evidenced in a letter from Catherine Dougherty, who wrote from Kilcar, Ireland, to her son Robert in Texas on December 10, 1865. Her children had all departed Ireland for

America, and her two sons Robert and James had fought in the Civil War after arriving here. In the letter, Catherine discusses the death of James and her thankfulness that Robert was alive and well. Private James Dougherty, 1st Texas Cavalry Regiment, Buchel's 1st Texas Mounted Rifles, Company "A" had died May 23, 1864, from wounds he received in the Battle of Marksville, Louisiana,[19] but months passed before the news of her son's death reached Catherine in Ireland. She tells Robert, "For my feeling, I think I do behold him constantly in my presence sometimes as if in bloom and next thoughts in the state of pain. . . . I am continually offering prayers for him." And then she tells of her experience when he died: "When in my house in Derrylahan I felt one night an exceeding shower of drops falling at my bed foot and I then asked Nellie and Robert your uncle if it was raining, they said not though they had felt weighty drops through the house, henceforth I took it for granted that James was to go."[20] Geography apparently does not hinder spiritual communication.

Catherine Dougherty's great-great-granddaughter Geraldine had her own vision when she was about eight years old. While Catherine was saddened by the vision she had, learning of her son's death in a foreign country's war, Geraldine's vision frightened her, probably because of her youth. This particular night, she was asleep in her grandmother's bed with cousin Rachel Timon, who was spending the night with the D'Ungers. Geraldine says, "I woke up and saw this woman who looked like she was in a negative, like reversed, sitting on the end of the bed looking at Rachel Timon. I swear it was Cousin Millie, and I was scared. I recognized her. . . . I was frozen until morning. . . . The woman had on this kind of granny gown like my grandmother wore that was flannel. My mother didn't wear them, and my grandmother was not home, and there was nobody else, so I went and asked my mother. She said, 'No, I did not [sit on the bed last night],' and I said, 'Well, I saw Cousin Millie' and [Mother] just pooh-poohed it.' "[21] The woman Geraldine saw was Rachel Emilia Sullivan Timon, mother of Rachel Timon, who slept in the bed with Geraldine that night. Rachel was a troubled young woman, and Geraldine surmises that

Cousin Millie had come to watch over her daughter.[22] Millie had died in 1947, some time prior to this vision.[23]

As a young bride, Millie Sullivan Timon had her own vision. With husband Harry "gone to market some cattle,"[24] Millie found herself alone in their ranch house, lying in bed, eyes closed, listening to the familiar sounds of the night. Suddenly, the sounds stopped. When she opened her eyes, she saw "the blurred figure of a man, tall and angular, facing the mantel clock as if he had come to see the time."[25] In her drowsy state, at first she thought the figure to be that of her husband, but she quickly remembered he was away. "Suddenly, she saw a band of flames, small in the beginning, encircle his waist. . . . The flames increased in height until they licked his shoulders. Instinctively, she breathed, 'Lord, have mercy on his soul' [and] the flames began to lower until they were no longer visible. And as they disappeared, so did the figure." She "mechanically reached for her rosary," and after a while, thought of the passage from Maccabbes, 'It is a holy and wholesome thought to pray for the dead, / That they may be loosed from their sins.' "[26] Millie then realized he had come to her for prayers, so she vowed "she would pray for this soul—always."[27]

Even my son J. Michael, who is now fifteen, has a vision story, albeit not of anyone in flames. On his first visit to Round Lake when he was about eight years old, J. Michael was down by the lake shore, checking things out like eight-year-old boys will do, while I was elsewhere on the grounds. Suddenly, he heard voices and laughter to his left. This got his attention because the only other people there that day were Catherine D'Unger and the caretaker, neither of whom was close by. J. Michael looked toward the voices and saw a group of adults and children gathered around a picnic table and the big brick barbeque pit. He said they were "laughing, having a good time." He said they were dressed "in old timey clothes," but he had no other details because the vision only lasted about ten seconds. He looked away for a second and when he "looked back over there, they weren't there really." He said he did see smoke from the pit as though the lid was being lifted to turn the meat when he plainly saw the group the first time. He said, "It's like I was there. It freaked me out. I ran inside." Discussing his experience with Geraldine, he asked her if they had had such parties at Round Lake, and she told him, "That was a gathering spot [the barbeque pit]" and that it was built in the 1950s. There had been a picnic table at that spot, as well. After hearing J. Michael's story, Geraldine said to him, "It just kinda runs in the family that people are aware of these things."[28]

The communications my family members and I have experienced have common elements. For one thing, they happen to level-headed, sensible people. Rachel Dougherty, even at her late age, had never heard voices or had visions, yet she acted upon her experience without a second thought, driving through the night by herself in a buggy. When J. Michael saw the people at the barbeque, he had never heard any of the family stories of this type. He has never been a fanciful child who fabricates stories for effect. And Geraldine McGloin is one of the most practical, reality-based people I have ever known. Yet, they believe what they experienced because they saw with their own eyes, heard with their own ears. The others whose stories appear here are the same—practical, no-nonsense people. They may like to tell a good story in the Irish tradition, but they take these spiritual experiences very seriously. When the experiences called for earthly action like Rachel's, "Those actions . . . were founded in love and caring. They cared about the subject enough to get up and do a darn hard thing."[29]

Another common thread is the attempt to bring comfort to us in this unsettled world. Jimmy Dougherty, no doubt, was trying to set his aunts at ease when he appeared to Aunt Mamie, just as Catherine D'Unger did when she came back to say she was okay. Even when the people/souls are seeking prayers, they are not bringing us grief. Instead, these experiences, as a whole, bring what Our Beeville Cousin calls "great joy, peace, and comfort." Prayer plays a significant role in many of these family stories and experiences, mostly involving prayers for the dead and saying The Rosary. As Geraldine points out, "In our Faith, we do believe in the eternity of the soul,"[30] and as Fr. Concetti pointed out, God allows the departed souls to guide us while we remain in this life, on this side. In one of my conversations with Robert, he also explained that these experiences are "our souls communicating with each other."[31]

Granted, a person does not have to be a Catholic or even Irish to experience communication from people "on the other side." What I am saying is that such experiences seem to be common among us Catholics of Celtic descent and that our family has an abundance of these stories. The stories retold here are only a representative sampling of the treasure trove we have to share. As Our Beeville Cousin so aptly summed it up: "Our family stories are the glue that keeps the family together."[32] If that's the case—and I believe it is—we must continue to tell the stories, no matter the subject matter or what skeptics may think.

## Endnotes

1. Rachel Bluntzer Hebert. *The Forgotten Colony: San Patricio de Hibernia.* Burnet, TX: Eakin, 1981. vi.
2. Victor J. Zammit. "A Lawyer Answers the Catholic Church's Attack on Spiritualism." *Victor J. Zammit: A Lawyer Presents the Case for the Afterlife.* http://www.victorzammit.com, Oct. 30, 2007.
3. Hebert. 368.
4. Ibid. 369
5. Ibid. 372.
6. Ibid. 373.
7. "Our Beeville Cousin." Letter, Feb. 15, 2006.
8. "Death of Miss Woods." *Corpus Christi Caller,* June 22, 1906. 4. *TXGen Web.* http://www.rootsweb.com/~txsanpat/Deaths/wood-ida.txt, Aug. 27, 2007.
9. Geraldine McGloin. Personal interview. Corpus Christi, TX, Aug. 25, 2007.
10. Bob Dougherty. Personal interview. Beeville, TX, Sept. 6, 2007.
11. Mary Catherine Dougherty Brown. Personal interview. Beeville, TX, Sept. 6, 2007.
12. Robert Dougherty. Personal interview. Beeville, TX, Sept. 6, 2007.
13. Hebert. 374.
14. "Our Beeville Cousin."
15. Ibid.
16. McGloin.
17. "Our Beeville Cousin." Telephone interview, Sept. 3, 2007.

18. Brown.
19. John D Dougherty. "Private James Dougherty, CSA." *TXGenWeb*. http://www.rootsweb.com/~txsanpat/military/dough-j-pvt.htm, Aug. 26, 2007.
20. Catherine Dougherty. Transcribed letter. Family Collection, Dec. 10, 1865.
21. McGloin.
22. McGloin. Telephone interview, Oct. 25, 2007.
23. McGloin. Personal email, Oct. 26, 2007.
24. Hebert. 385.
25. Ibid. 387.
26. Ibid. 388.
27. Ibid. 389.
28. J. Michael Sullivan. Personal interview. Corpus Christi, TX, Aug. 25, 2007.
29. McGloin. Personal Interview.
30. Ibid.
31. Robert Dougherty. Personal interview. Beeville, TX, Oct. 18, 2007.
32. "Our Beeville Cousin." Telephone interview, Oct. 7, 2007.

Carolyn Arrington

# CHIPITA RODRIGUEZ: THE ONLY WOMAN HANGED IN TEXAS *DURING* THE CIVIL WAR

by Carolyn Arrington

I was introduced to Chipita Rodriguez when I took a Texas history course in college several years ago. Our assignment was to pick from a list of subjects on which we would like to do a book report. Being a little bit of a history buff, and a songwriter and poet, Chipita's story fit my interests very well. I read various books and articles, and did well on the report. But all during my research for the report, I kept thinking the story could be taken to another level. Hence, the song came about. I performed it for a local junior high class, and one student told about a relative's land that borders the property that Chipita's ghost walks on. He said her ghost has even been seen in recent years. It seems that on nights when the sky is clear and the moon is full, you can hear her moaning and see her walking along the bank of the river, with the rope still hanging from her neck.

History books tell us that Chipita Rodriguez spent her early years in Mexico with her family and later, only her father. Chipita and her father, Pedro, fled Mexico when the Texas Revolution prompted Santa Anna to pledge attacks against the revolting Texians and settlers such as the Rodriguezes.

Native American paths and game trails are what most likely guided settlers to the McGloin-McMullen Colony, where Chipita's legend began. The original settlers had struck out from the Mission Refugio toward their new land in the spring of 1830. Where they stopped was at a low bank crossing off the Nueces River several miles north of the Refugio County Courthouse. Between the Native Americans, cutthroats, gringo bandits and, a little later, Federal troops that might raid the settlers such as Chipita and her father, it was hard to make a living or even survive. During this time it is said Chipta had an illegitimate son by a white man who stole the infant child and abandoned her. She was not to see her little one until many years later. And he would come into play with her fatal demise. Also, somewhere during this time, her father was killed in the Texas Revolution.

Chipita settled on the high bank of the river at the crossing and set up an "inn" for paying travelers in the late 1850s. Service consisted of a cot on the front porch and coffee and meals. Records show the land was actually owned by impresarios and Chipita was simply allowed to stake a living in such a lucrative location along the Nueces River. The inn was just a shack overlooking the bluff on the west bank near what was known as Aldrete's Crossing in San Patricio County. Land at the time was occupied by Mexican ranchers with grants from the Spanish and Mexican governments, and Irish impresarios who also lived by the stipulations of the Spanish and Mexican governments. It is speculated that Chipita was given permission by local officials or the Welder family to establish her "inn."

Chipita was an old woman when she gained notoriety in Texas history. She was thought to be about sixty years old in 1863. The paying traveler who gave her such notoriety was a man by the name of John Savage. He had sold a herd of horses in San Antonio and was carrying a nice pack of gold in his saddlebags. The horses were to be used by the Confederate Army. He was in transition to purchase more horses further south and bring them back to the army. Savage forded the river and settled in for a meal and a night's sleep at Chipita's inn.

A day or so later, a local family was setting up a picnic on the river, just south of Chipita's cabin. A servant with the family saw a gunnysack lodged under a log in the river. When she tried to retrieve it, the sack ripped and exposed an arm. The family fled to the closest ranch for help and to notify authorities. The sheriff and deputies found two gunnysacks with John Savage's remains; his head had been slashed open with an ax. Savage was carrying about $600 in gold, which was never found. The sheriff went to Chipita's cabin because it was the nearest facility to the crime, and found blood on her front porch. She said it was from a slaughtered chicken. Savage had been a boarder of Chipita's inn, and his body was found not far from her cabin. These facts along with the blood on the front porch led the sheriff to arrest Chipita and her hired hand, Juan Silvera, who was charged as an accomplice. Legends and stories say that Juan may have been her lost illegitimate son.

No actual date of the killing exists today. Fires in the courthouse where files were kept have destroyed the records. The killing probably happened between the first part of September of 1863 and when the trial started in October of 1863. She was hanged on November 13, 1863. During the entire trial and all interrogations, Chipita would never admit to the killing, anything about the murder or the gold (if she knew anything), or if she had an accomplice. It is said she never spoke a word about the incident, even to claim her innocence.

At her trial, Chipita was convicted by the jury; the judge sentenced her to hanging, although the jury had asked for leniency and all evidence was circumstantial. Why he followed through with the hanging is unknown. It is said the political times were a deciding factor. What was the jury's motivation to ask for a lighter sentence? Was she innocent, and did her illegitimate son/hired hand commit the crime? Only history knows the true facts and why they played out as they did. But it does make a good story, even if you don't believe in ghosts!

Soon after her hanging her ghost began to appear along the river, and some say it does to this day. Stories such as this often inspire me to find out more about them and, eventually, I set some of them to music. That's how the "Ballad of Chipita Rodriguez" came about. I accompany this song with my guitar, but fiddle embellishments would also enhance the spirit of the story.

**The Ballad of Chipita Rodriguez**
**by Carolyn Arrington**

This is the ballad of Chipita Rodriguez,
The only woman hanged in Texas,
Accused of a crime, too hideous, for anytime,
And her ghost still walks the banks of the Nueces,
They say her ghost still walks the Nueces.

At a very early age she was left motherless,
And was raised by her father Pedro Rodriguez,
They fled across the Rio Grande,
To escape the troops of Santa Anna,
But Pedro was killed in the Texas revolution.

She lived alone along the banks of the Nueces,
In a cabin with vine covered walls,
With a cot on the front porch for paying travelers,
Her last visitor was the man they say she murdered,
Her last boarder was the man she murdered.

He was hacked with an axe and stuffed in a sack,
The body found down stream from Chipita's cabin,
The story was told, he was carrying gold,
But not an ounce was found around him.

She was taken to trial for the murder,
The evidence strictly circumstantial,
Oh, the jury found her guilty, but asked for leniency,
But the judge sentenced her to hanging.
Yes, the judge sentenced to a hangin'.

She was chained to the wall of her jail cell,
The local children brought her candy and tobacco,
Her last visitor was a black woman,
Who braided her hair and brought her a dress for the
hanging.

She was taken to the hanging in an ox cart
Seated up on her own coffin,
The two wheels loudly creaked, not a word from Chipita,
Smoked her last cigarette, and they hanged her.

It was Friday the 13th, when they hanged her,
Buried ’neath her own hanging tree,
No cover to conceal the strangle,
Brutish jerks, and the car, was rolled forward.

It is said that the ghost of Chipita,
Walks slowly down the banks of the river.
She is pictured ’neath the full moon,
With a tattered hang man’s noose,
Hanging ’round the old woman’s neck,
Hanging down ’round the old woman’s neck.

**Ted and Gwen Sonnenburg, owners of the house where Oscar lived**

# OSCAR—THE FRIENDLY GHOST

by Edward R. Raasch

I never met "Oscar." I am convinced he existed because of my source—my daughter Jan and her friends Gwen and Ted, and their two children. Believing in ghosts or active spirits depends upon an experience one may encounter. I haven't had the pleasure or displeasure of any contacts with ghosts, so I always view the stories I hear concerning those ghostly meetings with a slight doubt. But golly, gee, my own daughter became a believer. That perked up my interest in checking out this friendly ghost named Oscar.

The background of this story is the Abilene house where Ted and Gwen first lived. Their home was one of many believed to have been built on an ancient Indian burial ground. In that area, there was a universal belief that the spirits were active. Ted and Gwen believed that Oscar truly was an active ghost in their Abilene residence.

Oscar first made his presence noticed in the children's room. Momma Gwen had felt Oscar's presence several times, and the children would say with no fear: "Momma, Oscar is here again." One night Ted was feeding their newborn son. Ted was resting comfortably in his favorite armchair, holding his son lovingly. He made sure the baby blanket covered the little guy. Ted fell asleep, and when he awoke, the blanket was spread on the floor and his baby son was sleeping peacefully. The bottle was carefully positioned by the little one. Ted is a heavy sleeper; he had not awakened. Checking with Gwen and the other children, Ted discovered they had been in another room during the night.

That left the other resident: Oscar. Gwen and Ted firmly believe that the friendly ghost Oscar had spread the blanket on the floor and placed the baby there. Who else? A friendly, caring apparition who had adopted the family and watched out for them, that's who!

Jan has been friends with these people for many years. Ted and Gwen are solid, successful citizens. I will vouch for my daughter, who had a wonderful career in the education field.

On one visit with Ted and Gwen in Abilene, Jan became a believer of her own accord. It seems that Gwen was in the back room of their home with the children and Jan was going down the hallway when suddenly she found herself in the center of a swirling, gentle wind. She stopped momentarily. She said she experienced no fear, and she could step out of and back into this wonderful, caressing atmosphere. Jan stood very quietly and the swirling, gentle breeze disappeared. At that moment, she knew she had met Oscar.

When Jan described this experience to Gwen, it was confirmed by her to be Oscar. As my daughter told this to me, I smiled and said: "Those old houses can have hidden openings allowing this gentle breeze to flow in the hallway."

Gwen said the house had been checked for leaks. They had checked the plumbing and all the heat and air conditioning registers. They found no problems. Regardless of the temperature inside or the weather outside, the gentle, warm, "feel good" breeze was there. And so Oscar became an integral part of the family life of Gwen and Ted. My daughter said to me, "Oscar also became a friend of mine, whenever I visited Ted and Gwen."

Years later, when Ted and Gwen moved to Arlington, Texas, Oscar moved with them. He stayed around for several months, and then suddenly he was gone. Ted and Gwen were positive that Oscar wanted to make sure the family was going to be all right in the new location. Then Oscar moved back to Abilene. The family missed him, but felt Oscar needed to be back in Abilene among his ghostly friends.

For many years, I doubted the existence of ghosts. Hearing about Oscar the friendly ghost opened my mind that there is a possibility these creatures are floating around. Well . . . maybe.

### "Hearse Song"
### or,
### "As the Hearse Goes By"

Did you ever think as the hearse goes by
That you may be the next to die?

They wrap you up in a big white sheet
And drop you down 'bout six feet deep.

All goes well for about a week,
And then your coffin begins to leak.

The worms crawl in, the worms crawl out,
The worms play pinochle on your snout.

They eat your eyes, they eat your nose,
They eat the jelly between your toes.

A big red worm with rolling eyes
Will crawl in your stomach and out your eyes.

Your stomach turns a slimy green,
And pus pours out like whipping cream.

You spread it on a piece of bread
But you never know it because you are dead.

[This version of the childhood song from Charles Clay Doyle's early days in Weimar, Texas (about 1956), was first printed in *What's Going On? (In Modern Texas Folklore),* Francis Edward Abernethy, Editor. Publications of the Texas Folklore Society Number XI, Austin: Encino Press, 1976. 175.]

# THOUGHTS, MUSINGS,

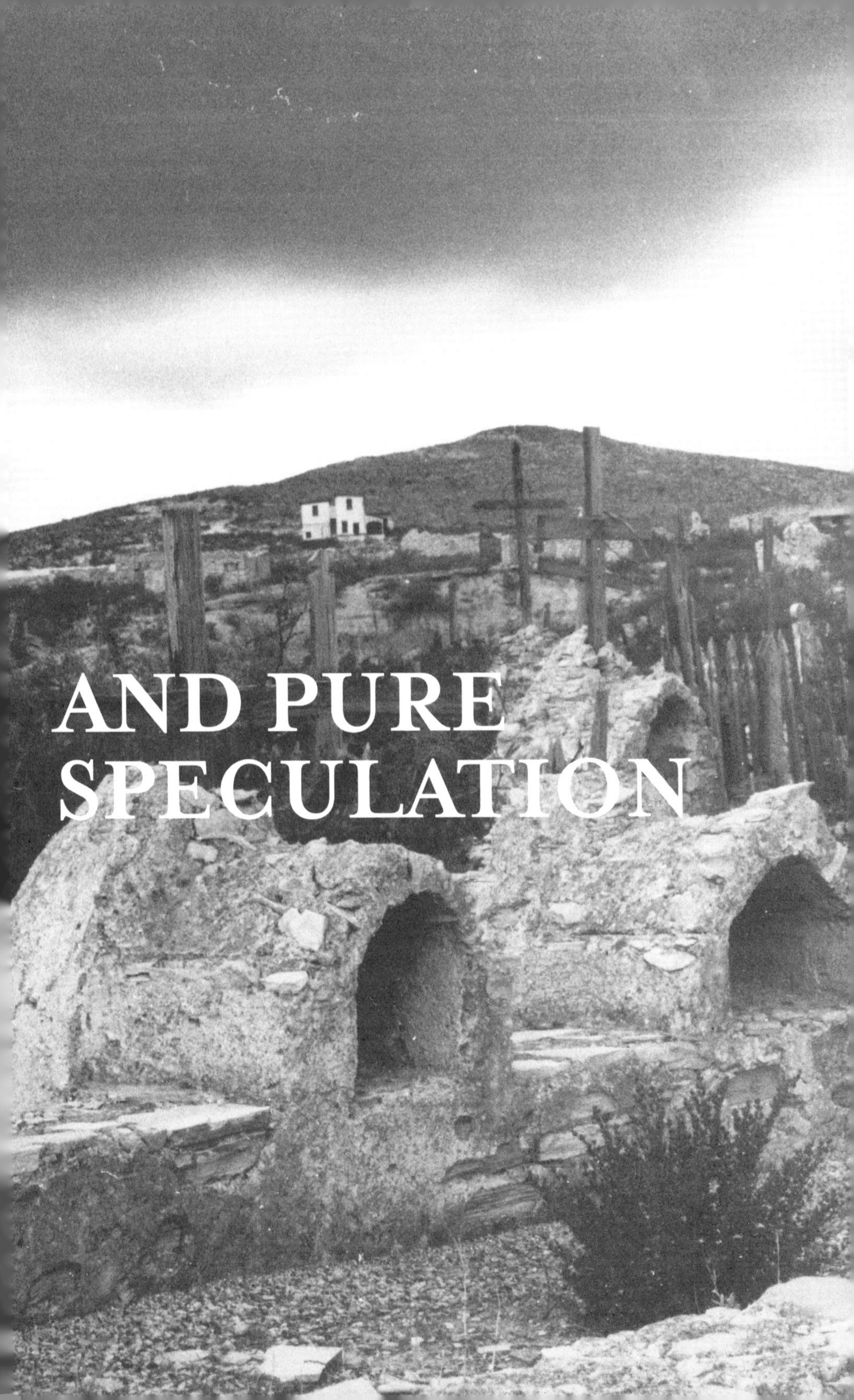
AND PURE
SPECULATION

**Leslie LaRo visiting an Irish cemetery**

# GRAVEYARD MEANDERIN'; OR, THINGS OF LIFE LEARNED AMONG THE DEAD

by Leslie LaRo

I have never been a particularly "normal" person, considering my unique quirks and "idiot-synchrasies" (yes, I know that's not a real word, but what is language if it won't do what we need it to do?). I get what my mom used to call "big ideas" as in, "what's the big idea, anyway?" Not all of them are fuzzy, warm, or particularly comfortable for others to consider, so some of them I keep to myself until I know a person better. One is my lifelong fascination with cemeteries, or graveyards. Most folks really don't understand this interest in walking, talking (to myself and whoever else may be listening), snapping pictures, and writing in a graveyard. I only know it has offered me images, ideas, and inspiration countless times. Oh, you may call it ghoulish, but there it is.

Never considered whistlin' past one, but I have also never driven past a country graveyard without wishing to go spend a few hours wandering around . . . just being. I am not talking about those manicured, devoid of standing stones, everything-at-ground-level jobs. No sir. I speak of the places where breezes tickle over-grown brush—where grasshoppers and grass burrs await your step with anticipation. This is true no matter where I find myself: Any-place, Texas, the South or Southwest, Washington state, Ireland, or Scotland. I really come alive in a graveyard.

I can recall many times in my childhood, which seemed fairly normal to me (but what do I know from "normal"?), daytrips to graveyards to visit family members who had "gone on to be with the Lord" or had "passed away to a better place." If when you died you got to spend lots of time in a graveyard, I wanted to do that, too. Die, I mean. Not in an everything's-dreadful-think-I'll-just-lie-right-down-and-die sort of way, but in a now-I-can-really-learn-something-important sort of way. An expression I heard as a child that has stuck with me all my days is this: "Whenever a person dies, an entire library of experience dies, too." While I have no idea who came up with this heartrending bit of wisdom, being a huge book lover and an avid reader, this idea still saddens me. Consider it: an entire library . . . gone, forever. Whether an Alexandrian treasure or a lifetime stuffed into a few hours on earth, each human spirit comprises a collection of memories, each unique to the one whose mind recorded it. I understood the gravity of this as I strolled within any number of cemeteries as a child, reading carefully each inscription, pondering the significance of the words or symbols that appeared in stone, weathered and often broken: lambs, crosses, open Bibles, hands holding doves, and lichen-covered rubble with all meaning lost. Occasions for mourning may bring me to these places of rest (or unrest), but curiosity beckons me back as often as I can grab a camera and go.

I must admit that many of the life skills that my blessed parents tried to instill in my sisters and myself were introduced, reinforced, and ingrained while wandering through graveyards. Let me explain. Beginning academic skills were built through sounding out names and inscriptions on stones. Those silent requiems to individuals immortalized by their contemporaries who erected the monument seen by generations of small children, forming syllables, working out basic math calculations—birth dates, death dates, wedding dates—all vitally important to lives of those who likely stood at the side of an open hole and wept. Surely these were worthy of my reading practice. The text was often difficult to decipher in that polysyllabic biblical names were frequently utilized in decades past, along with "archaic speech" of formal usage—the King James eloquence became my own. Sounds even better spoken aloud.

What were these people like? What thoughts filled their minds as they buried their dead? How did their voices sound? In my reverie, I learned silence. Scriptural references to being still and knowing "He is God" were made tangible to me, as I rocked on tennis-shoed feet with the blowing of warm Texas breezes in gardens of stone memory. There is a special softness to wind in cemetery silences. Did you ever notice this?

History speaks volumes in a graveyard. Plague, natural disaster, war, and famine have all left indelible marks on community life when dates appear in unison marking the passing of the brave, the unlucky, the weak and infirm of the day. Woodmen of the World, Masonic Brotherhood, and United States Armed Services . . . all lost beloved ones to the reality of life. I learned that while all must die, some die for a cause much bigger than the time in which it stood. And that some things are worth dying for. The faith of these generations screams loudest when I consider how it is taken for granted, sometimes discarded by the very ones who benefited most. Nothing makes me angrier than willful ignorance of history combined with an arrogant attitude.

I learned that throughout time, people have lost their babies, mourned their losses, and tried again, often to lose further children too young and too soon. Life goes on. Possibly a little slower, a bit more painfully, but it does go on. If they could take all of that hardship and keep on going, I can too. Perseverance, I guess you could call that lesson.

Creativity in memorializing loss is vast and touching. Angelic cherubim, carved crosses of many types, and heart-breaking verse are all ways to say farewell and leave a trace of the depth of grief. While Nature has taken a toll on the artistry that adorns the protected inside fences made of rock, iron, wooden slats, brick, chain-link, or simply stands of live oaks, vestiges of pride are found in stones sometimes over one hundred years standing, defiantly waiting for that final push from elemental enemies. Longevity has its limitations.

Lest you think I simply practiced mental math, learned historical lessons, sounded out difficult names, read love poems aloud and noted artistic ambiguities, science was never neglected. I can identify many natural grasses, trees, and types of flowers growing in the wilds of the Texas Hill Country and plains. I can tell a scrub jay call from a mockingbird and know that all things that buzz 'round your head aren't necessarily looking to sting. (Note: *never* wear good smelling stuff or brightly colored clothes to the great outdoors if you want to blend in with the wild.) Animals and all of the wonders of a bug's life were always available to offer entertainment and lessons in caution. Things that fly drop stuff and sometimes sting. Sticker burrs stick to everything, especially shoelaces, socks, and bottoms of shoes, and a tip for you city-types: they hurt like the dickens when you pull them off of anything they don't want to be separated from. Since mesquite trees are thorny devils, I wouldn't recommend holding onto one while you try to pry loose a burr—ouch! So, I guess between extraction exercises, insect bites and stings, and the swats I received for rebellious/disrespectful behaviors or risk-taking taught me something of the pain in life, as well. Come to think on it, some of the deepest laughter and fascination I can recall experiencing came from the antics of squirrels, field mice, cardinals versus scrub jays, and grasshoppers just doing what comes naturally.

Respect. Remembrance. Accountability. Gratitude. These I learned by reminders to stay off the grave stones, avoid walking on someone's final resting place (though we all knew the dead were not really there, but somewhere else, depending upon how well they had learned the lessons I speak of in their own lives). After Memorial Day, Veterans' Day, Independence Day, Thanksgiving, Armed Forces Day, Armistice Day, D-Day, and V-E/V-J Days, I learned that someone remembers even when I have not, the sacrifices made for me. Because of those tiny waving flags tucked lovingly into places only time remembers each day, I am touched by the past, humbled by the gifts of those who walked that hallowed ground. My ancestor who died at the Alamo left behind not only a grateful generation, but a mourning, beleaguered family. His final resting place is unknown, but he is remembered every year within the enshrined walls near where he likely fell for the last time.

I am reminded that all across the nation, indeed in nations across the world, my countrymen and women fell and were buried sometimes with public honor, sometimes in hidden fashion, known only to God. Places like Arlington or other national cemeteries put a very public and honored face upon our respect for our fallen—lessons learned from the times these sacred places are born must never be taken for granted. Yes, I cry in graveyards, even when I am not draped in somber dress, following a hearse.

I have searched the ground to find tiny rocks, shells, acorns, or chunks of wood to place upon the stones of those I visit and to whom I owe so much. So many tiny traditions like this may be remnants of pagan rites; I don't know. These tokens I leave in memory of those who lived as I do, day by day, imperfect but guided by a loving hand. Driven by a humility that makes me stand still and as tall as my short frame will allow, considering all I have learned among the places where the dead are sometimes remembered but more oft forgotten, I hope someday loved ones who follow me will stop and consider my final place of stillness, symbolizing the peace I will one day experience for eternity. Perhaps they, too, will place a seed of memory upon my marker, to say "We were here; we miss you."

In travel, I continue to indulge my fascination for the gardens of stone. I long to explore a community's values by peeking into their graveyards. My photographic eye finds a million images I wish to immortalize, but none do justice to what my senses record. I see well-kept grounds, lovingly manicured, and some not so well seen, where stones are broken, vandalized or looted. My heart breaks and my stomach clenches in anger. So much is revealed of the condition of a people by the condition of its memorials. Where is the treasure but in the heart? As I write these words, I can think of no more important life lessons than those I have learned where the dead once rested.

David H. Zimmermann

# THE WALKING DEAD: THE ROLE OF THE CORPSE IN WESTERN MYTHS

by David H. Zimmermann

Modern Westerns seem rife with dead cowboys. Of course the bodies are going to pile up with all of the gunfights, Indian battles, rattlesnakes, stampedes, stabbings, battles, and general ill will.

But a lot of them—the bodies that is—seem to malinger. Even John Wayne's characters seem to hop back and forth across the edge of life and death. In *The Cowboys,* the old rancher, Wil Anderson, is slain, but he is not fully dispensed with until the end of the movie—after an intense and lengthy gun battle and the wrap-up of a cattle drive when his cowboys establish their manhood by burying him. In *Big Jake,* Jake's appearance consistently prompts an "I thought you were dead" from friends, enemies, and passing acquaintances; Big Jake eventually embraces the comment before dispensing with the evil-doers. Clint Eastwood's preacher in *Pale Rider* may be the walking corpse or ghost of a gunfighter gunned down by a group of renegade marshals; it seems unlikely that anyone—even Eastwood—could survive the multiple wounds the ring of scars suggests: a pattern of wounds he visits upon the crooked marshal. And finally, and perhaps most importantly since it is set in Texas, McMurtry's summa, *Lonesome Dove,* concludes with the burial of both its main characters; Gus's corpse has been carried back to Austin from the high plains, and Call, having dug the grave, emerges from it if not as a ghost or apparition then at the very least an anachronism of a dead past (a role he fulfills in the novel's sequel *The Streets of Laredo*).

The narrative hinges on the role of the corpse; the embodiment of the legend, the story of the hero, it roams the countryside, forcing the narrative to continue. It must be returned home. This vivification of the corpse may be an extension of Joseph Campbell's notion of apotheosis: the hero acquires a god-like, transcendent stature.

Melquiades Estrada in *The Three Burials of Melquiades Estrada,* then, follows a clear tradition of cowboys whose importance is not tempered by death or the grave. Indeed, in this tradition, Melquiades' significance in the western is inextricably tied to his death, perhaps more accurately his corpse; the actual dying takes a secondary, supporting role; it is not as important as the questions posed by the presence of the corpse. Although the narrative thread is difficult to untangle, *The Three Burials of Melquiades Estrada* does appear to fit Campbell's theory of the monomyth, which would provide a structure for analyzing the transformation from mere mortal to deity and might provide some insight into the Western's—the West's—preoccupation with the walking dead.

The death of Melquiades confronts the Texas rancher, Pete Perkins, with Campbell's call to adventure—a call Perkins answers. He does not wait to be tricked or forced: he acts. At first he acts within the bounds of his own society, addressing his concerns to the sheriff and the head of the Border Patrol. When these attempts to resolve the issue fail, he takes the necessary steps to realize justice; the kidnapping of the Border Patrol agent, Mike Norton, marks his response to the call. As he prepares to cross the border into Mexico, he reflects a clear, systematic awareness of the implications of the journey he is about to make. He is leaving his society.

As he journeys through the desert of West Texas, with the body of Melquiades and the kidnapped border agent, Perkins is traveling in his world, what Campbell terms the world of the everyday. He knows the paths. He knows the sheriff and agents in pursuit. Indeed, he and the sheriff share the same lover. Perkins has responded to the call but has not yet crossed the threshold; he is still in the everyday. The river, still following Campbell's model, may mark the boundary, the threshold, of the two societies. The trucks remain behind, as he shifts to horses—animals of a different world and time. Appropriately, his horse is that of a dead man (Melquiades) and a Mexican, an inhabitant of the world he is about to enter. Mexico is the land of Melquiades, the land of the past, and apparently the land of the dead. For Campbell, it is the land of the quest—the otherworld. Although perhaps not fully aware of all of these possible readings, the Texan is attuned to the nature of the trip, the quest. He is methodically moving beyond the bounds of his world and he prepares accordingly.

The trip across the border is to bury a body, to return a soul to its home. The rancher is carrying a body to the land of a dead time and place. The Rio Grande may serve as the river Styx; that, though, is problematic. Mexico is a place of the past; people still ride horses, lack electricity; cowboys and shepherds and witches still emerge from the land across the river. It is also a place of origins, creating and recreating the myths and legends of Perkins's everyday world.

Significantly, society—as Campbell predicts—tries to prevent the crossing. The agents barricade the crossings, trucks line the river, and helicopters patrol it. Trapped, the rancher views the guardians from a ridge, looking at those who intend to capture him—literally imprisoning him in the everyday. Significantly, the Border Agents in their trucks and helicopters, with their electronics and semi-automatic weapons represent the modern, the contemporary—and perhaps, even the Northern—reinforcing the image of Mexico as a pastoral landscape of the past. The kidnapped agent is from a northern, industrialized city; indeed, the mounted Texas sheriff—a part of a dead past—has broken off the pursuit and gone on to other things; he is no longer a part of this. The agrarian is trapped and frustrated by the industrial; the Texan is bound in by the federal; the hero is baulked by the dictates, rules, and expectations of society. The guardians have accomplished their goal; the agents appear to enforce the boundaries of the everyday world, keeping the living in and the dead—Melquiades' people—out.

The Texan is unable to proceed until he sees a group of illegal immigrants crossing the river; the Mexicans represent an opportunity for him. The coyote becomes what Campbell would consider a helper who frustrates the guardians of society. The helper supplies passage; he also helps the rancher to overcome the first of his tests: curing the snake-bitten federal agent, who is in danger of not surviving the crossing. Buying the passage with one of the horses, the rancher has gained the help of an inhabitant of the other world that will enable him to complete his journey. Appropriately—within this

Jungian framework—the helper is a coyote, a trickster who knows and plays along the boundaries of society. He is a part of the everyday world and the other world. As a trickster, the coyote's presence provides a commentary on both worlds, understanding the values and behaviors of each: he knows the horse and rifle are of some value in the world of the Texas rancher. As trickster, he marks the boundary. His nature and his presence reflect the foolhardiness and necessity of crossing the threshold. The Mexicans must cross to realize economic opportunities; the rancher must cross to reconcile himself to Melquiades' death.

The trickster leads the rancher to the Mexican healer. The *curandera,* the wise and benevolent witch, the earth mother has the skills to cure the Border Patrol agent—the very agent who denied her access to the U.S., to the everyday. Slapping, punching the agent, she exacts her price for keeping him alive to continue his journey in the underworld. Just as he denied her access to his world, she has denied him access to her own, paradoxically, at the very same time that she enables him to continue moving through it. By curing the wound and sending him on his way, she has delegated him to the strange and discomforting twilight world of the quest which he has tried to escape. He does not belong. The boundaries are clear, but the inhabitants seem confused.

Having crossed the border into that other world, the rancher has disappeared from view until he calls the waitress. "Where are you?" The obvious and spontaneous question of the waitress suggests that the rancher has disappeared into the belly of Campbell's whale: he is no longer visible to his society. If so, and if the movie operates as a monomyth, a question is forced back upon the audience. As a myth—and hence an archetype adhering to a pattern independent of the writer, director, and audience—the film plays upon the collective unconscious. The audience is forced to wonder on some level, "Why can we still see him? Are we a part of that underworld?" In effect, the rancher has taken us across the border with him.

The photo of Melquiades's family, Campbell's totem, becomes the final means by which the quest can be completed. Relying on the photo and the description of the town, the rancher moves into the vicinity of Melquiades's family and home, approaching what would be the nadir of the journey. Once he has reached the town, the burial site, there is no need to continue on; he will have gone as far from home as possible. Confronting Melquiades's wife with the photo, the rancher is rebuked. She does not know Melquiades; in fact, he is on the edge of the photo, strangely disconnected from the other figures in the picture. The wife nervously, preemptively dismisses the rancher. Her behavior is confusing but clear. She does not want to discuss the photo. Her motives, though, remain uncertain.

Seemingly, the rancher has misjudged the focus of his quest. Perhaps returning the corpse to the dead man's wife might have served as a bride theft of sorts—claiming the attention, appreciation, and commitment of the feminine of the underworld. Perhaps by returning the body to her, home, the rancher might have achieved a sort of father atonement, making amends for the sins and failures of his world, of his fatherland, reconciling Texas and Mexico. Whichever it is, he fails; she does not admit to recognizing the man in the background of the photo, the man walking across the background eerily disengaged from those he claims to have been his family. Confused, disoriented, the rancher stumbles off, having failed his first attempt at the supreme ordeal.

Although this seems well suited to Campbell's structure, the limitations of such an approach become clear; the reading strips the text of its ambiguities by assuming, affirming, and even reinforcing a shared point of view; the audience must identify with the hero. Melquiades must serve as the other, the outsider, the idealized pastoral. Despite his assertions of friendship throughout the movie, or perhaps precisely because of the friendships, the rancher must construct a reality around Melquiades—friend, shepherd, cowboy, innocent, other. He is all that the rancher's world is not. The rancher is not equipped to view Melquidas as a liar or a cheat—a disillusioned loner who forces his dreams on an unsuspecting family. The rancher, Campbell's monomyth, and the audience's confused expectations do not leave room for these possibilities. Instead, Melquiades is coopted to fit the needs of a society working through its own views of death, immigration, industrialization, sex, marriage, commercialism, and violence. As the outsider, Melquiades becomes the canon by which each is measured. His halting English and quiet Spanish, his traditional and stylized Western attire, all serve as markers distinguishing him from Mexican Americans; the audience, the rancher, the everyday will not confuse Melquiades with the Hispanic Border Patrol agent. The two men are of different worlds. The Hispanic Border Patrol agent is firmly a part of the everyday world—he is gently corrupt, obtuse, dedicated. His place in the cafe, his U.S. uniform, his English, and his frustrations all mark him as a part of the everyday—they all mark him as one of us, an American, a Texan.

Melquiades, though, is different. He is marked by the film, by the agents, by the rancher, by the audience, as different. The application of Campbell's model relies on this projection of difference to structure the events. The quest, the inhabitants of the quest, and the goals of the quest all depend on the identification of Melquiades as something outside the norm. The differences, though, are clear, static, and imposed—they are expected. Perhaps most obvious are the scenes in Midland when Melquiades is in the truck meeting the agent's wife for a brief affair. His fascination with televisions and his quiet, shy innocence suggest that he is an innocent, a child of Rousseau.

The movie ends with Perkins and the Border Patrol agent building a home for Melquiades, the home he described to the rancher. They impose their view on the landscape of the otherworld. Just as he earlier burned off the ants and fixed Melquiades's hair, the rancher reshapes the world of Melquiades to fit his expectations, his needs. From the perspective of Campbell's theory, the rancher may have overcome the supreme ordeal—realizing an apotheosis of sorts. He becomes a god-like figure creating a new world, giving new life to the "dead" Border Patrol agent, and carrying the dead to their home. From Campbell's perspective, the rancher has completed the quest. He does not even need to return—the border agent riding off on the horse will presumably carry the story back with him, reviving the world with the story.

The quest, though, ends as a struggle to impose a world view, an identity on a place, on a person, on a land. The rancher is the very agent of the society he flees. He has sought to destroy the ambiguity and uncertainty of Melquiades's existence with the static, moribund myth of his death. The forms of the everyday world, the order of the everyday world, have been imposed on the chaos of the other: the Texan has defined the Mexican. The Mexican exists as a reflection of the Texan—the rancher's, the Border Patrol agent's, the audience's—needs. The views, values, and beliefs of the North have literally been transplanted into the South.

The cowboy's corpses, bones, and graves serve as an opportunity for the living—both their fellow characters and their audiences—to revisit the stories and myths of the West. It seems obvious that the legends, the stories of the western hero are somehow intricately linked to the hero's death. The corpses, though, hang about: the sign on I-40 marking the exit to see Billy the Kid's grave marks the West. Seemingly, the dead serve as texts for the living, texts that define, and limit, the stories the living are able to construct. The import and efficacy of the Western myth, then, may not be in its structure. It seems to reside in the context, in the viewing of the body—there is no need to look past Davy Crockett's crypt in San Fernando Cathedral. Standing next to it suffices.

A squash blossom, the "yellow flower of death"

# THE YELLOW FLOWER OF DEATH

by Hortense Warner Ward

*El muerto al poso,*
*El vive al negocio.*
(The dead into the hole,
The living to business.)

The late Sheriff William Shely of Christi was frequently heard to repeat the preceding proverb when viewing Latin-American funerals in the old days. It was a comment upon the alacrity with which mourners returned from graveside to normal pursuits of life. The saying intimates that feelings, as well as flowers, were left inside the cemetery gates. In reality, nothing is farther from the truth.

There is, however, a certain fatalism with which Latin Americans regard death. Such an attitude is frequently interpreted by others as careless acceptance of the event. Consequently, condemnation is sometimes called forth, and the family of the departed is accused of irreverence. Still it must be remembered that a people of mixed Spanish and Indian ancestry are but four-and-a-half centuries from that time when sacrificial death was embraced as the highest earthly honor to be achieved.

Before Cortez came to the New World, death was hardly considered an event for grief. Flower-decked youths, the most perfect and beautiful of their race, were chosen for sacrifice at the climax of ecstatic religious frenzies. Processions of flower-bearers accompanied them to an altar high upon the peak of a *teocalli*. The victims blew plaintive chants upon symbolic clay flutes, breaking the instruments upon the steep ascent of the shrine, even as their bodies were to be broken at the top.

Racial memories of these rites have been metamorphosed into a pale semblance of their former awful meaning. Significances have been sublimated until only flowers and pageantry remain. Death is no longer imposed, but comes as the natural termination of life.

Processions of white-clad youths and damsels, hand in hand and bearing flowers, still accompany on foot the dead to the grave. But instead of thin melodies played upon clay flutes, there is sometimes a loud and brassy band which precedes the cortege to its appointed destination.

So strongly identified with Christian ceremony have ancient customs become, that all trace of pagan practices seems to have been obliterated. Yet, the flowers carried to the graves are truly related to the past. They are still offerings to Coatlicue, to Tlacoteotl, Mictlantecuhtli, and Mixtlancihuatl, the ancient Aztec deities of love, death, and flowers. Dim racial memories of the gods persist among the Latin Americans, though the names of the deities are now foreign to the tongues of the people. And there are other blossoms than the yellow flower of death among the floral offerings at the graves.

To realize that these ancient memories still exist in the minds of men, there are several things to consider. There is first the connection of customs which are today observed in honoring the dead with those that existed in the past. Again to appreciate the full significance of this lore, the correlation must be pushed still further.

Even though such correlation at first glance may seem to be utterly divergent from the subjects under consideration, the reason for our consideration is soon apparent. I refer to the relationship between death observances and the symbolism expressed in cattle brand patterns still used by descendants of the ancient native races. The kinship is obvious when the sacred blossom that was the emblem of the god of death is seen pictured in these brand designs.

Now, any day in the week sees visitors on their way to the cemetery carrying flowers to the dead. Sunday, though, is a gala occasion in Corpus Christi. Then the lower social strata flock to God's acre to visit a while beside the narrow green couches. Busses are crowded with elderly *mamacitas*, accompanied by swarms of freshly scrubbed *niñitos*. At the end of the line, all are discharged upon a white-hot shell road. Rose Hill Cemetery can be seen blocks away, fluttering mysteriously through shimmering heat waves.

An informal procession arranges itself at once. There are first the plump *mamacitas,* black calico *rebosos* wound over head and throat, for protection against the sun. They roll along with the jerking gait of heavy Plymouth Rock hens. Next come the *niñitos,* clustering about the skirts of the old women, furthering the illusion of hen and chicks.

There is a good deal of chattering, but it is subdued. The children understand that this outing is an adult affair in which, by special dispensation, they are allowed to share. It is the bright pink hair ribbons, flying about on pigtails of little girls, that mark the height of the children's suppressed excitement.

All the pilgrims carry bouquets of flowers, Tuberoses, oleander blossoms from the hedge, roses, asparagus fern in liberal quantities—any flower at all that grows plentifully in the garden is plucked and carried to the sleeping loved ones. If no flowers are in the garden, then a week's wages may go over the counter at flower stalls on Leopard Street. The dead must be served, though the quick may have to pull in their belts in the serving.

If there has been little work of late, and there is no money at all, there are always paper flowers which one can make. The women are very clever with their quick, twinkling fingers. They fashion vivid red, pink, and yellow crepe paper into realistic roses. When dipped into paraffin, the flower petals acquire a velvety texture, and it is a comfort to know that though they lack fragrance, these substitutes will outlast the petals of real blossoms by many days.

But it is on All Saints' and All Souls' Days that Mictlantecuhtli and Mictlancihuatl, Our Lord and Lady of the Region of Death, come once more into their own. They are very much with the people, though it is under the guise of a Christian celebration.

Here at the cemetery, the first day of November promises to be warm, even hot, though under the trees it is still pleasant enough. A few cottony clouds float lazily in the soft blue sky. The feathery shade of mesquites and the deeper shadow of liveoaks form intricate patterns upon the grass. Daws creak like rusty hinges or whistle plaintively overhead through the branches. Mockingbirds flout each other in song.

**Jewelry that features the squash blossom motif**

Whole families turn out before the dew is off the grass. They arrive on foot, in broken-down cars, delivery trucks, taxis, the condition of their conveyances a revealing index to their economic status.

Now a shiny town car draws up, and a dainty, well-dressed girl gets out. She carries a cigarette in one hand, and an elaborate basket of flowers in the other. Her skirts swish enticingly as she teeters across the grass on three-inch heels. She places her basket at the foot of a large monument, pauses a moment to gather the effect of bright blossoms against grey granite. She puffs modishly on her cigarette, then, satisfied that duty is well done, trips back to her car and is gone.

From an adjoining plot a very old white-haired woman, dressed in the unrelieved black of mourning, squats upon her heels and watches the girl impassively. She too puffs a cigarette, but it is with the carelessness of long practice. Her sunken black eyes follow the movements of the young woman. Next year—six months from now—perhaps the young ones will be bringing flowers to honor this poor tired body. *¿Quién sabe?* Indeed, who knows?

Some folk carry galvanized buckets. Others have large brown paper bags from which they draw an endless supply of bottles, jars, and broken bits of garden tools. Occasionally a rake and spade are required to remove dead shrubbery. Then the men throw their arms and backs into this work with a will.

Fat middle-aged women, bending down to plant cuttings, expose shapeless, stump-like legs. It is, for all the world, like a rear view of the elephant line at the circus.

Children pull weeds and grass, or race back and forth between plot and water hydrant with slopping jars, trails of diamonds marking their routes.

There are many flowers today. There will be still more tomorrow. Chrysanthemums, calendulas, coxcombs, asters, zinnias, coral vine, tuberoses, mountains of asparagus fern—the gardens have been raped for the gods of love, death, and flowers!

Many women wear black, and while some few weep, the general atmosphere is one of subdued, pleasurable industry. Little children refrain from boisterous play and are quiet without having to be reminded of the day and place.

All is bustle in this lower part of the cemetery, but at the top of the hill, where Anglo-American dead look down upon their poorer Latin brothers, no one moves about. Only one grave is unforgotten. The name upon the stone is that of a Bohemian farm family. Flowers have been arranged there, but the living hands that placed them upon the grave have departed.

Down below, there is continuous motion. Men and women walk about through the graves visiting old friends, greeting relatives both quick and dead. Now one pauses to lay his work-gnarled hands upon a carved stone cross, to stroke gently the replica of a compassionate Christ, to bow reverently before the Blessed Virgin. Little knots of folk talk quietly. There is even a trickle of low laughter, for it is hard to be sad amid such beauty and peace.

Towards noon some leave, walking hand in hand. At the gate, they pass small boys who have thrown themselves down in the bottom of a drainage ditch beside tubs of garden-grown chrysanthemums. The children roll and tumble with each other like puppies and have scant time to spare for the more serious business of selling their blossoms. They have no time at all to reverence Coatlicue, that ancient patron deity of Aztec flower vendors.

Where the road turns into the cemetery between tall brick pillars, a woman has set up a couple of boxes. Upon one of these is a small coal-oil stove over which she is making *tacos.* Upon the other box stands a great yellow bowl piled high with shredded lettuce, beets, carrots, and tomatoes. From this she deftly fills crisp, crimped *tortillas,* lifting them hot from a smoking kettle of fat. Over each tidbit she drips a spoonful of the concentrated crushed fire of chiltipín peppers.

The *dulce* vendor is there also. He sits in the shade of a palm beside his little glass case of sweet candied pumpkin and yams. He calls his wares in a cheerful, low voice to the passers-by. Business is good, for there is a constant stream of arrivals and departures.

Now a mystery begins to solve itself. All afternoon a small, low platform, centrally located, has stood bare and uninteresting in the hot strong sunlight. It is only after rosary is said that it blossoms with lighted candles. The good folk who have come to watch all night by the side of their dead lay offerings of food and drink upon it. Traditionally these foods are for the dead to partake of, but in reality they are to be eaten by the watchers themselves.

The platform groans under its load of *tamales, tortillas, tacos, pan dulce,* jugs of coffee, and chocolate. By morning, little of its gifts will remain. The body, as well as the soul, needs sustenance through the long night hours.

All Souls' Day dawns bright and sultry. The crowd doubles and trebles that of yesterday. There is an air of fiesta about God's acre, and tears are so few as to be remarked. The Anglo-American part of the cemetery remains deserted and bare except for its one grave. The Bohemian family is here now, and kneels in grief-stricken prayer about their dead.

If one climbs the low, rolling hill at the back of the cemetery, he finds a soft cooling breeze at the top. From this point, a full appreciation of the view is had. What seems to be a miraculously blooming garden is spread out in a wide carpet below.

Much more has been done to beautify the graves since last night. A flag has been spread out over one of them as a coverlet. Near this same spot, bright red, green, and yellow crepe paper streamers twist down from a headstone to the earth. Wreaths and crosses of paper flowers in vivid colors lean against others.

By noon the sun has walked laboriously up the sky and rests at the zenith in broiling intensity. Every bit of shade, down to that of the scantiest shrub, has its crouching occupant. Some visitors have had the forethought to bring folding chairs, and now sit comfortably fanning themselves with bits of paper. The majority, however, squat on their heels or sprawl full length. Oblivious of the heat, they eat the heavy rich food they have brought along in paper sacks.

Bright orange shucks, peeled from *tamales,* are strewn everywhere underfoot, attesting the fact that vendors at the gate have done a roaring business. These last have increased in number since yesterday. *Chile* and *enchiladas,* in addition to *tacos,* may now be bought. The pungent odor of chopped onions and garlic mix pleasantly with the cloying scent of tuberoses and other heavily perfumed flowers.

This visiting with the dead, however, is not confined to the city of Corpus Christi. In San Antonio, All Saints' and All Souls' Days are observed in similar fashion, but the occasion is a livelier affair. Outside the gates of the cemetery, trucks are parked thickly, giving the scene an air of a marketplace. Vendors of oranges, foods, candy, flowers, and souvenirs vie noisily with each other to coax coins from the pockets of visitors. Inside, many graves are set with foods and flowers, while watchers sit upon the ground or kneel in prayer, as their temperaments dictate.

Observing an elderly woman weeping as she kneels at a graveside, another approaches and asks, "Why do you cry? You know that your son is better off, and that he is happy."

"No, *Madama,* that cannot be," replies the old woman, wiping her eyes.

"But surely you believe . . . "

"*Ay!* But he was not called; he was sent!" the woman wails.

"And how is that?"

"He was sent! He was killed! *Ay-ay-ay!*" The kneeling woman weeps afresh.

Bit by bit, the story is drawn out. The boy had died as the result of a stab received in a fight, and so had been sent to an unnatural death instead of being summoned at his rightful time. Now the old woman has set bread, fruit, and wine upon his grave, because in life her son liked them. "And I know he must enjoy the wine," she finishes, naïvely, "because when I come in the morning, the bottle is always empty."

The celebration of All Saints' and All Souls' Days in San Antonio is a pale thing beside the observance of these days in Mexico. There the visit with the dead is a real fiesta. It is even more closely related to the past than are the customs north of the Rio Grande. One sees a profusion of flowers—the yellow flowers of death. In addition to the conventional food, sugar skulls and bones are offered for sale and consumed with more relish than thought of their pagan significance. Somehow Mictlancihuatl and Mictlantecuhtli have found their way into the confectioners' shops. These sublimated emblems of the human bones once worn by the Aztec deities at the peak of their power, now go to satisfy an appetite for sweets in profane worshipers.

But flowers are not reserved for the cemetery alone. On lesser occasions—in fact, on any day in the week—Tejanos carry a flower or two about with them. Men, with no thought of frivolity, will place a rose in the hatband, or wear it jauntily behind the ear. In tomato and lard cans, upon tiny verandas of the humble shacks in which they dwell, geraniums and gay-leaved coleus brighten squalid surroundings. Dooryards are neatly swept; fences are built around them from discarded shingles or beer bottles. Frequently there is a minute yard, with an equally minute garden glowing like a jewel. No patch of ground is too poor or too small to lack growing things when care will bring them forth. The old reverent love for flowers still remains a passion with these people, though their symbolism of the gods of love and death has long been forgotten.

It is very clear that the flower gods still play an unsuspected, though important, part in the lives of these folk. And if documentary proof were needed to substantiate this statement, that is avail-

**The petals of the squash blossom are a vibrant yellow**

able also. Such proof is seen, of course, in the designs of the old stock brands which descendants of this mixture of Spanish and native races use to this day.

Many of the queerly patterned stock brands incorporate a flower in the designs. This flower is similar in appearance to the representation of the Aloseka, or bud of the squash blossom, as drawn by the Indians of the San Franciscan mountains. It is regarded by them as a rain symbol. Furthermore, it is almost identical with that symbol seen upon the face of Ekchuah, the Maya god of peddlers and traveling merchants, whom those ancient peoples called the Black Calabash.

It will be recalled here that blossoms of squash and calabash are similar in appearance, but a more interesting, and significant, fact is that both are *yellow.* The deities for which this flower symbol stood performed multiple offices; not only were they patrons of travelers and gods of death, but also gods of fertility. *Tauitas*[1] that are in themselves symbols of fertility emphasize this particular meaning of the blossom.

And why should the early *mestizo* cattleman have chosen the yellow blossom of death for his brand design? Because, if the reference were to Ekchuah, for instance, or to one of his counterparts among the other native religions, there would be direct connection between the rancher's needs and the powers of this god. During periods of drouth, cattle have been known to roam far from their unfenced home range in search of food and water. It is logical to think that the watch Ekchuah exerted over human travelers was extended to wandering stock entrusted to his care. In due time he would return them safely home again. Aside from this, the blossom was a rain symbol. Surely Ekchuah would not neglect to furnish food and drink for his charges.

In a Cameron County brand this squash—or gourd—blossom springs from a representation of the mythical cosmic pot, that vessel from which emerged the primal pair. This particular brand shows a *media luna vaciada,* or half moon emptied, as the lip of the pot.[2] Now the gourd, according to the belief of many ancient races, including some of those in the New World, was a form of the cosmic pot. The conventional blossom used in connection with such pot-shaped designs emphasizes the original meaning of the symbol. Combined with the inverted crescent, an additional guarantee of fertility and rain, this brand design just about covers the entire category of any cattleman's needs.

Another Cameron County brand shows the same blossom design. It springs from a recognizable earth symbol and has a similar blossom accompanying the figure, which is probably the *venta* or counter brand. In the *venta,* however, the flower arises from the cosmic pot much like that in the preceding illustration.[3] There is a possibility that here is intended a reference to Coatlicue. She was an earth goddess, as well as being at the same time one of death, war, love, and the patroness of dealers in flowers. Both earth and cosmic pot are but means of saying the same thing in different terms. As an earth goddess, Coatlicue would not only be the one from whom all things spring, but also the provider of sustenance for all. Her symbol on a herd of cattle would be excellent insurance for the fertility not only of the herd, but also of the lands upon which they grazed.

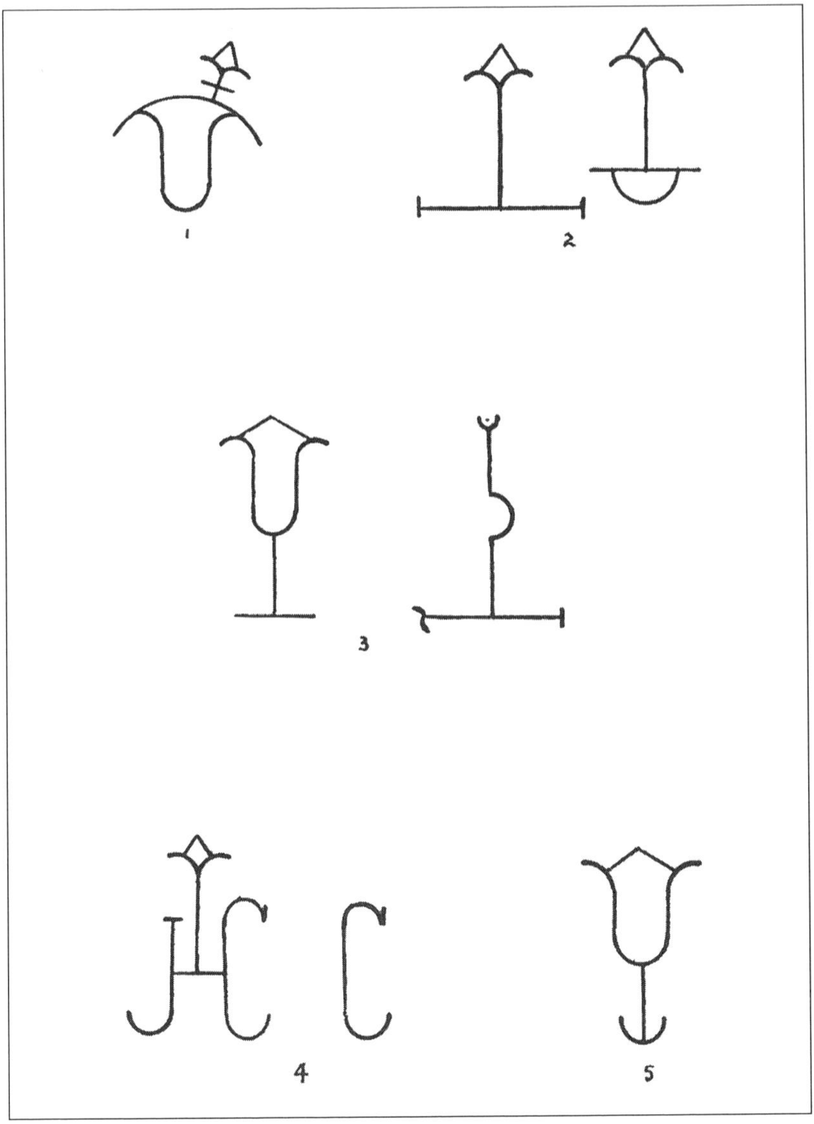

Fig. 1—Squash or gourd blossom springing from the mythical cosmic pot, with half moon emptied as the lip of the pot.

Fig. 2—Blossom springing from the earth, and counter brand of blossom springing from the cosmic pot.

Fig. 3—Blossom springing from the earth, and counter brand made of fertility symbols—crescents, serpent, earth, and double-headed thunder axe.

Fig. 4—Combining blossom design with owner's initials J. C., and counter brand repeating the C, or crescent.

Fig. 5—Blossom springing from an upturned crescent.

A third brand, likewise from Cameron County, has an entirely different *venta*.[4] However, its value as a related symbol is at once apparent. The latter figure is constructed entirely from symbols recognized universally as those of fertility—crescents, the serpent, the earth, and a double-headed thunder axe. Again a reference to Coatlicue may well be intended.

Josefa Carrasco de Arizpe of the Districto del Centro, Mexico, has combined the blossom design with her first two initials to form her stock brand.[5] The *venta* repeats the C, or crescent, while the flower, in the brand pattern of Refugia G. Falcon of Rancho del Chiltepin in Nueces County,[6] springs from an upturned crescent.

This list could be prolonged indefinitely, but to no further advantage, for the brands repeat the same petitions to the ancient deities over and over again.

It is strange how the symbols have persisted while their meanings have become obscured in their passage through time. With patience, though, their messages can be read as clearly today as four hundred fifty-odd years ago when Cortez ravished the Aztec temples and threw down their gods.

In spite of the fact that the gods have been so discredited, never have the deities of love, death, and flowers relaxed their hold upon the peoples who once abjectly served them. These deities watch and wait. Their patience is unsurpassed, but in the meantime they demand their annual tribute. Simple folk still carry yellow flowers of death to the graves of their loved ones.

## ENDNOTES

1. *Tauitas,* colloquial Spanish. There is no exact translation for this word, but the term is used in reference to the decorative flourishes applied to the main brand design.
2. Fig. 1, Ed M. DuBose, personal brand record, manuscript.
3. Fig. 2. ibid., op.cit.
4. Fig. 3. ibid., op.cit.
5. Fig. 4. Planilla General de Fierros del Estado de Coahuila, de Zaragoza, Tipografia del Gobierno en Palacio, Dirigida por Severiano Mors, 1897.
6. Fig. 5, Nueces County Brand Records, Book C., June 8, 1877.

## GRANDMOTHER'S UNCLE

**by Brenda Black White**

He chose his fate,
holding up the stagecoach
that carried payroll.
He was left in the desert to die
        an ignoble death—
bullet through the gut,
his horse shot from under him.

The parched sand's
only moisture was the pool of blood
        he lay upon.

Later, his bones were found,
        dry and white—
bleached by the sun,
after the flesh was stripped
by wolves and vultures,
the only meal they'd had in days.

**Tony Clark**

# A GIFT OF TIME

by Karen Clark Ristine

[I wrote this story on Dec. 7, 2005, after traveling with my family on a car trip across Texas that really seemed like a magic realism trip across time. My father, Tony Clark, died after heart surgery on Dec. 15, 2005. I have always appreciated that I recognized this day as a gift in the moment, while my father was still alive. And what a gift, too, that he read this before he died—and that through this writing we shared our love of family and our love of words, and now continue a legacy of sharing our family folklore with the Texas Folklore Society.—*Ristine*]

The last time my "original family"—my mother, my father, my brother and I—took a car trip together, I was twenty years old. We were headed for Creede, Colorado. It was our first trip to a place that would become an annual summer vacation destination for my parents, but it was our last car trip together as a family.

Some twenty-five years later, we took an unexpected journey together that moved us geographically across south-central Texas, from Houston to Austin, but our travels also moved us across time as we recalled and shared memories of past family times together, while also creating a new and indelible memory of celebrating the family we were and the family we have become.

The car trip was an unexpected gift, though none of us would have said so at its outset. We were gathered in Houston expecting that Dad would have surgery at the Texas Heart Institute. We had already been together for twenty-four hours. When I had arrived from San Diego, Dad was in recovery from a procedure to help his doctors determine how best to approach their surgical efforts to repair an aortic aneurysm. We all still thought he might have surgery the next day, but, at ten p.m., the hospital sent us back to our motel to await word from the doctors. That word came the next morning,

December 7—the surgery would be the following Monday. So we packed my parents' car and prepared to take them home.

Though we had been with each other for a day, even acknowledging how rare it is for just the four of us to be together, we were still in our twenty-first-century roles of grown-up adult children, with older parents appreciative of their children's assistance and even leadership. But there was something about being in the car together, covering the miles with nothing to do but talk, that threw us back into (functional) family road trip dynamics. The only thing different was that my brother was driving and I was riding shotgun, and my parents were in the back seat.

It didn't take long for us to revive the past.

There was the time my brother, Todd, had announced to the family that he was not really part of our family. He knew we had adopted him and that his real father was Marlin Perkins of Mutual of Omaha's *Wild Kingdom*—an ancient precursor to Animal Planet. When Marlin Perkins died years later, I had called my brother and offered my condolences.

Todd told a story of a trophy that had traveled from dorm room to dorm room each week after the Friday night Battling Tops competition during his freshman year at The University of Texas. My father countered with a story about a trophy that traveled between his office and a colleague's after (what I suspect was more frequently than weekly) gin rummy games they played during down time as teachers at Paris Junior College. Neither Dad nor Todd had heard the other's story before, but they were delighted to know that they had each created a similarly silly tradition with friends.

I introduced a new family car game—a discussion starter I learned from a youth pastor—to replace past games of "I spy something. . . ." If you could have anyone serenade you, I asked them, who would it be? This simple question took us through a journey of all the music that had been meaningful in our lives together as a family, and also the music that had helped define us as individuals.

"Well we all know who my choice would be," my mother said.

And we did.

"Willie," I said without a question mark.

While mother's choice of Willie Nelson as a serenader did not surprise me, her choice of song did. I had expected she would pick "Blue Eyes Cryin' in the Rain." Instead, she chose another classic: "I Never Cared for You." It's not as odd a selection as its title suggests. "The sun is full of ice and gives no warmth at all / The sky is never blue / The stars are simply raindrops with no place to fall / And I never cared for you." It's a song about a man working hard to persuade the woman he loves that she can trust his love.

My father worked through an intriguing set of possibilities before landing exactly where I had expected him to. His progression was this:

Elvis—"Even though Elvis died for me several years before he actually died."

The Drifters—Singing, of all things, "White Christmas."

The song by the fool in Shakespeare's play *Twelfth Night*.

But finally, he said, what he would really want to hear would be Beethoven's Ninth Symphony—specifically the fourth movement with its four soloists and 200-voice chorus. I knew it would be Beethoven. I knew it would be the Ninth Symphony. (And I suspected his preferred conductor would be Leonard Bernstein—but he didn't say.)

And then, as an odd and surprising little coda, my father said he would like to hear the final hymn sung at the Last Supper.

My brother struggled with the question the same way I had when I first heard it. First, he worked his way through all the bands he really respects—U2, Garbage, Foo Fighters, Nickel Creek. Then he said that, as a teenager, he would have wanted a serenade from Linda Ronstadt, but he doesn't have the same needs now that he had then and he can't get her sixty-something look out of his head to be serenaded by the Ronstadt of the 1970s. I took comfort in his struggle because it was so similar to mine. We both love music. We both respect artists with a message, talent, *and* creativity. How do you choose? Finally, Todd also landed in a predictable and touching place. He said he would take his wife, Kristi, back to the time of U2's *Rattle and Hum* album and go to a concert with her.

I said if I were picking someone to serenade me and my husband, Jeff, it would be Bonnie Raitt. But I told my family of my choice of Paul Simon to serenade me and how it had been ridiculed as "dorky" by my friends on the road trip where I had first heard the serenade question. "Well, he is dorky," my mother said, "but his music is good." My Dad said that Paul Simon and Bob Dylan were really the best wordsmiths of their eras, that it would be hard to beat either of them in that category. I told my family that I had almost picked Dylan—earliest Dylan—but was afraid he would be ridiculed, too. And that launched us into a discussion of Dylan, who has been a formative part of each of our lives in relation to music. For my brother and me, it was our parents who brought Dylan into our awareness, but—not unlike religion and faith—we came to respect and embrace him and his music and its message through our own perspective and experience.

We stopped for lunch at a café in a small Texas town, the kind of place where the fact that the parking lot is full at two in the afternoon lets you know the place has a good reputation and the food must be good. We were also drawn in by the name. It was called "Tony's Family Restaurant." We were with Tony, and we were his family, so it seemed the place to eat. We each ordered the gigantic chicken-fried steak from the handwritten list of lunch specials. (Dad was the only one who could eat it without guilt, since he had just been told that his sixty-nine-year-old arteries had no blockages. My brother and I could only hope that trait was hereditary.) Our lunch led us to talk about all the great cafes we have eaten in, starting, of course, with the Green Frog Café in Jacksboro, Texas, where my father grew up and his mother lived until her death fifteen years earlier. My brother and I both ordered fried okra and black-eyed peas. Even the food on our journey was nostalgic.

Back in the car, I brought up the most fascinating family discussion I had ever witnessed. My brother remembered it vividly, too. My father has no siblings, but his best friend, Randy, had become like a brother over the years. One night, my Dad shared with us his belief that he was the center of the universe. This unusual philosophy was not really as self-centered as it literally appears. His contention was that—to himself—he was the center of the universe, but every other sentient being experienced the same center-of-the-universe sensation. Randy rejected this philosophy, and the debate went on into the evening. I don't remember contributing much at all to the discussion. My brother chimed in from time to time on Randy's side, but mostly he did so to be a contrarian to my dad, which I suspected at the time and Todd admitted on this trip. My father still held this philosophy, and it has begun to make more sense to his grown children.

But there had been another conversation that long-ago evening in our living room that was equally fascinating. Dad was a new convert to Catholicism and, somewhere in the discussion, Randy told him that Roger Staubach, legendary quarterback of the Dallas Cowboys who really shouldn't need an appositive here, was Catholic, too. My dad immediately rejected this concept. Staubach was too born-again to be Catholic. Randy was certain he was. So Dad bet Randy $20 and Todd took the same bet for a dollar. They agreed to research the question and pay off the bet in a "mutual bar." Recalling that evening, my brother and I pointed out to Dad that now the bet could be settled in an instant with a Google search, but at the time Dad had gone to the periodical section of the junior college library to do his research.

Dad lost. And the mutual bar selected was The Miner's Inn in Creede, on that last family vacation. I was the designated driver that afternoon because I was old enough to drive in Colorado but not old enough to drink. When we returned to our cabin at Broken Arrow Ranch, my father and I leaned on the front of the family car, a Ford Fairmont station wagon, and looked across the meadow at Bristol Head. My father, who up to that point had never been very demonstrative about his emotions, told me just how much he loved me, how proud he was of me, and how much hope he had for my future. I remember the moment with a clarity as crisp as the Rocky Mountain evening air. I have never regretted or resented that this confession of his faith in me and love for me came while Dad was less than sober. Perhaps it is because it was a message he had offered freely and consistently ever since. The next morning, we packed the car and left Creede. On Wagon Wheel Gap, one of the most treacherous stretches of mountain road leading home, we had a flat. My Dad, hungover from paying off his bet in a mutual bar the night before, unloaded all our belongings from the back of the station wagon to get to the spare tire. Thus began the last leg of our last family road trip.

Until today.

I realized, even as we continued our travels to my parents' home, that the return trip to Houston would not be this jovial. We had been given a brief reprieve from our worries about Dad's health. We had been given a little time to just be family together. I knew that when we returned to Houston we would carry again the burden of our anxiety.

But on that last trip before his surgery, we were given a gift. We celebrated our family as it was. We celebrated what our family has become. We celebrated and affirmed one another. It was an amazing journey into our life and love as a family. I knew as it was happening that it was magical, but it was more than magical. It was a blessing.

It was a gift of love and a gift of time.

Linda and Tony Clark at the 2000 TFS meeting in Nacogdoches

**Faye Leeper**

# SUPER REALITY

**by Faye Leeper**

Must not the question be asked before the answer comes?

If a person owns an experience that the general population accepts as out of the realm of common, it could be considered well-named, "supernatural." Yet, is it not "natural" only because all persons do not claim one?

Most of us have gone near enough to the supernatural that we are willing to listen to another tell of some strange experience. When we are watching a television show that we know could not have been true according to our reality, we will still be disappointed if someone turns it off before we see the cause or consequence of the supernatural.

My father would never have stepped on a grave. He had more respect for the dead than that—and he had heard folks tell of strange consequences of such behavior. Still, he was not above telling jokes on the dead. He told of a man who died in Tennessee, and two friends were digging his grave. One friend needed to leave before the job was finished, so the other friend assured him he would finish it. About dark he measured and decided that the dimensions were about standard, so he tried to get out. He kept sliding back in on the loose dirt. He finally realized he could not make it, so he sat down in the corner of the grave and wrapped his coat around himself, resigned to spend the night. He fell asleep.

Later, a couple of teenage boys were trying to show off for their girlfriends that they were not afraid to cross the cemetery at midnight. One of the boys, half paralyzed with fright, accidentally fell into the open grave. He made several frantic attempts to get out. The man sitting in the corner woke up and realized what was happening. He tapped the boy on the back and said, "You cannot get out of here. I have already tried."

Well, he got out!

Why fear a cemetery? And why at midnight? Can fear create a chemistry that can create for one's consciousness an image that he assumes his eyes detected? After scoffing at folks for years who claimed to have seen a ghost, I saw one. I had never lost a loved one, until I was a student at UT one summer when I was called home to grieve with the family. My father had overdosed on insulin. He was seventy-five years old. I rushed back to summer school after a couple days and was then called home again. After seeing the horrible state my mother was in, the last thing I could do was to go back to class. I was in total denial of my father's death—so much so that I did not even cry. I actually seemed to feel that he would rise up anytime to show me he was not really dead. Then, two weeks later, I was standing at the ironing board and he appeared for a split second before me in the suit he was buried in, grinning and saying, "But you thought I was dead!" Strange, indeed, how a split-second experience can affect one's life. I never actually saw my mother after her going; but one day she touched me on the shoulder from behind. I was shocked as I turned to see that she was not actually there.

Now, as I am writing this, I realize that the only other supernatural event I recall is the one shortly after my husband died, although it carries a stranger consequence. I had started going to our little cabin in the rustic hills in New Mexico. How I was able to go then, when I was never brave enough to go alone ever before, I cannot explain. Grief, I suppose, can sometimes just push reality out the back side of one's skull. Anyway, I was drinking a new-made strong cup of coffee there in the living room about 2:30 a.m. with my eyes shut. I saw down a dark tunnel with daylight at the end of it. I identified it as the birthing canal. I think I was agreeing to death.

I do not know exactly how to explain this. It was one of those few times I had admitted to the darkened world that I thought I was not "going to make it," like a sort of contract to go—or consent to go. When I saw the tunnel I sharply changed my mind. I jumped up and whispered hurriedly, "Not now!" Then suddenly I asked myself, "Why did you choose to stay here in this misery?"

Immediately I concluded, "I choose only to stay and accept the challenge." However noble I have made this sound, I believe I have told it exactly the way I experienced it. I had never read one of the LIFE AFTER DEATH books, so I did not learn until about a year later that the tunnel with daylight at the end of it was a common trait in these experiences. I still feel that I was about to be born into another life.

Another puzzle I am pondering as I write is that my husband never claimed to have any such experiences, but our son did. Could this be hereditary? We had left our birthplace in Texas to spend a year in California. The boy was five years old and in kindergarten. One Sunday night we went through all the goodnight rituals, and he went in to his bed—I thought. After about twenty or thirty minutes, he called, "Mootther." I went into his room and experienced one big shock. He was not there, and both twin beds looked still untouched. I immediately called out, "Where are you?" I followed his voice into our bedroom. "What are you doing in here?"

"Mother, why did Grandmother die?" I asked which grandmother. He said, "The one that makes me popsicles." That was my mother. I told him both his grandmothers were very much alive. Then he asked why she rode in the ambulance. Then, "Why did the kids think she was dead?" I had mixed feelings about all this, but I do not remember being greatly distressed.

Wednesday, four days later, I got a letter from my mother. She said she had stepped off the curb at church and broken her ankle. She had the whole leg in a cast, so the fellows brought her home in an ambulance. When they brought her inside, she asked why all the children from the apartment complex were crying. One of the attendants went outside and came back in with the news, "They thought Grandma was dead." My mother asked them to prop her up on the sofa and bring the kids in and she would read them a story.

Our son has never shared another experience of this scope with us. I remember telling long-time TFS member Paul Patterson about this, and he said that he felt some of us were born with this talent, but if we do not know how to exercise that skill and train it, then we lose it.

In some cases, we may be better off to lose it when we understand it so little. One day a couple of weeks later, there was a beautiful glow across the sky about one o'clock in the afternoon as we were driving to the store. My son exclaimed, "Mother, who is Jesus coming for?" I nearly wrecked the car. I feared for a split second that He could be coming for us. We never learned that He came for anyone we knew just then, but even one of Shakespeare's characters knew that could happen: "The Heavens blaze forth the death of princes."

Once as I told a story to a friend who had directed our Great Books Club, she reciprocated with her own. She said that as she sat on her bed one evening, dressing for sleep, she looked up at her father in an oil portrait of him. He was weeping and the tears were rolling off the frame and falling to the floor. As she was adjusting her covers, the phone rang. Her mother told her that her father had just died of a heart attack. He was in St. Louis. She answered the phone in Midland, Texas.

Dr. Ralph Houston, a long-time staunch member of TFS, introduced me to Franz Werfel's *Song of Bernadette*, a very popular novel of the young Catholic girl who was directed by the Virgin Mary to uncover the magic spring in Lourdes where so many have reportedly been healed by bathing in the waters. Several years later, he brought me an article about the many samples of its water that had been sent round the world for testing from the springs. All the tests came back identical. The samples had every kind of bacteria, but it was all inert, and none of the labs knew where the water had come from. Seeing the millions of books that were sold and the millions who saw the movie, it seems that many wanted to believe in the magical cures.

Strangely today, with no threat of Bedlam, psychiatrists tell us that these stories are plentiful. They were only afraid to admit them earlier. The *Wall Street Journal* reported that in 1993, the favorite topic in published books was "life after death."

But what is our question?

If one can see an event without being present in body and mental awareness, or if one is cured of a disease with no assistance except desire, or if one can move solid objects from one place to another, from where does this power come? Is this source out of the ordinary, or out of nature's common course? As I ponder and write, I cannot think of a word that seems to define it.

Dear reader, please remind me if our question is of religion or science, now that our physicists and metaphysicists can sit down to tea together. Most of us will acknowledge that as we see the world, so the world is; and what we cannot see clearly with our eyes, we can ad lib with our imaginations. In fact, our imaginations can create things like dragons which God himself forgot to make. And, as Mark Twain says, "You can't depend on your eyes when your imagination is out of focus." We feel that the eye enlightens us empirically, but we cannot always tell which is directing us. We are not all in agreement about which of the two has discovered the Loch Ness Monster nor the Abominable Snowman.

When we consider that so many persons have had an experience beyond what is classified as *common* reality, is there really such a realm that we can designate as *supernatural,* or are those experiences really natural to anyone with a special talent for awareness beyond the common, physical world?

Castaneda, like most of us, realizes that our common vocabulary on this topic is inadequate. As he struggles to tell of such things, he wants to call them *separate realities,* whether the images come from dreams or drug-induced vagaries. Andrew Weil likes to refer to them as *altered states of consciousness.* If we do not even have a vocabulary in common to discuss this matter, how can universities claim to have set up separate disciplines of parapsychology?

In the late 1980s a great series of topics came into being for show on television. I saw only four of the videos of the *Thinking Allowed* series. It was the topic "Roots of Consciousness," hosted by Jeffrey Mishlove. All four of the scientists said that we have no word to define "consciousness." What is its source, and how is it powered?

Saul-Paul Sirag, the last physicist on that panel, from San Francisco, said he thought that what we designate as our consciousness is that field of energy we have overlooked. He thinks it is perhaps the greatest, strongest field of energy, but like all the other fields, we will have to learn its laws before we could harness that energy and make it work for us. Man saw for years what electricity could do, but until we learned what could safely conduct it to the wall plug, we could not make use of it. He thought he could prove this in about two decades. While I am fairly good at research, I find little he has written. He appeared on the show to find great difficulty explaining his theories—a total recluse, perhaps, as many are.

Does this suggest the beginning to the answer for which we are looking? What is consciousness, and how is it navigated? By our own intent, or by mere happenstance? Are some of us even compelling it now in some ways that we are still unaware? Is there anyone who has never heard of mind over matter? Telepathy? Foretelling actual events? Or communicating with someone on another continent?

Many well-known Christian writers have called Albert Einstein an atheist. I do not get the idea that he denied a god. Like many other topics, our words do not seem to carry the same meanings for all of us. He acknowledged that everything that was here in the beginning is still here. "From dust thou art, to dust returneth." "Recycle" is a relatively new word. And the concept of a loved one making this kind of transition is actually traumatic in this country. It is not everywhere. As some scientists and other scholars see it, Einstein just took the notion of recycling one step further. He felt that a great Consciousness created "all this." He borrowed his consciousness from that source, and like his physical self, his consciousness would go back to join the parent source. Here, again, word choice becomes troublesome.

Stephen Hawking, the renowned scientist of the Black Hole, has lived with ALS (Lou Gehrig's disease) since he was twenty-six. A TV announcer asked him if he could go back to the physical state that he enjoyed at that age, would he go. He replied with energy only from his computerized correspondence apparatus, "No, because leaving the physical has allowed my mind to go beyond the bounds of human thought." How does thought relate to "consciousness"?

Since our major field of study is "folklore," we might review our definition. W. J. Thoms coined this word in 1849 to distinguish the learning of the common folk from the formal learning of the academic world. Their collections of "strange old stories" were called "antiquaries," and they were very popular. While we have all enjoyed some humorous cures and folk stories that we feel could not have been documented, we must admit that many held great substance. They were not lies nor manufactured tales. Today, many home cures have now been clinically tested and proved to be efficacious for exactly the cure the folks had claimed it to be. However, until we have a satisfactory word and a good definition for out-of-the-common, ordinary, natural kind of seeing and feeling, I will just call it "supernatural."

We may have to wait a little longer for Saul-Paul and his scientists to help us with this question so that we can come closer to our meaning of the all-encompassing word we call "consciousness." Meanwhile, the question stands tall in my pondering. I strive to learn why some folks can attest to being able to leave their bodies or predict events that are yet to happen, or see all these interesting ghosts and things such as future events. However, I do hope gaining that knowledge will not take away all those marvelously fascinating stories and their suspenseful thrills—unless we can find or concoct something to take their places.

## Contributors' Vitas

**Jim H. Ainsworth** authored three business books and co-authored a fourth (all published by John Wiley & Sons) before leaving the profession that had chosen him. At fifty-three, he planned to pursue the abandoned dreams of his childhood—to be a cowboy and an author. He made a trip by covered wagon and horseback across Texas to retrace the journey his ancestors had made two generations earlier, and wrote *Biscuits Across the Brazos* to chronicle the trip. He traveled the team roping circuit as an amateur and worked roundups on big ranches. Working beside *real* cowboys sent him back to writing. Using lessons he learned from more than 10,000 client interviews over thirty years and memories from his rural Texas roots, *In the Rivers' Flow*, his first novel, was published in 2003. *Rivers Crossing* followed in 2005. *Rivers Ebb*, a Writers League of Texas contest finalist and Writers Digest International Book Competition finalist, is the third novel in his *Follow the Rivers* trilogy.

**Carolyn Arrington** willfully admits to being a songwriter, poet, substitute school teacher, mother (grandmother), and wife. She enjoys playing all the stringed instruments, as well as others: guitar, banjo, mandolin, fiddle, mountain dulcimer, hammer dulcimer, dobro, mouth bow, penny whistle, saxophone, harmonica, and probably some others she just can't think of right now. Her musical preference is Old Timey music, bluegrass, and folk, but she also plays alto sax in the local community band. She writes a lot of songs about other historical events and whatever else comes into lyrical play. She says she is an *ethnohistoricalmusicologist*.

**Mary Margaret Dougherty Campbell** holds a B.A. and an M.A. in English from Texas Tech University and an M.S. in Educational Administration from Texas A&M University, Corpus Christi. She has published articles in *English in Texas*, *South Texas Traveler*,

*South Texas Catholic*, and *Cowboy Magazine*, as well as *The Family Saga* and *Folklore: In All of Us, In All We Do*. Her poems have appeared in *English in Texas*, *American Cowboy*, *Rope Burns*, and three volumes of the *Texas Poetry Calendar*. In November 2008, she will become the Executive Director of George West Storyfest. Currently, she serves TFS as a Director.

**Margaret A. Cox** of Austin grew up in Eden, Texas, fourth generation of 1886 Concho County pioneers. She maintained close ties to Eden while working for thirty-five years with the University of Texas library. Besides the Texas Folklore Society, Margaret's memberships include the Texas State Historical Association and the Society for Children's Book Writers and Illustrators. She's presently busy compiling dozens of untold stories.

**Jennifer O. Curtis** moved to Texas in 1979 with her husband and six children. She has taught English at San Jacinto College in Houston. She enjoys writing, history and storytelling, and has told stories for local schools and groups for many years. She is currently pursuing a Ph.D. in Composition and TESOL at Indiana University of Pennsylvania.

**Kenneth W. Davis**, a professor emeritus of English at Texas Tech University, is a past-President of the Texas Folklore Society and of the Texas/Southwest Popular Culture Association, the American Studies Association of Texas, and of the West Texas Historical Association, of which he was named Honorary Life Member in 2007. He has also been Sheriff of the Lubbock Corral of Westerners International, and is currently a member of the Lubbock Country Historical Commission. He remains interested in traditional oral narratives in Texas and the Southwest.

**Robert J. (Jack) Duncan** was born in Pilot Point on Pearl Harbor Day 1941, the seventh grandchild on each side of his family. He grew up in McKinney and has lived there most of his life. Jack is a writer/editor/researcher for Retractable Technologies, Inc., a manufacturer of safety needle medical devices in Little Elm. He is also a widely published freelance writer, in both scholarly and popular periodicals, including *Reader's Digest*. He has written several hundred newspaper and magazine articles over the past quarter century. He helped write and edit the screenplay for a major motion picture, *Lethal Alliance*, soon to be filmed in Shreveport. Author Bill Porterfield calls him "a root hog who digs up the damnedest truffles!" Jack has taught at Collin County Community College and Grayson County College, and has worked for Richland College as well as Collin. As a lifelong learner, he continues to take graduate courses in a variety of disciplines. Jack was President of the TFS once upon a time, and has attended the last thirty-five annual TFS meetings, often taking part in the programs. He has contributed to eight previous TFS volumes. Jack is a life member of the Texas State Historical Association and former Sheriff (president) of the Dallas Corral of Westerners International. He has been married to his high school sweetheart, the former Elizabeth Ann Harris, since 1963. They have two grown sons (who live in Texas) and five grandsons who think they're grown.

**Sue M. Friday**, a native of Houston, lives on a farm outside Charlotte, North Carolina. She and her husband have spent the last few years rescuing her grandparents' dogtrot house in Hemphill and spend at least a month there annually. A former columnist for the *Charlotte Observer*'s "Viewpoint" page, she has also taught high school English and published numerous short stories, some with a Texas theme (*New Texas* 2002). She earned an M.A. in English from the University of North Carolina at Charlotte. Descended from a family of East Texas outlaws, she is currently working on a novel about their exploits in the late 1800s.

**L. Patrick Hughes** is a Professor of History at Austin Community College, where he has served on the faculty since 1977. A graduate of the University of Texas, he is also a guest lecturer for UT's

Elderhostel and Road Scholar programs. An active member of numerous state and regional organizations, he is the current President of the Texas Folklore Society.

**David LaRo** spent most of his working years as a financial and budget advisor to the Base Commander of Kelly AFB, Texas. He was born a "pistol shot from the Alamo" and continues to live almost that near it. A full-time job in a field that concerns itself with money does not allow one much time to pursue the finer things in life, such as books. After retirement in 1988, he became a volunteer at the University of Texas San Antonio's Institute of Texan Cultures, where he came into contact with such cultured gentlemen as Clyde Hester, Al Lowman, and "Ab" Abernethy. It was through such contacts that he really began to cultivate a lifelong love of Texas, its history and its folklore, and books. After approximately one year as a volunteer, he joined the Institute staff on a part-time basis, doing mostly what came naturally: traveling and just talking with people. He still loves to talk with people, and has been told he loves it too much! He is married to his wife, Margie, and they have three daughters and six grandchildren.

**Leslie LaRo** is the youngest kid of a multi-generational Texan and an Illinois-born-again Texan, who regularly used to drag their three daughters from place to place, in an effort to **ed-ju-cate** them proper. She is the only one who picked up the curious love of cemeteries and other tranquil (but not necessarily quiet) places where she could contemplate the workings of the world and her tiny but unique place within it. Her preferred uses of time (pleasure reading, writing, traveling, snapping photographs, thinking about God's purpose for her life, and taking a truly superb nap, all to an eclectic musical score in shuffle mode) are frequently inconsistent with the demands upon her. These days you can find her either teaching children with visual impairments in her professional world, working on a paper for a post-graduate degree, listening intently to pieces of other people's narratives, or reading just about anything interesting she can put her hands on. Though proudly born more than forty years ago in the Piney Woods of East Texas, she now lives in San Antonio, Texas, in a petite house containing her books, treasures, music, and photographs of people and places she knows—all of which pretty much symbolize the great loves of her life.

**Faye Leeper** has a B.S. and an M.A. in English, and a few stray courses from the University of Edinburgh, Scotland, and Cambridge, England. She taught English for twenty-five years at Lee High School in Midland, Texas. She says some of us have been schooled and some have been educated, but she thinks that the rest of her life will be well spent if she can only re-learn the things that she has been wrongly taught or that she has wrongly interpreted. That would certainly be a re-schooling, since technology alone has tripled since she was thirty years old, and folklore might soon indicate as much progress. Grandma's recipe (home remedy for nasal congestion) has been clinically tested and found to be the best after all. It can now be bought over the counter in any drugstore.

**Jerry B. Lincecum**, a sixth-generation Texan, is Emeritus Professor of English at Austin College. He holds a B.A. in English from Texas A&M University and M.A. and Ph.D. degrees from Duke University. A past-President of the Texas Folklore Society, he has presented many papers at annual meetings of the Society, and co-edited *The Family Saga: A Collection of Texas Family Legends* for the TFS in 2003. Since 1990, he and Dr. Peggy Redshaw have directed "Telling Our Stories," a humanities project at Austin College that aids older adults in writing their autobiographies and family histories. Volume 7 in the TOS series of books is scheduled to appear soon, and major festivities are planned for the twentieth anniversary.

**Dr. Charles B. Martin** is Professor Emeritus of English at the University of North Texas in Denton. He is a former President of the Texas Folklore Society, and has been a member since the late

1960s. He has read several papers, most on Hispanic folklore and customs gathered during the two years he taught in Spain.

**Ruth Massingill** has more than twenty years experience in journalism, public relations, and advertising, both as a professional communicator and as a university administrator and faculty member at Sam Houston State University in Huntsville. Recent awards include the Research Achievement in Mass Communication Award for Outstanding Research and Scholarship (SHSU College of Humanities and Social Science, 2007), Outstanding Educator (American Advertising Federation, 2002), and Outstanding Faculty (University of Phoenix-Houston, 2003). She is a published author who regularly presents papers dealing with communications topics at national and international conferences. She holds an M.A. in journalism from the University of Wyoming and is currently working toward a Ph.D. in social marketing from the University of Teesside in Middlesbrough, England.

**Charlie Oden** is a folklore addict. He was born into a storytelling family in 1918, a time before radio and television changed the home lives—and the storytelling and music—of the American people. He became addicted to folklore when he began reading the writings of J. Frank Dobie and found they were like the Oden family stories. During his working life on the T&NO (SP) Railroad, he mixed and mingled with switchmen, enginemen, trainmen, and other railroaders. Most of them had stories to tell; some were master spinners of yarns. Charlie's addiction continued after his retirement, and he joined the Houston Folklore Society. (Founded by John Lomax, HFS is now Houston Folklore and Folk Music Society.) Oden is or has been a member of the Canadian Folk Music Society, the Texas Folklore Society, the Southwest Celtic Music Association, and the Central Texas Storytelling Guild. He has told stories with the *crème de la crème* of storytellers, none other than TFS members Doc Moore and Tim Tingle with Uncle Roy. Joseph Campbell would say that Charlie is following his bliss.

**Edward R. Raasch**'s last retirement—from the lumber business—was at age eighty. He was a radio station manager in the 1940s. He has one daughter, one son, three grandchildren and three great-grandchildren. During his retirement, he has written essays that have appeared in six books, won the Hastings top award twice, and written two mystery novels. He believes writing is like medicine—it keeps the mind alert. He also feels computers are a joyous challenge. At age ninety-three, he lives alone.

**Karen Clark Ristine** is a fifth-generation Texan and fourth-generation journalist, who has spent the past three years in seminary at Claremont School of Theology, where she graduated in May 2008 with a Master's of Divinity degree. Her work in journalism included editing assignments at *The San Diego Union-Tribune* and *The Dallas Times Herald*. She spent her childhood in Fort Worth, Texas, her teenage years in Paris, Texas, and graduated in 1981 with a B.S. in journalism from the University of North Texas. She is the daughter of Linda and Tony Clark, a poet and educator active in the Texas Folklore Society until his death in 2005. She is the mother of Ryan Ristine, who, at six, loves fishing and baseball and writing as much as his grandpa did.

**J. Rhett Rushing** is the staff Folklorist and Oral Historian for UTSA's Institute of Texan Cultures. A proud Aggie, husband, and father, he has been with the Texas Folklore Society for twenty-five years now, and has contributed a number of articles and papers to the Society's publications.

**A. C. Sanders III** arrived on this earth March 11, 1941, in Lubbock, Texas. His father, A. C. Jr., was born in Lubbock and his mother, Crystelle, in Plainview, Texas. The Sanders family owned Sanders Funeral Home, established in 1929. A. C. studied piano under his musician mother, and played football and baseball. Throughout high school and college, he worked at the family funeral home, which would provide fodder for stories in later years.

He attended Lubbock High School and then Texas Tech, where his studies included philosophy, history, and government. He also participated in varsity swimming and water polo. After college, A. C. entered the army. In 1965, he married Mary Kindle. The army moved them to El Paso, Germany, Oklahoma, Georgia, and North Carolina. The couple was blessed with two sons. Tired of a revolving door to Vietnam, he left the military in January 1972. He owned several businesses during the 1970s and '80s. In 1985, A. C. returned to school at the University of Texas at El Paso to study kinesiology and exercise physiology. He now structures exercise programs for folks with special needs. In the late 1980s, A. C. began journaling to confront old Vietnam demons and put them in perspective. After much editing and help from writer friends, he wrote his first short story, "He Never Knew Her Name," in 1994. It won a short story award from the El Paso Writers' League. Buoyed by success, he jumped into the writing game with both feet and has won several regional awards for short stories, nonfiction, and poems. A. C. presently writes a monthly column on El Paso history and folklore for the *El Paso Magazine*.

**Herbert H. Sanders** was born and raised in Dallas, Texas. He was educated in the Dallas Independent School District and at Southern Methodist University. After tours of duty with the U. S. Navy, he was employed with Southwestern Bell Telephone Company for thirty-two years, filling several positions in craft and management. After his retirement in April of 1981, he and his wife moved to their summer home on Lake Texoma. In Grayson County, he spent ten years with Grayson County Community College and five years as director of the Pottsboro Area Public Library. Herb and Pat celebrated their golden wedding anniversary March 31, 2000. They have two sons and three grandsons.

**Mildred Boren Sentell** was born in Post, Texas, and reared in Post and Crane. She married B. J. Boren while at Texas Tech University in 1953, and after his death in 1972, moved to San Angelo to attend

Angelo State University, where she began teaching in the English Department in 1976. In 1992, she married Joe Sentell and retired and moved to Snyder. After Joe died in 2002, she moved back to Post in 2007, where two of her three children live, as well as most of her other relatives. She now divides her time between family, her home in town, and her home on the ranch on Lake Alan Henry.

**Hortense Warner Ward** contributed articles on cattle brands for *From Hell to Breakfast* (1944) and *The Sky Is My Tipi* (1948). She also wrote extensively about the lore and history of Corpus Christi for journals such as the *Southwestern Historical Quarterly*. Two of her major publications include *Cattle Brands and Cowhides* (1953) and *A Century of Missionary Effort* (1960).

**Brenda Black White** has read her poetry at the annual "Hootenanny" of the Texas Folklore Society, at "open mike" nights at bookstores, and at writers' conferences across Texas and in Florida, New York, and Virginia. Those who've heard her have been affected by her range, insights, and magnetism. With West Texas roots in Baird, Callahan County, where she was born and in Cisco, Eastland County, where she grew up, she obtained her oxymoronic name when she married Ken White, a physician, and moved to Commerce. Her poetry has appeared in *McCall's*, *Sulphur River*, *Riversedge*, *A 150-Year Anthology* (1994), *Texas in Poetry2* (2002), and in other publications. Her first collection of poetry was *Callahan County* (1998), followed by *The Thing About Me* (2007). She is currently completing a sequel to *Callahan County* and a volume of new poetry.

**Henry Wolff, Jr.** has been a Texas journalist for five decades—most of his adult life. He has worked for the *San Angelo Standard-Times*, the *Abilene Reporter-News*, and the *Victoria Advocate*. He joined the *Advocate*, the second oldest existing newspaper in Texas, in 1963 as a reporter and photographer. As a full-time columnist from 1979 to 2007, he wrote more than 6,000 of his "Henry's Journal" columns. Now semi-retired, he continues to write a Sunday column. He is a former President of the South Texas Historical Association and of the Texas Folklore Society.

**David H. Zimmermann,** a native of San Antonio, completed his B.A. and M.A. at Saint Mary's University. After a stint in the Catholic seminary, he married before heading north to complete a doctorate at the University of North Texas under Jim Lee's watch. Having taught in San Antonio, the Metroplex, and the Panhandle, David has now hunkered down to teaching English and chairing the ESOL/Languages and Speech Department at Lone Star College–Montgomery, while helping his wife, Daniza, raise twins in The Woodlands, a task equal to that of Pete Perkins' quest. His odes to small town living continue to fall on deaf ears.

# INDEX

## C



## D

## L



## M

## S



## T